The Art of Negotiation

Preparation for Successful Negotiations

LUIS TEJADA

Table of Contents

Introduction

Negotiation is an ancient art woven into the very fabric of human history. From the ancient Silk Roads to the modern steel and glass skyscrapers, the ability to negotiate has been a defining factor in success, both personally and professionally. In this book, we will delve into the fundamentals of "The Art of Negotiation," a fascinating journey through the concepts, strategies, and skills that underlie every exchange and agreement we forge in life.

Negotiation is a multifaceted process, a dance of wills, needs, and ever-evolving interests. Throughout these pages, we will break down thirty crucial topics that will help you understand and master this art. We will begin by establishing the basic concepts of negotiation, demystifying its complexity and exploring the various approaches that can be adopted in different contexts. From the world of business to personal relationships, the tactics and strategies for achieving effective agreements are equally applicable.

Effective communication is the foundation of any successful negotiation. Therefore, we will dedicate a chapter to essential communication skills, exploring how words, tone, and body language can influence the outcome of a negotiation. Preparation is also paramount, and you will learn to set clear goals and strong boundaries to guide your negotiation efforts toward success.

At the heart of any negotiation lies the creation of value, a process through which both parties can gain mutual benefits. But, of course, there will be times when you need to make concessions to reach an agreement. You will learn when and how to make concessions effectively, avoiding common pitfalls.

Negotiation can be viewed from different perspectives. We will discuss win-win and win-lose strategies, as well as the difference between competitive and collaborative negotiation. We will also explore the various types of power in negotiation, from informational power to emotional power.

Psychology plays a crucial role in negotiation, and we will analyze how emotions and decision-making influence the process. Additionally, we will address intercultural negotiation, highlighting key aspects for success in global and diverse environments.

In the upcoming pages, we will immerse ourselves in a variety of negotiation scenarios, from the business world to situations of crisis and personal disputes. We will also reflect on ethics in negotiation, the role of empathy, and the importance of active listening and nonverbal communication.

As you progress in your reading, you will discover how to confront challenging situations, overcome impasses, and negotiate effectively in teams and groups. We will also explore dispute resolution and mediation as essential tools in the negotiator's toolkit.

As you venture further into the world of negotiation, you will uncover long-term strategies, the impact of the digital age, and the significance of ethical decision-making. Along the way, you will encounter case studies of successful negotiations that illustrate the discussed principles and strategies.

Finally, we will consider the development of negotiation skills over time, providing you with the tools to become a master negotiator as you advance in your career and personal life.

1. Introduction to Negotiation: Basic Concepts and Approaches

Negotiation is a fundamental process in human interaction, whether in personal or professional contexts. In essence, negotiation involves seeking a mutually acceptable agreement between two or more parties with divergent interests, goals, or viewpoints. Here, I will introduce the basic concepts and approaches to negotiation.

At the heart of any negotiation are the interests of the involved parties. Interests are the needs, desires, concerns, or goals that each party seeks to satisfy or achieve in the negotiation.

Before entering into a negotiation, it is essential for parties to identify and understand their own interests, as well as the interests of the other party. This involves conducting a deep analysis of what is genuinely important to each party.

Often, underlying interests are more significant than stated positions. Understanding these underlying interests allows parties to find creative solutions that satisfy both sides.

Not all interests are equal in terms of importance. Some are "critical," while others may be "negotiable." The ability to prioritize and distinguish among them is key to effective negotiation.

During negotiation, it is important to communicate one's interests clearly and effectively. This facilitates mutual understanding and can help parties work together to satisfy those interests.

Interests may evolve over time, so it is important to be willing to adapt as the situation changes. Flexibility in negotiation can be essential for achieving successful agreements.

Parties may discover that they have common or overlapping interests. Identifying these shared interests can pave the way for a more collaborative and effective negotiation.

In some situations, keeping certain interests confidential can be strategic. Parties may choose not to reveal all their interests right away and instead disclose them gradually as the negotiation progresses.

Interests are the driving force behind a negotiation. Understanding, communicating, and managing them effectively are essential components of reaching agreements that satisfy the needs and goals of all parties involved.

Positions are the specific demands or proposals that one party makes in the negotiation. Positions are often presented as a starting point for negotiation but may not align with the parties' real interests.

Positions are concrete statements of what a party wants or demands in the negotiation. They can include demands, proposals, prices, conditions, terms, and other elements that a party considers essential for reaching an agreement.

Positions are used as a starting point in a negotiation. Each party presents its own initial positions, which may be based on their interests but are often not fully disclosed from the beginning.

Positions can be either rigid or flexible. Rigid positions imply that a party is less willing to compromise or make concessions. Flexible positions allow room for negotiation and the pursuit of intermediate solutions.

It is important to understand that positions may conflict with underlying interests. Sometimes, parties may maintain extreme positions to gain an initial advantage in negotiation but may be willing to accept alternatives if their interests are met.

In some situations, negotiation primarily focuses on positions. Parties may haggle and make concessions on specific terms of an agreement. This approach is more common in distributive negotiations.

As the negotiation progresses, it is beneficial for parties to move away from positions and focus on underlying interests. This can open the door to more creative solutions and mutually beneficial agreements.

Communication and mutual understanding of positions are essential in negotiation. This involves active listening and asking questions to clarify the demands and proposals of the other party.

Parties must manage their expectations regarding positions. It is not always possible for both parties to get everything they want, and negotiation often involves a compromise to reach an acceptable agreement for both parties.

Positions are an integral part of negotiation, but it is important to recognize that they do not always fully reflect the parties' real interests. The ability to manage and negotiate positions effectively is a key component in the pursuit of successful agreements.

It is crucial that each party keeps their alternatives to a negotiated agreement in mind. Alternatives represent what a party will do if the negotiation does not lead to a satisfactory agreement.

Alternatives are the options or courses of action available to each party if the negotiation does not result in a satisfactory agreement. These alternatives can include agreements with other parties, internal solutions, or even the absence of an agreement.

Knowing their alternatives strengthens a party's position in negotiation, as they are not entirely dependent on an agreement with the other party.

Alternatives help establish an upper limit for the concessions a party is willing to make. If the alternatives are more attractive than the proposed agreement, the party will have less incentive to concede in the negotiation.

Alternatives allow parties to assess whether a proposed agreement is genuinely better than the options available outside of the negotiation.

In some cases, parties may work to improve their alternatives before the negotiation. This can include seeking new business partners, developing internal solutions, or investing in resources that enhance the attractiveness of the alternatives.

Alternatives also serve as a basis for comparison. Parties can evaluate proposals based on how they compare to their alternatives. This can help determine whether an agreement is fair and beneficial.

If the alternatives are more attractive than the proposed agreement, one party may choose to withdraw from the negotiation. On the other hand, if the alternatives are less desirable, there may be incentives to seek a negotiated solution.

In some cases, parties may choose not to fully disclose their alternatives to the other party. This can be a strategy to maintain a stronger negotiating position.

Alternatives are a critical element in decision-making in a negotiation. Knowing and carefully evaluating available alternatives allows parties to make strategic decisions that lead to agreements that best satisfy their interests and needs.

The Zone of Possible Agreement (ZOPA) is a central concept in negotiation that represents the space in which parties can reach a mutually acceptable agreement.

It is an imaginary region on the spectrum of positions and demands of the parties in the negotiation. It is the area where the positions and interests of both parties overlap and allow the possibility of reaching an agreement.

It is created when parties find areas in which their interests, although they may differ in some respects, overlap or complement in some way. This means there are elements on which both parties can agree.

Successful negotiation involves identifying and expanding the ZOPA. As parties work together and consider creative solutions, they can overcome some of their initial differences and expand the area of possible agreement.

The goal of negotiation is to move toward the ZOPA and find a point within this zone that is acceptable to both parties. This generally involves a willingness to make concessions and seek solutions that satisfy the interests of both parties.

It is not infinite; it has limits. These limits are determined by the positions, interests, and alternatives of the parties. If the parties cannot find a solution within the ZOPA, the negotiation could fail.

In a distributive negotiation (often competitive), parties may be more focused on determining how limited resources within the ZOPA will be divided. In an integrative negotiation, parties seek to expand it by creating value and satisfying mutual interests.

Successful negotiation involves effective communication and creativity in finding solutions that maximize it. This may require exploring different scenarios and considering innovative approaches. It is a key concept in negotiation that represents the space where parties can reach an agreement. Understanding and expanding the ZOPA are essential for achieving mutually beneficial agreements and resolving differences in negotiation.

During negotiation, parties often make concessions, meaning they give up something to reach an agreement. The ability to manage and balance concessions is crucial in negotiation.

Concessions are a central element in the negotiation process and play a fundamental role in reaching mutually acceptable agreements.

Concessions refer to the waivers or commitments that a party is willing to make during a negotiation to move closer to an agreement with the other party. These concessions may involve changes in initial positions, terms of the agreement, or additional commitments.

Making concessions can help build trust between parties. It shows goodwill and a willingness to find mutually beneficial solutions.

Concessions allow parties to move toward the Zone of Possible Agreement (ZOPA) by seeking intermediate points that satisfy the interests of both parties.

Concessions are often necessary to resolve differences and overcome obstacles in negotiation.

The ability to manage and balance concessions is essential to avoid one party conceding too much and maintain a fair balance in the negotiation.

These are concessions that one party makes without expecting an equivalent concession from the other party. They can be a gesture of goodwill.

In many negotiations, parties make concessions in exchange for concessions from the other party. This may be part of a strategy to maintain a balance.

To manage concessions effectively, it is important to set limits and know when to concede. It is advisable to have a clear negotiation strategy and be aware of which concessions are "critical" and which are negotiable.

Keeping a record of concessions made by both parties can be helpful for proper negotiation tracking and ensuring that concessions are balanced.

Sometimes, concessions are used strategically to gain certain advantages or to make the other party feel more committed to the agreement.

Parties should constantly assess whether the concessions they make and receive align with their interests and overall objectives in the negotiation.

Concessions are an essential component of negotiation and play a crucial role in building successful agreements. The ability to manage and balance concessions effectively is fundamental to achieving mutually beneficial and satisfactory solutions for all parties involved.

In this approach, resources are considered finite, and one party gains what the other party loses. Common tactics include setting hard limits, haggling, and competition. It is typical in win-lose situations.

Distributive negotiation is an approach where resources are perceived as finite, based on the idea that one party gains what the other party loses. This approach is characterized by a zero-sum mindset, where one party's gains are achieved at the expense of the other party.

In distributive negotiation, it is assumed that the resources at stake, whether money, time, goods, or any other resource, are limited. As a result, one party seeks to maximize their share of those resources, often at the expense of the other party.

Parties often maintain rigid initial positions and firmly defend their demands. This can lead to a bargaining process where concessions are difficult to achieve, and parties tend to maintain hard limits.

Competition is a distinctive feature of distributive negotiation. Parties often view negotiation as a competition in which one party "wins" what the other party "loses." This can result in a win-lose approach, where one party achieves its goals at the expense of the other.

Common tactics in distributive negotiation include setting hard limits, using minimal concessions, and resisting giving ground. Bargaining is a common strategy where parties negotiate over every aspect of the agreement to gain advantages.

Due to the zero-sum mindset and competition, distributive negotiation tends to produce limited results in terms of mutual satisfaction and relationship building. Often, one party feels they have gained an advantage at the expense of the other party.

Distributive negotiation is more suitable in situations where resources are scarce, and parties have opposing or conflicting goals. It can be effective in business negotiations, auctions, and competitive situations.

While distributive negotiation focuses on competition and profit maximization, it is not the only negotiation approach. In many situations, a more collaborative approach, such as integrative negotiation, which seeks to create value and mutually beneficial agreements, may be preferable for building long-term relationships and meeting the interests of both parties. The choice of the negotiation approach depends on the nature of the situation and the goals of the parties involved.

In contrast, integrative negotiation seeks to create additional value through cooperation. It focuses on expanding the Zone of Possible Agreement (ZOPA) and satisfying the interests of both parties. Parties collaborate to find solutions that benefit both.

Integrative negotiation is an approach to negotiation that focuses on creating additional value through cooperation and the pursuit of mutually beneficial solutions. Unlike distributive negotiation, which is based on competition and zero-sum thinking, integrative negotiation is oriented towards expanding the Zone of Possible Agreement (ZOPA) and satisfying the interests of both parties.

Integrative negotiation focuses on creating value, which means finding opportunities to increase the size of the pie rather than simply dividing it into larger portions. Both parties collaborate to identify areas where they can mutually benefit.

In integrative negotiation, the interests of both parties are central. Parties seek to understand and satisfy the interests of the other party while protecting their own.

Collaboration is an essential element of integrative negotiation. Parties work together to seek creative solutions that take into account the needs and goals of both. This promotes the building of long-term relationships.

Instead of fighting for the largest possible piece of the pie, parties seek to expand the ZOPA by considering multiple dimensions and variables for the agreement. This allows for intermediate and equitable solutions.

The ultimate goal of integrative negotiation is to achieve an agreement that satisfies the interests and needs of both parties. This approach tends to result in longer-lasting and more satisfying agreements for all parties involved.

Open and effective communication is key in integrative negotiation. Parties must express their interests, needs, and concerns transparently, which fosters a deeper understanding and enables innovative solutions.

In integrative negotiation, parties often explore creative solutions, such as package deals that address multiple issues at once, conditional agreements, or solutions that efficiently leverage available assets and resources.

Integrative negotiation seeks to create agreements in which both parties feel they have won. This promotes stronger cooperation and can lay the foundation for future collaborations.

It is especially effective in situations where parties have common or interdependent interests, and where building long-term relationships is valuable. Although it requires time and effort, it often leads to more sustainable and mutually beneficial agreements.

In most real-world negotiations, distributive and integrative approaches intertwine. Parties may compete in certain aspects and collaborate in others. The key is to determine when to apply each approach effectively.

Mixed negotiation is an approach that recognizes that in most real-world negotiations, distributive and integrative approaches intertwine. Parties may employ both competition and collaboration in different aspects of negotiation, depending on the situation and specific objectives.

In mixed negotiation, parties are flexible and adapt to changing circumstances. They acknowledge that different approaches may be necessary at different times in the negotiation.

The key to mixed negotiation is identifying when it is appropriate to apply a distributive or integrative approach. For example, when establishing initial terms, parties may compete and haggle, but when dealing with more complex or interdependent issues, they may collaborate to create value.

In mixed negotiation, interests remain fundamental. Parties continue to focus on satisfying their own interests but also consider how to address the interests of the other party constructively.

As negotiation progresses, parties may choose to transition from a distributive to an integrative approach or vice versa. This can be an effective strategy for overcoming obstacles and moving toward an agreement.

Mixed negotiation also involves recognizing and capitalizing on common interests when possible. These can serve as starting points for collaboration and value creation.

Parties should manage expectations effectively and clearly communicate their intent to shift their approach when necessary. This can help avoid misunderstandings and conflicts.

In mixed negotiation, communication and negotiation skills are essential. Parties must be able to alternate between competition and collaboration effectively.

Despite the alternation between approaches, the ultimate goal in mixed negotiation remains reaching a mutually beneficial agreement. Parties seek to balance their interests with value creation when possible.

Mixed negotiation recognizes that in complex, real-world situations, there is no one-size-fits-all approach. The key is to be flexible and strategic, applying the approach that best suits the situation and the specific objectives of the negotiation.

This approach is based on open communication, trust, and cooperation. Parties work together to maximize mutual outcomes and build long-term relationships.

Collaborative negotiation, sometimes also referred to as "principled negotiation" or "win-win negotiation," is an approach in which parties work cooperatively to maximize mutual outcomes and build long-term relationships. This approach centers on open communication, trust, and joint value creation. The key aspects of collaborative negotiation are as follows:

Open and candid communication is fundamental in collaborative negotiation. Parties strive to express their interests, needs, and concerns clearly and transparently. This fosters a deeper mutual understanding.

Trust is essential in collaborative negotiation. Parties endeavor to build a trusting relationship based on integrity, honesty, and commitment. Trust enables more effective collaboration.

In collaborative negotiation, the interests of both parties take center stage. Parties seek to identify and satisfy their mutual interests and needs rather than focusing on rigid positions.

Parties in collaborative negotiation explore creative solutions and win-win solutions that efficiently leverage available assets and resources. This can include package deals that address multiple issues at once.

Collaborative negotiation often focuses on building long-term relationships. Parties seek solutions that not only satisfy their immediate interests but also lay the groundwork for future collaborations.

Instead of striving to win at the other party's expense, collaborative negotiation aims for equitable agreements in which both parties feel they have won.

Parties continue to assess and adjust their approaches as they progress in negotiation. This ensures that the agreement is beneficial and meets the needs of both parties.

In some cases, parties may turn to mediation or facilitation by impartial third parties to assist in collaborative negotiation, especially when significant differences exist.

The goal in collaborative negotiation is for both parties to benefit and feel that they have achieved their objectives. The final agreement should be mutually beneficial.

Collaborative negotiation is suitable in situations where parties have common or interdependent interests, and where building long-term relationships is valuable. This approach can lead to strong and sustainable agreements that promote cooperation and trust in the future.

In this case, parties view themselves in a zero-sum situation and seek to maximize their gains at the other party's expense. This approach often results in conflicts and resource depletion.

Competitive negotiation, also known as "zero-sum" or "win-lose" negotiation, is an approach in which parties perceive themselves in a situation where resources or benefits are limited and, therefore, believe that one party's gains are achieved at the expense of the other party. This approach can generate conflict and resource depletion.

In competitive negotiation, it is assumed that the available resources are finite, which means that one party's gains come at the cost of the other party. This mindset often leads to a struggle for the largest slice of the pie.

 In competitive negotiation, the parties often maintain rigid positions and staunchly defend their demands. This can lead to a bargaining process where concessions are hard to achieve, and the parties tend to hold firm boundaries.

Competition is a distinctive feature of competitive negotiation. The parties view the negotiation as a competition in which one party "wins" what the other party "loses." This often results in a perception of "winner" and "loser," which can lead to conflicts.

Common tactics in competitive negotiation include setting hard limits, using minimal concessions, and resisting giving ground. Bargaining is a typical strategy where the parties negotiate over every aspect of the agreement to gain advantages.

Due to the zero-sum mentality and competition, competitive negotiation tends to yield limited results in terms of mutual satisfaction and relationship building. Often, one party feels it has gained an advantage at the expense of the other party.

Continuous competition can lead to resource exhaustion and, in some cases, may result in the breakdown of the negotiation without an agreement.

Competitive negotiation is more suitable in situations where resources are scarce, the parties have opposing or conflicting goals, or there is no long-term relationship at stake.

Competitive negotiation is just one of the possible approaches to decision-making in a negotiation. In many situations, a more collaborative approach, such as integrative negotiation, which seeks to create value and mutually beneficial agreements, may be preferable for building long-term relationships and meeting the interests of both parties. The choice of the negotiation approach will depend on the nature of the situation and the goals of the parties involved.

Negotiation is a complex process that involves seeking mutually beneficial agreements. The approaches and strategies vary depending on the situation and the parties involved. A solid understanding of the basics and the choice of an appropriate approach are crucial for success in any negotiation process.

2.Communication Skills in Negotiation

Communication skills are essential in negotiation, as effective communication is fundamental to understanding the parties involved, expressing your own interests, and reaching satisfactory agreements. Here is a list of key communication skills in negotiation:

Active listening involves giving full attention to what the other party is saying, asking questions to clarify, and demonstrating genuine interest in understanding their viewpoints and needs.

Active listening is a fundamental communication skill that involves giving complete and engaged attention to what another person is saying. It's about more than just hearing the words; it's about understanding, empathizing, and showing a genuine interest in what the other person is expressing. Here are some key aspects of active listening:

When practicing active listening, you focus on the person who is speaking. You eliminate distractions, such as electronic devices or internal thoughts, to be fully present in the conversation.

It's essential to show the other person that you care about what they are saying. This is achieved through body language, facial expressions, and verbal responses that indicate interest and empathy.

You can ask questions to gather more information or clarify what the other person is saying. This demonstrates your desire to better understand their perspective or needs.

Interruption can be a barrier to active listening. Allow the other person to finish speaking before responding or asking questions.

An effective active listening technique is to reflect what the other person has said, which helps confirm that you've understood correctly. You can also summarize their key points to show that you are following the conversation.

Try to put yourself in the other person's shoes and understand their feelings and perspectives. This helps build a stronger connection and communicate more effectively.

Active listening is crucial in interpersonal communication situations, such as personal relationships, the workplace, and conflict resolution. By practicing it, you can improve your communication skills and strengthen your relationships with others, as it demonstrates respect and consideration for others' opinions and needs.

Clear and concise communication is essential to avoid misunderstandings. Expressing your ideas and proposals in an understandable manner helps the other party understand your position.

It is a fundamental element in any type of interaction, whether personal, professional, or social. When you communicate clearly, you ensure that your messages are easily understood, which helps prevent misunderstandings and effectively convey your ideas. Here are some key principles of clear communication:

Before communicating, organize your thoughts and structure your message logically. This facilitates the transmission of information coherently.

Avoid ambiguity and redundancy. Express your ideas concisely and directly to make the message clear and easy to follow.

Adjust your language and terminology to your audience. Use language that is understandable to the other party, avoiding unnecessary jargon or technical terms.

Leave no room for misinterpretation. Be specific in your communication and provide details when necessary.

Effective communication is not one-way. Listen attentively to the other person to ensure you understand their viewpoints and needs.

At times, using concrete examples can help illustrate your ideas and make them clearer to the other person.

After communicating, it's helpful to ask the other party if they clearly understood your message and if they have any questions or concerns.

Body language, facial expressions, and tone of voice are also part of communication. Ensure that they align with your message.

Clear communication is essential in professional contexts, as it helps avoid misunderstandings in the workplace and make informed decisions. It is also vital in personal relationships, promoting empathy and mutual understanding. Practicing clear communication will help you become a more effective communicator and build stronger relationships with others.

Empathy involves the ability to put yourself in the other party's shoes, understand their emotions and perspectives, and show consideration for their needs and concerns.

Empathy is a fundamental skill in communication and interpersonal relationships. It involves the ability to understand and share the feelings and perspectives of another person while also showing consideration for their needs and concerns. Here are some key aspects of empathy:

It involves making an effort to understand how the other person feels and seeing things from their perspective. This doesn't mean you have to agree with their viewpoints, but you should be able to understand them.

Empathy starts with active listening. When you listen attentively to someone, you can pick up on their emotions and concerns. This demonstrates that you care about what they are experiencing.

Recognizing the other person's feelings is an important part of empathy. You can express understanding and empathy by saying something like, "I understand that this may make you feel frustrated" or "It seems like you're going through a tough time."

Being empathetic involves suspending personal judgments and criticisms. Instead of judging, show understanding and compassion toward the other person.

Empathy goes beyond understanding; it also involves being willing to offer support if necessary. Asking how you can help or simply being there for the person can make a difference.

Body language, facial expressions, and tone of voice are important in empathetic communication. Your nonverbal language can show emotional connection with the other person.

Empathy is essential in many situations, from consoling a friend during a difficult time to resolving conflicts in the workplace. By practicing empathy, you can strengthen your relationships, improve communication, and foster mutual understanding. It is also a fundamental component of emotional intelligence, which is valuable both in personal and professional contexts.

Making effective questions is crucial for obtaining relevant information and exploring interests and solutions. Open and closed questions can be useful in different contexts.

The skill of asking questions is essential in effective communication and problem-solving. Proper questions can help you gather relevant information, better understand others' needs and perspectives, and explore solutions. There are two main types of questions used in different contexts: open questions and closed questions.

Open questions invite the other person to provide a detailed and expansive response.

These questions often begin with words like "What?", "Why?", "How?", "When?", or "Where?".

They are useful for obtaining in-depth information, promoting conversation, and allowing the other person to express their thoughts and feelings.

Example: "Can you tell me more about your project?"

Closed questions typically have short and specific answers, such as "yes" or "no" or choices that require a simple selection.

These questions are used to obtain specific information or confirm facts.

They are useful for clarifying information, making quick decisions, or steering the conversation toward a specific topic.

Example: "Are you ready to start the meeting?"

Some tips for asking effective questions include:

Before asking a question, listen carefully to the other person to understand the context and what has already been said.

Formulate your questions clearly and directly to avoid confusion.

Choose the type of question (open or closed) that best suits the situation and your goals.

Avoid leading the other person's answers with questions that suggest a specific response.

Use open questions to promote meaningful and deep conversations, especially in situations where mutual understanding is crucial.

While closed questions can be helpful at times, avoid overusing them as they can limit the conversation.

The ability to ask questions effectively is valuable in a wide range of situations, from job interviews to group discussions and personal relationships. It helps gather accurate information, demonstrate interest, and facilitate informed decision-making.

Nonverbal communication, including body language, facial expressions, and tone of voice, is important in negotiation. These elements can convey emotions and attitudes that can influence the dynamics of the negotiation.

Nonverbal communication plays a crucial role in negotiation and in any human interaction. It includes elements such as body language, facial expressions, tone of voice, and other signs that do not rely on spoken words. In the context of negotiation, nonverbal communication can significantly influence perception and conversation dynamics. Here are some ways in which nonverbal communication is important in negotiation:

Facial expressions can reveal emotions and attitudes. A genuine smile can indicate kindness and a willingness to cooperate, while a furrowed brow or a serious expression may suggest disagreement or dissatisfaction.

Posture, gestures, and physical proximity can communicate power, confidence, submission, or even aggression. For example, standing upright and maintaining eye contact can demonstrate self-confidence, while crossing your arms or moving away can signal reservation or disagreement.

Tone of voice and intonation can change the meaning of words. A calm and serene tone can convey calm and patience, while an angry or aggressive tone can create tension in the negotiation.

Proper eye contact can indicate interest, sincerity, and trust. Avoiding eye contact or looking away may suggest dishonesty or discomfort.

Gestures can add emphasis to what you're saying and help convey your points. For example, pointing to something or nodding can indicate agreement or importance.

In addition to tone of voice, speaking rate, pause, and rhythm are also important aspects of nonverbal communication. A fast pace can demonstrate enthusiasm or anxiety, while a deliberate pause can emphasize a statement.

Although not strictly a form of nonverbal communication, your attire and personal appearance can influence how others perceive you in a negotiation.

Nonverbal communication in negotiation can be powerful because it often reveals underlying emotions and attitudes that words may not fully express. It's important to pay attention to both what is said and how it is said to fully understand the dynamics of a negotiation and achieve better results. It's also useful to be aware of your own nonverbal communication to ensure you are conveying the right signals and fostering a positive negotiation environment.

The ability to manage your own emotions and respond to the emotions of the other party in a calm and constructive manner is essential for maintaining a productive negotiation environment.

Emotional management is a crucial skill in negotiation and any human interaction. It involves the ability to recognize, understand, and handle both your own emotions and the emotions of the other party in a calm and constructive way.

When both parties in a negotiation can effectively manage their emotions, the chances of emotional conflicts and heated arguments are reduced. This allows for a more peaceful environment focused on finding mutually beneficial solutions.

Intense emotions can cloud judgment and lead to impulsive decisions. Emotional management allows you to make decisions based on logic and factual analysis instead of being driven by anger, frustration, or other negative emotions.

Effective emotional management enables you to be more empathetic and understanding towards the other party, as you can view their emotions and needs from an objective perspective. This facilitates bridge-building and conflict resolution.

Maintaining calm and composure helps you stay focused on the negotiation's objectives and seeking mutually beneficial solutions. Uncontrolled emotions can divert attention from these objectives.

Effective emotional management contributes to the building of trusting and respectful relationships. People appreciate those who can remain composed in emotionally charged situations.

Key practices for effective emotional management include:

Recognizing and labeling your own emotions.

Taking breaks when necessary to calm yourself.

Practicing empathy and trying to understand the other party's emotions.

Using effective communication techniques, such as active listening and asking questions, to avoid misunderstandings.

Fostering collaboration instead of confrontation.

Avoiding aggressive or provocative language and behavior.

Emotional management in negotiation is a skill that can be developed through practice and self-awareness. When applied effectively, it contributes to a more productive negotiation environment and the achievement of mutually beneficial outcomes.

Summarizing and paraphrasing the other party's statements is a useful technique to confirm mutual understanding and demonstrate active listening.

Summarizing and paraphrasing the other party's statements is an effective technique to ensure both parties have a clear understanding of what has been said and to show that you are actively listening. When summarizing, you briefly restate the key points of what the other person has expressed. When paraphrasing, you rephrase their words in your own words, which demonstrates your understanding and provides additional clarity. These actions are crucial in communication, especially in negotiation situations, to avoid misunderstandings and promote more effective conversation.

The strategy involves rephrasing in your own words what the other person has expressed to verify shared understanding and evidence attentive listening.

Being able to express your interests, needs, and goals clearly and specifically helps the other party understand what is important to you in the negotiation.

Certainly, expressing your interests, needs, and goals clearly and specifically is essential in any negotiation process. Here are some reasons why this is important:

By expressing your interests and needs clearly and specifically, you ensure that the other party understands exactly what you are seeking. This reduces the possibility of misunderstandings or misinterpretations.

Transparency in communication strengthens trust between the parties. When both parties feel that they are being honest and direct about what they want, they are more likely to feel secure in the negotiation.

By expressing your interests and needs, you can discover areas where both parties have similar goals or desires. This can pave the way for finding mutually beneficial solutions.

If a conflict arises during the negotiation, clearly expressing your interests and needs can help address and resolve the issue more effectively. It can help identify the source of the conflict and work together on solutions.

Clear communication saves time and effort. When both parties understand what is important to each other, they are more likely to reach an agreement more efficiently.

By understanding the needs and interests of both parties, a variety of options and solutions that meet those needs can be explored. This expands the set of possible agreements.

Clearly and specifically expressing interests, needs, and goals in negotiation is essential to facilitate an effective and constructive negotiation process. It helps build strong relationships, find mutually beneficial solutions, and achieve agreements that satisfy both parties' goals.

When discussing positions, the ability to present your arguments and proposals logically and persuasively is important for advocating your case.

Position negotiation is a fundamental part of any negotiation process, whether in personal, professional, or business settings. In this approach, the involved parties openly express their positions, demands, and initial proposals. Here are some key guidelines for presenting your arguments and proposals logically and persuasively during position negotiation:

Research and fully understand your position and the other party's position.

Identify your objectives and potential points of compromise.

Gather solid data and arguments to support your proposals.

Communicate your position clearly:

Be clear and concise when stating your demands and proposals. Avoid ambiguities.

Use simple and direct language to prevent misunderstandings.

Actively listening to the other party is essential to understand their arguments and needs.

Ask questions to clarify points and demonstrate interest in their concerns.

Highlight mutual benefits:

Emphasize how your proposal benefits both parties, which can increase persuasion.

Show empathy toward the other party's needs and desires.

Use logic and reasoning:

Base your arguments on concrete facts and data rather than emotions.

Use logical reasoning to support your proposals and explain why they are beneficial.

Maintain composure and respect:

Remaining calm and respectful is crucial for a constructive negotiation environment. Avoid aggressive or provocative language and behavior.

Expressing your arguments and proposals logically and persuasively is vital for advocating your case in position negotiation.

Keep a calm and respectful tone at all times.

Avoid aggressive or confrontational language that can hinder communication.

Be flexible and willing to compromise:

Negotiation involves give and take. Be willing to make concessions if necessary to reach an agreement.

Emphasize the points where you are willing to be flexible.

Build relationships:

Negotiation is not just about reaching an agreement but also about building long-term relationships.

Show willingness to collaborate and find mutually beneficial solutions.

Handle objections effectively:

Anticipate possible objections from the other party and be prepared to address them reasonably.

Offer solutions or alternatives when possible.

Be patient:

Negotiations often take time. Don't rush into impulsive decisions. Give both parties time to consider their positions.

The ability to present arguments and proposals logically and persuasively is essential in position negotiation. Clear communication, the use of logic, respect, and a willingness to reach mutually beneficial solutions are key elements for success in this process.

Providing feedback in a constructive and diplomatic manner can help the other party understand how their proposals or actions can be improved.

Providing constructive and diplomatic feedback is essential in any context where the goal is to improve another person's proposals, actions, or behaviors. Here are some guidelines for offering feedback effectively:

Instead of making vague or general comments, provide specific examples that support your feedback. This helps the other person better understand what you mean.

Use an "I" approach rather than a "you" approach: Instead of saying, "You always do this wrong," you can say, "I noticed it could be more effective if..." This prevents the feedback from sounding like a personal attack and focuses on the action or behavior in question.

Maintain a positive attitude: Start with what is working or what you appreciate before pointing out areas for improvement. This creates balance and makes the feedback more receptive.

Avoid using vague or ambiguous language. Be direct and objective when providing your feedback.

Don't just point out the problems; also offer solutions or suggestions for improvement. This shows your commitment to finding solutions.

After providing your feedback, allow the other person to respond and share their perspectives. Listening is an important part of any feedback conversation.

Keep a calm tone of voice and avoid aggressive or accusatory language. The idea is to encourage communication, not conflict.

Acknowledge the other person's emotions and show empathy. Some people may be sensitive to feedback, so try to be understanding and respectful.

Don't expect the other person to immediately accept your suggestions. Give them time to reflect and consider how to apply the feedback effectively.

If the feedback involves long-term changes, periodically check progress and provide ongoing support.

Remember that constructive feedback is about helping the other person grow and improve, not criticizing or judging. By following these guidelines, you can provide feedback effectively and constructively, which, in turn, contributes to a healthier and more productive work environment or relationships.

Maintaining control of the conversation and avoiding excessive interruption is important for maintaining a respectful and efficient negotiation environment.

Pay attention to what the other party is saying before responding. Active listening allows you to fully understand their views and concerns.

Do not interrupt the other party while they are speaking. Wait for them to finish their argument or comment before responding.

After the other person has spoken, take a pause before responding. This allows you to carefully consider what has been said and respond more thoughtfully.

Your body language also plays a significant role in controlling the conversation. Maintain eye contact and use gestures and expressions that show your interest and respect for what is being said.

You can agree on communication rules with the other party at the beginning of the negotiation. For example, you may agree that each person will have a specific time to express their views without interruptions.

If you are in a situation where several people are participating in the conversation, you can request speaking turns to ensure that each person has the opportunity to express their opinions without being interrupted.

In formal situations, such as negotiation meetings or debates, a moderator can help maintain control of the conversation and prevent excessive interruptions.

When it's your turn to speak, respond constructively and relevantly to the points raised by the other party. Avoid changing the subject or diverting the conversation.

If you have questions or need clarification about what the other person said, instead of interrupting, wait for them to finish and then ask questions for more information.

Show empathy toward the concerns and perspectives of the other party. This can help create an atmosphere of mutual respect and openness.

Maintaining control of the conversation and avoiding excessive interruption is essential for effective negotiation and ensuring that all parties feel heard and respected. Additionally, it contributes to a more efficient and collaborative communication environment.

In the virtual negotiation environment, written communication skills and proficiency in communication platforms are essential to ensure smooth negotiation. Written communication skills and competence in handling communication platforms play a crucial role in the success of negotiation.

Clarity in written communication. Use clear and concise language to avoid misunderstandings.

Structure your messages logically, breaking them into paragraphs and using bullet points or numbers when necessary.

Review and edit your messages to correct grammatical and spelling errors before sending them.

Respect for time and availability:

Coordinate virtual meeting schedules in advance and confirm the availability of all parties.

Be punctual for meetings and respect agreed-upon deadlines.

Familiarize yourself with the communication platform you are using (e.g., email, video conferencing, chat, etc.).

Ensure you are aware of key features such as screen sharing, file attachments, and chat.

Effective use of video conferencing:

Turn on your camera and ensure your environment is professional and free from distractions.

Look directly into the camera to maintain effective eye contact.

Files and documentation:

Share relevant documents and files in an organized manner and ensure all participants have access to them.

Use descriptive file names to facilitate document identification.

Assertive communication:

Express your views and opinions clearly and assertively, without being aggressive or passive.

Listen attentively to the opinions of others and show respect for them.

Information management:

Organize important information in an easy-to-follow format, such as summaries or key point lists.

Use labels or tags to categorize and archive important conversations or emails.

Protect the security of confidential information and ensure the platforms used comply with privacy regulations.

Before important meetings, conduct technology tests to ensure that your equipment, internet connection, and software are functioning correctly.

If technical issues arise, remain calm and work on alternative solutions. You can consider alternative forms of communication, such as a phone call if video conferencing fails.

Effective communication and technology management are essential in virtual negotiations. Focus on clarity, punctuality, and respect for the preferences and needs of the parties involved will help ensure that the negotiation flows smoothly and is successful.

Being able to adapt your communication style to the personality and preferences of the other party can enhance communication effectiveness.

Adaptability in communication style is a fundamental skill in various interactions, including negotiations. By tailoring your communication to the personality and preferences of the other party, you can significantly enhance the effectiveness of the conversation. Here are some ways you can be more adaptable in your communication style:

Begin by listening carefully to the other person to understand their communication preferences. Pay attention to their tone, style, and keywords.

Some people prefer a direct and concise communication style, while others may value more casual and friendly conversation.

Notice whether the other person focuses on facts and data or on emotions and personal relationships.

Once you've identified the other party's communication style, adjust to it as much as possible.

Use a tone and language that suits their preferences. If they are formal, be formal; if they are informal, be more relaxed.

Some people prefer quick and efficient conversations, while others value a more deliberate and thoughtful pace.

Adjust your speaking speed and the length of your responses according to the other person's preferences.

Asking open-ended questions invites the other party to express their thoughts and feelings in more detail. This can help you adapt your communication more effectively.

Show empathy toward the other person's emotions and concerns. This can help you build a stronger and more open relationship.

If you realize that the other party responds better to a particular approach, be flexible and adapt to that communication style.

Adaptability in communication is a skill that improves with practice. Practice with different people and in various contexts to develop your adaptation skills.

Being able to adapt your communication style to the personality and preferences of the other party is essential to enhance communication effectiveness and build strong relationships. Adaptability allows you to establish a stronger connection and facilitates mutual understanding in negotiation situations and in life in general.

Communication skills play a critical role in negotiation as they facilitate mutual understanding, relationship building, and the search for mutually beneficial solutions. Practicing and developing these skills can improve your performance in any negotiation context.

3.Preparation for Successful Negotiation

Preparation is fundamental to achieving a successful negotiation. Before starting any negotiation, define your objectives and expectations. What do you want to achieve? What are your priorities?

Establishing clear objectives is a crucial step in preparing for a successful negotiation. Instead of vague goals like "I want a good deal," be specific. For example, "I want a 10% discount on the purchase price" is much clearer. Recognize which of your goals are the most important and which ones are more flexible. This will help you know where you're willing to compromise and where you should maintain a firm stance.

Set your boundaries before the negotiation. How far are you willing to go in terms of price, deadlines, conditions, etc.? Knowing your limits helps you avoid agreements that aren't beneficial to you. In addition to your objectives, consider the needs and desires of the other party. Often, finding mutually beneficial solutions involves understanding what is important to both parties.

Make sure your goals are realistic and attainable. Setting unattainable goals can lead to frustration and a deadlock in the negotiation. Consider how you would feel if the negotiation doesn't result in an agreement. Having a "plan B" provides you with a safety net. List your goals in order of importance. This will help you focus on the most critical aspects of the negotiation.

While having clear objectives is important, it's also crucial to be willing to adapt if the situation requires it. Flexibility can be key to reaching a satisfactory agreement. Clarity in your objectives not only benefits you but also facilitates communication with the other party, as they will know what you're looking for and can adjust their own proposals accordingly. Establishing clear objectives is a crucial first step for effective negotiation.

Research the other party involved in the negotiation. Understand their interests, needs, goals, and constraints. The more information you have, the better you can tailor your strategies.

Researching the other party in a negotiation is essential to understanding their position and adapting your strategies effectively. Find out who the key people in the other party are who will be involved in the negotiation. This includes identifying the person with the authority to make decisions and those who will influence the process.

Conduct online research and gather publicly available information about the other party. This may include their history, corporate values, recent news, and any information that may be available on their website, social media, or annual reports.

If possible, reach out to people who may have information or prior experiences with the other party. Professional networks and contacts can provide valuable information and additional insights. If the other party has been involved in previous negotiations, research the outcome of those negotiations. This can offer clues about their approach and typical strategies.

Try to find out the other party's objectives and needs in the negotiation. What are they trying to achieve? What is important to them?

Determine the restrictions or limitations the other party may face, whether in terms of budget, timelines, regulations, or any other factor that may influence their ability to make decisions.

Observe how they communicate and present their arguments. Some people may be direct and data-focused, while others may focus more on relationships and empathy.

Understand the culture and values of the other party's organization, as this can influence their approach to the negotiation.

Examine any past history of relationships with the other party, including previous agreements or disagreements. This can provide valuable information about their current position.

Consider the current context, such as changes in the industry or economic circumstances, that may influence the negotiation.

Research is not just about collecting information but also about analyzing and understanding what you have gathered. The more information you have about the other party, the better prepared you will be to adapt your strategies and approach the negotiation effectively.

Determine the range of acceptable outcomes for both parties. This will help you set boundaries and be prepared for concessions.

Identifying your BATNA (Best Alternative to a Negotiated Agreement) is a key step in preparing for a negotiation. The BATNA represents the range of outcomes in which both parties can reach a mutually acceptable agreement. Here's how to determine your BATNA:

First, establish your ideal position (upper limit) and your minimum acceptable position (lower limit). The ideal position is what you want to achieve, while the minimum limit is the least you are willing to accept.

As mentioned earlier, research the other party to understand their interests and needs. This will help you estimate their upper and lower limits.

Knowing your limits and having an idea of the other party's limits will allow you to identify the BATNA. This is the range of outcomes that falls between your minimum limit and the other party's maximum limit, or vice versa.

Based on the BATNA and your objectives, set realistic goals for the negotiation. Your goal should be within the BATNA to have a high probability of reaching an agreement.

As you approach your minimum limit, be prepared to make concessions. It's important to know in advance what concessions you're willing to make without compromising your main objectives.

Although knowing your BATNA is essential, it's also important to maintain some flexibility during the negotiation. Circumstances can change, and being willing to adapt within the BATNA may be necessary to reach an agreement.

During the negotiation, communicate your limits clearly and respectfully. This helps set expectations and can guide the other party toward a mutually beneficial agreement.

Identifying your BATNA provides a solid framework for managing the negotiation and helps you avoid agreements that fall below your minimum limits. Effective negotiation involves finding solutions within this range where both parties can feel satisfied with the outcome.

Anticipate possible arguments and objections from the other party and prepare to respond in a logical and persuasive manner. The preparation of arguments and responses is essential for a successful negotiation. Here are some guidelines for anticipating and addressing possible arguments and objections from the other party in a logical and persuasive way:

Try to understand the perspective of the other party and what arguments they might present. This will help you anticipate their concerns.

Make a list of objections or questions that may arise during the negotiation. This could include issues related to price, deadlines, quality, terms and conditions, among others.

For each potential objection, prepare strong arguments that support your position. Use data, examples, and concrete evidence whenever possible.

Practicing your responses will help you feel more confident during the negotiation. You can do this on your own or with a friend or colleague acting as the other party.

While it's important to be prepared, you should also be flexible. Negotiation is a dynamic process, and unexpected objections may arise. Being willing to adapt is crucial.

During the negotiation, maintain composure and courtesy, even when facing challenging objections. Politeness and patience can help persuade the other party.

Actively listening to the other party allows you to understand their concerns and objections in real time. This provides an opportunity to respond in a more specific and persuasive manner.

When responding to objections, don't just defend your position; also offer solutions or alternatives that can meet the needs of both parties.

Acknowledge points of agreement with the other party and reinforce those aspects. This can help build a foundation for collaboration.

If you find that certain arguments are not effective or persuasive to the other party, be flexible and adjust your responses accordingly.

Preparation and the ability to respond effectively to objections are fundamental to a successful negotiation. The skill of communicating your arguments logically and persuasively can make a difference in achieving your goals in the negotiation.

Design a plan that outlines the sequence of the negotiation, including the topics to be discussed and the order in which you will address them. Creating a negotiation plan is essential to keep the negotiation focused and structured. Here's a step-by-step approach to designing an effective negotiation plan:

Before creating the plan, make sure you have clear objectives and well-defined priorities. Knowing what you want to achieve is crucial.

Make a list of the topics and points that will be addressed in the negotiation. This could include aspects such as price, deadlines, terms and conditions, quality, quantity, legal terms, etc.

Prioritize the topics based on their importance and relevance to your objectives and priorities. This will help you determine the focus to give to each one.

As mentioned earlier, research the other party to understand their interests and needs. This will help you anticipate their positions and objections.

Based on your objectives and your knowledge of the other party, establish a general strategy for each topic. What will be your initial position? What concessions are you willing to make?

Decide the order in which you will address the topics during the negotiation. You can start with the less controversial topics and move on to the most critical ones.

Set a time frame for the negotiation. This includes the estimated duration of the negotiation as a whole and the time you plan to dedicate to each topic.

Think about different possible scenarios and how you would handle them. What will you do if you can't reach an agreement on a particular topic?

As mentioned earlier, be prepared for possible objections and counterproposals. Having strong arguments will help you maintain control of the negotiation.

Consider how you will communicate with the other party. This includes how you will present your arguments, listen to their responses, and handle difficult conversations.

During the negotiation, make sure to include scheduled breaks and moments of reflection to assess your progress and adjust your approach if necessary.

Keep a detailed record of what has been discussed, offers, and concessions. This will help you remember what has been agreed upon and track progress.

At the end of the negotiation, prepare a summary of the agreements reached, next steps, and any pending matters.

A solid negotiation plan provides you with a roadmap and a framework to guide the discussion effectively and strategically. However, it's important to be flexible and willing to adapt as the negotiation evolves.

Consider what your position will be if an agreement is not reached. This will give you a safety net and make you feel more confident during the negotiation. Establishing a "plan B" is an important part of preparation for a negotiation. It is also known as your "Best Alternative to a Negotiated Agreement" (BATNA). Here's how to create an effective plan B:

Start by identifying what your options are if you don't reach an agreement with the other party. What other solutions or alternative agreements are possible? This could include seeking other suppliers, considering different terms or conditions, or exploring other sources of financing, among other alternatives.

Once you have identified your options, evaluate how attractive or realistic they are. Are they feasible and practical? What are their pros and cons? Make sure your alternatives are viable and beneficial compared to a negotiated agreement.

Rank your alternatives based on their priorities and objectives. What would be your preference if you can't reach an agreement with the other party? Having clarity about your priorities will help you make informed decisions.

Set your limits or thresholds for each alternative. At what point does an alternative become unacceptable? Knowing your limits will help you make quick and effective decisions if the negotiation is not successful.

During the negotiation, you can mention your plan B, but do so carefully. Don't threaten or pressure the other party, but communicate honestly and respectfully that you have viable alternatives.

Although having a plan B is important, you should also be willing to adapt and consider creative solutions that may arise during the negotiation. Your plan B is your safety net in case you can't reach an agreement. Knowing that you have alternatives will make you feel more secure and less pressured during the negotiation. As the negotiation progresses, you may need to adjust your plan B based on how the conversations unfold and new circumstances. Having a plan B provides you with confidence and helps you make informed decisions in case the negotiation is not successful. However, the best option will always be a mutually beneficial agreement, so it's important to strive to achieve it before resorting to your alternatives.

Although having a plan B is important, you should also be willing to adapt and consider creative solutions that may arise during the negotiation. Your plan B is your safety net in case you can't reach an agreement. Knowing that you have alternatives will make you feel more secure and less pressured during the negotiation. As the negotiation progresses, you may need to adjust your plan B based on how the conversations unfold and new circumstances. Having a plan B provides you with confidence and helps you make informed decisions in case the negotiation is not successful. However, the best option will always be a mutually beneficial agreement, so it's important to strive to achieve it before resorting to your alternatives.

Work on your communication skills, including active listening, empathy, and clear expression of your viewpoints. Improving your communication skills is essential for a successful negotiation. Here are some strategies to strengthen your communication skills:

Active listening is crucial in effective communication. Pay attention to what the other party is saying instead of planning your response while they speak. Ask questions to clarify and demonstrate that you are interested in understanding their viewpoints.

Empathy involves understanding and acknowledging the emotions and perspectives of the other party. Show empathy by validating their feelings and concerns. This can help build a trusting relationship.

Your body language, facial expressions, and tone of voice are key elements in communication. Maintain open and friendly body language and use an appropriate tone of voice for the situation.

Communicate your thoughts and arguments clearly and concisely. Avoid using jargon or confusing language. Use examples and exercise clarity in presenting your ideas.

Learn to ask effective questions. You can use open-ended questions to encourage discussion and closed-ended questions to obtain specific answers. Questions can be a powerful tool for directing the conversation and delving into important issues.

Assertiveness involves expressing your needs and opinions in a respectful but firm manner. Practice assertiveness to effectively advocate for your interests without being aggressive.

Conflict resolution skills are essential in negotiations. Learn to handle disagreements constructively and seek mutually beneficial solutions.

If much of your communication in the negotiation is written, make sure to write clearly and professionally. Review and edit your messages before sending them.

As mentioned earlier, be adaptable in your communication style. Adjust your approach to meet the other party's preferences. Some people may respond better to direct and data-focused communication, while others may prefer a more friendly and personal approach.

Practice is crucial for improving communication skills. Engage in role-playing exercises, seek feedback from colleagues or friends, and continue learning and improving your communication skills over time.

Effective communication is two-way, so also pay attention to how the other party communicates and adapt your approach accordingly. Strong communication skills can make a significant difference in building strong relationships and achieving successful outcomes in a negotiation.

Building strong relationships can be key in a negotiation. Work on establishing an atmosphere of trust and respect. Building solid relationships is essential in a successful negotiation. Here are some strategies to establish relationships based on trust and respect:

Promote open and honest communication from the outset. Be transparent about your goals and expectations, and encourage the other party to do the same. Honesty contributes to building trust.

Pay attention to what the other party is saying and show that you value their viewpoints. Active listening is crucial to demonstrate respect and understanding.

Understand the concerns and needs of the other party. Show empathy toward their emotions and perspectives, even if you disagree with them.

Seize opportunities to build a personal relationship with the other party. You can engage in conversations about personal topics unrelated to the negotiation to establish stronger connections.

Courtesy and respect are essential. Use respectful language and avoid derogatory or aggressive comments.

Keep your promises and commitments. Reliability is crucial for building and maintaining trust.

Instead of taking a zero-sum approach, work on finding solutions that are beneficial for both parties. This demonstrates your willingness to collaborate and build long-term relationships.

Conflicts can arise in a negotiation. Instead of avoiding them, address disagreements constructively and seek solutions that can satisfy both parties.

Express appreciation and gratitude for the efforts and cooperation of the other party. Small gestures, such as sending a written thank-you, can strengthen relationships.

If appropriate, look for ways to collaborate in the future. This may include joint projects, partnerships, or ongoing agreements.

If you are negotiating with people from different cultures, invest time in learning about their customs and cultural values. Cultural sensitivity can contribute to building stronger relationships.

In challenging situations, such as disagreements or conflicts, stay calm and avoid impulsive emotional responses that may damage the relationship.

Good relationships can be a valuable asset in negotiation, as they can facilitate mutually beneficial agreements and build a foundation for future collaborations. Building relationships is based on trust, respect, and a willingness to work together to achieve common goals. If relevant, make sure to have all the necessary documents and evidence to support your arguments.

Gathering relevant documentation and evidence is essential to support your arguments and strengthen your position in a negotiation. Here are some steps you can follow to ensure you are well-prepared in this regard:

Determine what documents, data, and evidence are needed to support your arguments and positions in the negotiation. This may include contracts, prior agreements, financial reports, market data, evidence of past performance, among others.

Classify and organize your documents in a clear and systematic manner. You can use physical or electronic folders to keep everything orderly and easily accessible.

Verify the authenticity of the documents and evidence you plan to use. Ensure they are accurate and up to date.

It's always prudent to keep backup copies of your documents as they can get lost or damaged. Store electronic and physical copies in secure locations.

Familiarize yourself with the content of your documents and evidence. This will allow you to explain them and defend your position effectively.

For some complex documents, it may be helpful to prepare a summary highlighting key points. This makes it easier to communicate relevant information during the negotiation.

If the negotiation involves legal or regulatory aspects, make sure you understand the applicable laws and regulations. Compliance with legal requirements is crucial.

You don't need to share all your documents and evidence immediately. Instead, present information selectively as it becomes relevant in the conversation. This can be useful in effectively supporting your arguments at the right moment.

When presenting documents and evidence, make sure to do so logically and persuasively. Explain how they support your viewpoints and benefit both parties.

Anticipate possible questions or objections from the other party regarding your documentation and evidence. Have clear answers backed by the available information.

If the other party requests to review your documents, show willingness to do so, as long as it's within reasonable limits.

Gathering appropriate documentation and evidence is an essential component of preparing for an effective negotiation. Information supported by strong evidence can strengthen your arguments and help you achieve more favorable agreements.

Think in advance about the concessions you would be willing to make and under what conditions.

Considering concessions in advance is an essential part of negotiation preparation. Here are some guidelines for thinking about your concessions effectively:

Before the negotiation, categorize your concessions based on their importance. Determine which concessions you are most willing to make and which are less important.

Set clear limits for your concessions. How far are you willing to go in terms of price, deadlines, conditions, etc.? Knowing your limits helps you avoid agreements that are not beneficial to you.

Recognize which of your objectives are more critical and which are more flexible. This will help you understand in which areas you are willing to compromise and in which you should hold a firm position.

Evaluate the relative value of your concessions compared to what you are getting in return. Ensure that your concessions are proportional and fair in the context of the negotiation.

Think about when you will make your concessions during the negotiation. You can choose to withhold some concessions for the right moment or to obtain reciprocity from the other party.

Create a list of the concessions you are willing to make and what you are willing to offer in exchange. This allows you to respond quickly and effectively during the negotiation.

Don't concede on all aspects indiscriminately. Instead, select the concessions that are genuinely necessary to move towards an agreement.

When making a concession, effectively communicate the value you are offering. This can help persuade the other party and foster a spirit of collaboration.

Also, consider the concessions the other party may be willing to make. Being prepared to recognize and respond to their concessions is important for progress in the negotiation.

As the negotiation progresses, circumstances may change. Be willing to adjust your concessions as necessary.

Concessions are a natural part of negotiation and should not be seen as a weakness. A well-planned and strategic concession can be beneficial in achieving a mutually satisfactory agreement. The key is to know when and under what conditions you are willing to concede.

Negotiations can take time, and hasty decisions can be detrimental. Stay calm and be patient.

Patience is a virtue in negotiation. Maintaining composure and being patient can make a difference in securing a beneficial agreement. Here are some reasons why patience is essential in negotiation and how to practice it:

Patience allows you to build strong relationships with the other party. Showing patience demonstrates respect and a willingness to listen, which can contribute to creating an atmosphere of trust.

Taking the time to consider all options and evaluate key aspects of the negotiation can result in more informed and beneficial decisions.

Impatience can lead to hasty decisions that are not advantageous. Being patient allows you to negotiate strategically and obtain more favorable agreements.

Disagreements are common in negotiations. Patience gives you the necessary space to address disagreements constructively and seek mutually beneficial solutions.

Patience is essential for active listening. By giving the other party the time to express their viewpoints, you can better understand their needs and concerns.

Impatience can lead to impulsive emotional responses that can harm the negotiation. Patience allows you to stay calm and respond more effectively.

To practice patience in negotiation, consider the following tips:

Recognize that negotiations can take time and may not be resolved immediately.

If you feel frustrated or anxious, take a moment to breathe deeply and regain your composure.

Allow the other party to express themselves and their views without excessive interruptions.

If you're facing an important decision, don't feel pressured to make it immediately. Take the necessary time to reflect on the implications and possible consequences.

During the negotiation, take moments of reflection to assess progress and consider if adjustments to your approach are necessary.

Patience is related to maintaining a positive attitude. Confront challenges with an open and constructive mindset.

Patience can be a powerful tool in negotiation, as it enables you to manage complexity, maintain emotional control, and make informed decisions. Practicing patience will help you achieve more successful long-term agreements.

If the negotiation will take place online, ensure that your team, internet connection, and software are in optimal condition.

Preparing your technological environment is crucial for a successful virtual negotiation. Here are some steps to ensure everything is in optimal condition:

Ensure you have a stable and high-speed internet connection. Slow or intermittent connections can disrupt communication and delay the negotiation.

Use a reliable computer or device that functions properly. Ensure that the hardware is in good condition and up-to-date.

Make sure all applications and software you will use in the negotiation are up to date. This includes video conferencing software, presentation programs, messaging platforms, etc.

Choose a quiet and well-lit location for the virtual negotiation. Ensure your environment is professional and free of distractions.

Before the negotiation, perform audio and video tests to ensure everything is working correctly. Verify that your webcam, microphone, and speakers are in good working order.

Keep an extra device charged and ready in case an issue arises with your primary equipment during the negotiation.

If you plan to share documents or presentations during the negotiation, make sure they are ready and organized on your device.

If you're using a video conferencing or messaging platform, choose one that is secure and protected against unwanted intrusions.

Ensure you follow best online security practices, such as using strong passwords and protecting your personal information.

In case of unexpected technical issues, have a backup plan. This could include an alternative phone number for communication or an alternate location for the negotiation.

If possible, schedule a test meeting on the video conferencing platform that will be used for the negotiation. This allows you to familiarize yourself with the features and ensure everything works correctly.

If the primary communication platform fails, have an alternative means of communication available, such as a backup phone number or email address.

Preparing your technological environment is essential to ensure a smooth virtual negotiation. By performing these checks and preparations in advance, you'll reduce the possibility of technical interruptions and can focus on the negotiation itself.

If the negotiation is in-person, choose an appropriate location that is neutral and comfortable for both parties.

When negotiation is in-person, selecting the right location is essential to create an environment conducive to dialogue and decision-making. Here are some tips for establishing a suitable setting:

Opt for a location that is neutral and comfortable for both parties. This can be a conference room at a neutral location or an office that is equally accessible to both parties.

Ensure that the location provides privacy for confidential conversations and is free from unwanted interruptions.

Choose a comfortable environment so that people feel relaxed. Ensure there are adequate seating arrangements, and if necessary, provide beverages or snacks to keep everyone comfortable.

Control the lighting and room temperature. Proper lighting and a pleasant temperature contribute to a more agreeable atmosphere.

Before the meeting, remove any distractions that might disrupt the negotiation. This includes turning off unnecessary electronic devices and ensuring there are no annoying noises.

If you plan to use presentations, graphics, or other audiovisual media, ensure the location is equipped with the necessary devices that are in good working order.

If relevant, have a whiteboard or large paper for visual annotations during the negotiation. This can help clarify concepts and track the progress of the discussion.

If the negotiation requires the arrival of guests, ensure you greet them cordially and provide a brief introduction to the location and available amenities.

Before the meeting, check that everything is in order in the negotiation location, from the availability of writing materials to internet connectivity, if necessary.

You can establish rules of conduct at the beginning of the negotiation, such as speaking times and turn-taking, to ensure an orderly and respectful dialogue.

The in-person negotiation environment plays a significant role in creating a conducive atmosphere for decision-making and building solid relationships. Carefully choose the location and pay attention to details to ensure everything is prepared for a successful negotiation.

Ensure your body language reinforces your words and aligns with your objectives.

Your body language plays a crucial role in communication during a negotiation. Ensuring that your body language aligns with your words and objectives can contribute to more effective communication.

Eye contact is essential for conveying confidence and showing that you are engaged in the conversation. Avoid looking down or averting your gaze excessively, as this can be interpreted as lack of interest or distrust.

A genuine smile can help create a friendlier and more relaxed atmosphere. However, ensure that your smile is appropriate for the situation and doesn't appear forced.

Maintain an open and relaxed posture. Avoid crossing your arms or legs, as this can be interpreted as a defensive attitude. Instead, keep your arms at your sides or in your lap.

Use natural and controlled gestures to emphasize your words. Excessive or nervous gestures can be distracting, so practice moderation.

Leaning slightly forward shows interest and engagement in the conversation. However, avoid leaning too much, as it can seem intrusive.

Gestures such as frowning, rolling your eyes, or sighing can be interpreted as signs of disagreement or frustration. Try to maintain a neutral or positive body language.

While listening to the other party, nod occasionally to show that you're following the conversation and understanding what they're saying.

Excessively touching your face can give the impression that you're nervous or insecure. Try to keep your hands on the table or in your lap rather than near your face.

The speed of your speech is also part of your body language. Speaking too fast can make you appear anxious, while speaking too slowly can seem indecisive. Find a pace that is clear and comfortable.

Ensure that your body language aligns with your words. If you're expressing agreement, make sure to nod or use positive gestures. If you're expressing disagreement, your body language should appropriately reflect it.

Being authentic in your body language is essential. Try not to force gestures or facial expressions; instead, let your body language naturally reflect your emotions and attitudes.

Body language is a skill that improves with time and awareness. During the negotiation, pay attention to your own body language and that of the other party to adjust your approach effectively and establish stronger communication.

As the negotiation progresses, continually assess the situation and adjust your strategy as needed.

Evaluating and adapting your approach during a negotiation is essential to maximize your chances of success. Here are some guidelines for doing so effectively:

During the negotiation, listen carefully to what the other party is saying. Pay attention to their needs, concerns, and non-verbal cues. The information you gather can help you adapt your strategy.

If you're unsure about something or need more information, don't hesitate to ask questions. Questions can help clarify important points and better understand the other party's perspective.

Observe how the other party reacts to your proposals and arguments. Signs of approval or disagreement can indicate the direction in which you should adjust your strategy.

Don't cling rigidly to your initial position. If new information arises or the situation evolves, be flexible and consider adjusting your terms and conditions to achieve a more favorable agreement.

As the negotiation progresses, expect the other party to present counterproposals. Be prepared to assess and respond to these counterproposals effectively.

If necessary, review your goals and priorities based on current information and circumstances. You can adjust your goals as you progress to ensure they remain realistic and achievable.

Keep track of the negotiation's progress and assess whether you're moving towards a mutually beneficial agreement. If you feel the negotiation is stalled or not progressing satisfactorily, consider changing your approach.

If you notice that a specific strategy isn't working as expected, recalibrate your approaches. You can try different communication approaches, arguments, or tactics to see if you get more favorable results.

If you're negotiating on behalf of an organization, it's helpful to consult with your team or superiors when necessary. They can offer additional information and insights to help you make more informed decisions.

The ability to stay calm and not react impulsively is essential when adapting your strategy. Don't let emotions hinder your ability to make rational and effective decisions.

While it's important to be flexible, it's also crucial to set clear boundaries and know how far you're willing to concede. Don't overcommit in an attempt to reach an agreement.

Adaptation is an important skill in negotiation. Being able to evaluate and adjust your strategy as you progress can help you achieve more successful and satisfying agreements. The key is to maintain a balance between flexibility and firmness in your objectives.

Preparation is essential, but it's also important to be flexible and willing to adapt as the negotiation unfolds. A combination of strong preparation and adaptation skills can be the key to a successful negotiation.

4.Setting Goals and Boundaries

Establishing goals and limits is a fundamental part of the art of negotiation. Before entering into a negotiation, you should have a solid understanding of what you are trying to achieve. Define your goals clearly and specifically. For example, what outcome do you want to achieve? What are your priorities?

Defining your goals clearly is essential before entering any negotiation. Setting specific goals provides you with a clear direction and helps you maintain focus during the negotiation process.

Start by determining what the desired outcome of the negotiation is. Ask yourself what you are trying to achieve, whether it's a sales agreement, a contract, mutual commitment, etc.

It's important to be as specific as possible. For example, instead of saying "I want a good deal," you can say "I want a 10% discount on the purchase price" or "I want the contract to include a penalty clause for late delivery."

Not all goals are equally important. Prioritize your goals based on their importance. This will help you make decisions if you need to make concessions on some aspects to achieve what's most important.

Define your limits, meaning the point at which you are willing to concede or accept compromises. It's also helpful to have alternatives in case an agreement with the other party is not reached.

Consider the goals and concerns of the other party. Understanding their needs and perspectives can help you design proposals that are more appealing to them and ultimately facilitate a mutually beneficial agreement.

Ensure that your goals are achievable and realistic. Setting unattainable goals can lead to frustration and a lack of agreement.

Develop strong arguments and strategies to support your goals. Consider how to address possible objections or counterproposals from the other party.

During the negotiation, communicate your goals clearly and respectfully. Explain why they are important to you and how they relate to the interests of both parties.

By defining your goals clearly and specifically, you will be better prepared to conduct a successful negotiation and achieve results that align with your goals and priorities.

If you have multiple goals, prioritize them based on their importance. This will help you focus and adjust your approach during the negotiation.

Prioritizing your goals is a fundamental practice in negotiation, as it allows you to focus your efforts and resources on what matters most to you.

Identify your most important goal in the negotiation. This could be something fundamental, like the price you're willing to pay or the desired outcome you cannot compromise on.

Then, rank the goals that are important but not critical. These may include aspects you want to achieve but are not essential to closing a deal. For example, delivery times, additional warranties, or other contractual terms.

Set a category for goals that would be nice to achieve but are not essential. These goals are flexible and subject to concessions if necessary to achieve your primary goals.

Finally, identify goals that are of low priority or can be sacrificed without significantly affecting your interests. These may be aspects that, while good to achieve, are not crucial to the success of the negotiation.

Once you have prioritized your goals, you can make informed decisions during the negotiation. Focus on achieving your primary goals and, if necessary, use secondary goals as bargaining chips to reach an agreement. Prioritization provides you with a clear guide for making real-time decisions and helps you avoid premature concessions on critical aspects.

Ensure that your goals are realistic and achievable. Don't set unrealistic goals that may jeopardize the negotiation or create unreasonable expectations.

Yes, it's essential to be realistic when setting your goals in a negotiation. Establishing unrealistic goals can have negative consequences, such as jeopardizing the possibility of reaching an agreement or creating unreasonable expectations that can lead to frustration. Here are some guidelines to ensure that your goals are realistic and achievable:

Before entering the negotiation, research and fully understand the situation, circumstances, and limitations involved. This will help you set goals that are in line with reality.

Consider the other party's interests and needs. Make sure your goals are reasonable and that there is room for compromise and cooperation.

Take into account your own resources, time constraints, and capabilities. Ensure that your goals are attainable within your means.

If possible, seek references or comparisons with similar agreements or negotiations. This will provide you with a clearer idea of what is realistic in your situation.

Instead of having a rigid goal, consider setting a range where you'd be satisfied. This provides flexibility to adapt to circumstances and make concessions if necessary.

If you're unsure about the realism of your goals, seek advice from experts or advisors in the field of negotiation. They can provide valuable insights and help you make more informed decisions.

As the negotiation progresses, keep an open mind and be flexible. If you realize that your original goals are not realistic, be willing to adjust them or reevaluate them as new data or information arises.

Setting realistic and achievable goals is essential for effective negotiation. It allows you to maintain a strong stance without compromising the possibility of reaching a mutually beneficial agreement. Additionally, it contributes to building a trusting relationship with the other party, as it demonstrates that you are an honest negotiator willing to find practical solutions.

Before the negotiation, set clear boundaries. How far are you willing to go in terms of price, deadlines, conditions, etc.? Knowing your limits helps you avoid agreements that are not beneficial to you.

Knowing your limits is a crucial part of effective negotiation. Establishing clear boundaries helps you maintain control over your interests and avoid agreements that do not benefit you.

Before entering the negotiation, reflect on what your limits are in terms of price, deadlines, conditions, or other aspects that you are not willing to exceed. Establish these limits in a specific and quantitative manner whenever possible.

Evaluate your options outside of the negotiation. What would you do if an agreement is not reached? Understand your alternatives and how favorable or unfavorable they are compared to the negotiation.

Be honest about your own needs, constraints, and desires. Knowing your limitations will help you avoid commitments that may be detrimental to you in the long run.

During the negotiation, it's important to communicate your limits clearly but without being inflexible. You can express your limitations as a matter of necessity or priority rather than as an ultimatum.

Instead of having rigid limits, consider setting a range within which you are willing to move. This provides you with flexibility to adapt to circumstances and make concessions within certain limits.

During the negotiation, it's important to remain calm and not let emotions lead you to cross your limits. Excessive emotionality can lead to unfavorable agreements.

As the negotiation progresses and new circumstances or information arise, be flexible in reevaluating your limits. You can adjust them if necessary, but do so consciously and strategically.

Knowing your limits provides you with a solid guide during the negotiation and helps you make informed decisions. It also allows you to maintain control over your interests and avoid agreements that are not beneficial to you. However, it's important to balance firmness in your limits with the flexibility necessary to reach a mutually beneficial agreement.

Determine the range of acceptable outcomes for both parties. This will help you identify areas where an agreement can be reached and areas where there is less room for maneuver.

The ZOPA, or Zone of Possible Agreement, is a fundamental concept in negotiation that helps you identify the range of acceptable outcomes for both parties. Determining the ZOPA is essential for finding areas where an agreement can be reached and recognizing areas with less room for maneuver.

Before the negotiation, thoroughly research the other party and their interests. Share information openly and honestly to better understand their needs and priorities.

Determine your goals and limits, as mentioned earlier. This will provide you with a solid foundation for determining your ZOPA.

Identify the interests and needs of both parties in the negotiation. This will allow you to identify areas of overlap and collaboration opportunities.

Based on the information you have gathered, establish an initial range of acceptable outcomes for both parties. This may include a price, deadlines, conditions, or other relevant terms.

Look for areas within your range and that of the other party where there is an overlap. These are the areas where the ZOPA is most likely to be found.

As the negotiation progresses, consider creative options that can expand the ZOPA. This may include alternative business terms or mutual concessions that benefit both parties.

During the negotiation, keep an open mind and seek solutions that fit within the ZOPA. Always strive for a balance between your goals and those of the other party.

Work to reach an agreement within the ZOPA, as this maximizes the chances of satisfaction for both parties.

Determining and using the ZOPA effectively is essential for a successful negotiation. It helps focus your efforts on areas where an agreement is more likely, fostering a mutually beneficial resolution of differences and promoting long-term relationships.

For each goal, be prepared to present logical arguments and justifications that support your position. The more information and evidence you have, the better.

Preparing strong arguments and justifications supported by information and evidence is essential to support your goals in a negotiation. Here is a step-by-step approach to prepare effective arguments:

Start by listing all your goals in the negotiation. These may include aspects such as price, deadlines, conditions, and other relevant terms.

Before preparing arguments, make sure you thoroughly understand your own underlying interests and needs. This will help you articulate your goals more effectively.

Research the situation and gather data and evidence that support your goals. This may include market research, price comparisons, financial data, technical reports, and any other relevant information.

For each goal, create a list of logical arguments that support your position. These arguments should be backed by facts and concrete data. For example, if you want a specific price, you can present data that demonstrates it is reasonable and competitive in the market.

Accompany your arguments with clear justifications. Explain why your goals are important and how they relate to your interests and needs. This helps the other party understand your perspective.

Consider possible objections that the other party may raise and be prepared to respond to them in a logical and convincing manner. This shows that you have considered different perspectives and are willing to address them.

Practice presenting your arguments so that you can communicate them clearly and persuasively during the negotiation. This will help you remain calm and confident at the critical moment.

During the negotiation, make sure to communicate your arguments effectively and listen carefully to the other party's arguments. Open and respectful communication is essential.

If new information arises or circumstances change during the negotiation, be flexible and adjust your arguments as needed.

Preparing strong arguments supported by information and evidence gives you a significant advantage in negotiation. It shows that you have done your homework and that your goals are reasonable and justified. It also allows you to effectively communicate why your goals are important and how they benefit both parties in the pursuit of a mutually beneficial agreement.

Before starting the negotiation, establish your limits and conditions. This includes financial limits, deadlines, and conditions that you are not willing to modify.

Setting boundaries before a negotiation is a fundamental practice to protect your interests and ensure you do not compromise your position unfairly. Here are some guidelines for establishing clear boundaries before entering a negotiation:

Setting boundaries before a negotiation is a fundamental practice to protect your interests and ensure you do not compromise your position unfairly. Here are some guidelines for establishing clear boundaries before entering a negotiation:

Determine the maximum you are willing to pay or the minimum you are willing to accept in financial terms. Set these limits based on your budget, market analysis, and financial goals.

Establish specific deadlines for the negotiation and consider critical dates that may be important to you. Make sure the deadlines are realistic and achievable.

Identify conditions that are fundamental and that you are not willing to modify. This could include aspects such as product or service quality, warranties, payment terms, confidentiality clauses, among others.

Ensure that your limits do not compromise your primary goals in the negotiation. If a limit is crossed, it should be for a reason that justifies a compromise based on your fundamental interests.

During the negotiation, communicate your boundaries clearly and respectfully. Explain why they are important to you and how they relate to your goals and interests.

While it's important to have clear boundaries, you should also be willing to be flexible in areas where there is room for compromise. Flexibility can be essential for achieving a successful agreement.

Anticipate possible objections or challenges the other party may present regarding your boundaries and be prepared to respond logically and convincingly.

Always keep the end result in mind and whether the proposed agreement, even if it crosses some of your boundaries, is still beneficial overall.

Setting boundaries before negotiation helps you maintain control of your interests and avoid detrimental compromises. However, it's important to balance firmness in your boundaries with the ability to be flexible in areas where a mutually beneficial agreement can be reached.

During the negotiation, communicate your boundaries clearly and respectfully. Make sure the other party understands your restrictions and why they are important.

Communicating your boundaries clearly and respectfully is essential for effective negotiation. Here are some guidelines on how to do it properly:

Choose the right time to communicate your boundaries. It may be appropriate to do so at the beginning of the negotiation or when a specific issue related to those boundaries arises.

Avoid ambiguity or vagueness when communicating your boundaries. Use clear and direct language to prevent misunderstandings.

Communicate your boundaries in a respectful and professional manner. Avoid being confrontational or aggressive, as this can hinder communication and cooperation.

Don't just set your boundaries; explain why they are important to you. This helps the other party understand your motivations and underlying needs.

When relevant, provide specific examples that support your boundaries. This can help illustrate your points and make them more understandable.

After communicating your boundaries, listen carefully to the other party's response and concerns. Communication should be a two-way process.

If possible, offer solutions or alternatives that allow both parties to find common ground. This shows that you are willing to collaborate.

Maintain composure and patience, even if the other party disagrees with your boundaries. Excessive emotionality can hinder negotiation.

If the negotiation continues and your boundaries are questioned again, reaffirm your position consistently and patiently.

Seek a balance between being firm in your boundaries and being willing to be flexible in other aspects of the negotiation. Flexibility can be essential for reaching a mutually beneficial agreement.

Communicating your boundaries clearly and respectfully helps establish clear expectations and promotes open and constructive communication with the other party. It also contributes to building a solid foundation for negotiation and the possibility of reaching a satisfactory agreement for both parties.

Maintain firmness regarding your boundaries, but also show flexibility when necessary. Flexibility can be useful in finding mutually beneficial solutions.

Being firm yet flexible is an important strategy in negotiation. While it's crucial to maintain firmness in relation to your boundaries and goals, flexibility allows you to adapt to changing circumstances and find mutually beneficial solutions. Here are some guidelines on how to balance firmness with flexibility in a negotiation:

Define your boundaries and goals clearly and specifically before entering the negotiation. This provides a strong foundation for your position.

During the negotiation, communicate your boundaries clearly and respectfully, as mentioned earlier. Ensure that the other party understands your restrictions and why they are important.

Pay attention to the needs and goals of the other party. Active listening helps you understand their concerns and identify areas where you can be flexible.

Instead of simply defending your positions, work together to find creative solutions that satisfy both parties. Flexibility in seeking alternatives can be valuable.

In some cases, you may be willing to make strategic concessions in areas where you have room to do so. This can foster reciprocity and help build a trustful relationship.

While you can be flexible in certain aspects, make sure your primary goals are not compromised. Do not yield on fundamental areas for you.

During the negotiation, continually assess the balance between firmness and flexibility. Make sure you are protecting your interests while seeking opportunities for compromise.

As mentioned earlier, work to identify and expand the Zone of Possible Agreement (ZOPA) where both parties can find common ground.

Negotiation can be a lengthy and sometimes challenging process. Maintain composure and patience, even when obstacles arise.

Being firm yet flexible is an essential skill in negotiation. It allows you to advocate for your interests while seeking opportunities for mutually beneficial agreements. The ability to adapt to circumstances and be creative in finding solutions can make a difference in a successful negotiation.

As the negotiation progresses, try to understand the other party's boundaries. This can help you find areas of compromise that benefit both parties.

Evaluating the other party's boundaries is an important part of effective negotiation. By understanding their constraints and needs, you can identify areas where both parties can find common ground and reach mutually beneficial agreements.

Pay attention to what the other party is saying and try to understand their goals and concerns. Active listening is key to gaining insight into their boundaries.

Ask open and strategic questions to gather more information about the other party's boundaries. Questions like "What are your priorities?" or "What are your financial constraints?" can reveal valuable information.

Pay attention to non-verbal cues, such as body language and facial expressions from the other party. These signals can provide clues about their emotions and comfort levels with certain topics.

Consider the other party's history in previous negotiations, as well as their behavior during the current negotiation. This can help you understand their patterns and limitations.

Understand the current situation of the other party, including any challenges or changes they may be facing. These factors can influence their boundaries.

Observe the concessions the other party has made in the negotiation so far. This can provide insights into their boundaries and priorities.

Promote open and constructive communication with the other party. The more open the communication, the easier it is to gather information about their boundaries.

As you learn more about the other party's boundaries, look for areas where mutual compromise may exist. You can explore solutions that take into account their constraints and yours.

Throughout the process, demonstrate respect and consideration toward the other party. Mutual respect contributes to building a trusting relationship and facilitates the exploration of mutually beneficial solutions.

Evaluating the other party's boundaries is a valuable skill in negotiation. It allows you to better understand their needs and constraints, which, in turn, helps you find solutions that benefit both parties and build strong business relationships.

If the situation changes or new information emerges during the negotiation, do not hesitate to reassess your boundaries. Sometimes, adjusting them may be necessary to reach a satisfactory agreement.

Reassessing your boundaries during a negotiation is a sensible and strategic practice. Circumstances can change, new data or relevant information may arise, and adapting your boundaries can be essential for achieving a satisfactory agreement. Here are some guidelines on how to effectively reassess your boundaries:

Stay informed and attentive to any changes in the situation or negotiation dynamics. This could include new market information, the other party's needs, or external factors.

Evaluate the importance of your boundaries in light of the new information. Are they still fundamental to your interests, or do they need adjustment based on the circumstances?

If you decide to reassess and adjust your boundaries, communicate your intentions openly and transparently to the other party. Explain why you are considering a change and how it would benefit both parties. Reassessing your boundaries demonstrates adaptability and a willingness to find mutually satisfactory solutions.

Make sure that any adjustments to your boundaries do not compromise your primary goals in the negotiation. If a change negatively affects your fundamental interests, you should consider whether it is acceptable.

As you reassess your boundaries, remember to keep flexibility in mind. Flexibility allows you to adapt to changing circumstances and find solutions in a constantly evolving negotiation environment.

When reassessing your boundaries, consider how they fit into the overall agreement. Ensure that any change contributes to a more satisfactory overall outcome.

Keep your alternatives outside the negotiation in mind. If you adjust your boundaries, consider whether you still have viable options if an agreement cannot be reached.

Reassessing your boundaries during a negotiation demonstrates adaptability and a willingness to find mutually beneficial solutions. However, it's important to do so strategically and with a focus on achieving an agreement that aligns with your primary interests.

When communicating your boundaries, do so with composure and confidence. Do not let pressure or emotions lead you to compromise on important limits.

Maintaining composure and confidence when communicating your boundaries is essential for effective negotiation.

Before the negotiation, prepare thoroughly, as mentioned in previous tips. The better you prepare, the more confidence you will have in your arguments and boundaries.

During the negotiation, if you feel under pressure or emotionally tense, take a moment to breathe deeply and regain your composure. Keep control over your emotions to make rational decisions.

Communicate your boundaries clearly and unwaveringly. Speak with a firm and confident voice to convey your determination.

Maintain a respectful tone and avoid unnecessary confrontation. Calm and confidence do not equate to aggression. You can be firm without being confrontational.

Your body language also communicates calm and confidence. Maintain an upright posture, eye contact, and composed gestures.

Keep your primary goals in mind and remember why they are important to you. This will help you maintain composure and confidence when defending your boundaries.

Assertiveness involves communicating your boundaries in a respectful yet firm manner. Practicing these skills will improve your ability to express your needs effectively.

Listen attentively to the other party's responses and concerns. Empathy and active listening can contribute to more effective communication and a more satisfactory resolution.

Remember that calm and confidence in negotiation pertain not only to the immediate outcome but also to building strong, long-term relationships.

After the negotiation, reflect on what worked well and what you could improve in terms of maintaining calm and confidence. Past experiences can be valuable lessons. Calm and confidence are powerful attributes in negotiation. They help you advocate for your interests effectively and build strong business relationships. Practicing these skills will enable you to face challenges with determination and maintain control in high-pressure situations.

5.Creating Value in Negotiation

Creating value in negotiation refers to the process of finding ways to increase the mutual benefits of the parties involved, rather than simply dividing or distributing a fixed value. In other words, it seeks to maximize the total value available to both parties instead of focusing solely on obtaining a larger share for oneself. Here are some key strategies for creating value in negotiation:

Instead of focusing on rigid positions, work to understand the underlying interests and needs of both parties. You will often discover areas of overlap where mutual interests can be met.

Identifying shared interests and needs is a fundamental step in creating value in negotiation. Here are some tips on how to go about this process:

During the negotiation, use open-ended questions to encourage the discussion of interests and needs. Questions like "What are your main concerns in this negotiation?" or "What is most important to you in this agreement?" can help uncover underlying interests.

Listen carefully to what the other party is saying and show genuine interest in their perspectives. Pay attention to keywords and recurring themes that may indicate hidden interests and needs.

When the other party presents a position or request, inquire about the "why" behind that request. Ask about the motives and reasons that lead them to take that position.

As the conversation progresses, look for areas of overlap between your interests and those of the other party. It can be helpful to note these points of agreement.

It's not just about discovering the other party's interests but also sharing your own. The more open the communication, the easier it is to find areas of overlap.

Underlying needs are often more fundamental than stated positions. Ask yourself and the other party what needs they are trying to satisfy through the negotiation.

Try to put yourself in the other party's shoes to understand their perspectives and feelings. Empathy can help identify shared interests and needs.

Once you've identified shared interests and needs, work together to find creative solutions that satisfy them. Creativity can be a powerful tool for value creation.

Focus on shared interests and needs as a starting point for the negotiation. This can help build common ground for decision-making.

Throughout the negotiation, regularly reaffirm shared interests and needs to maintain a focus on value creation.

Identifying shared interests and needs is essential to finding solutions that benefit both parties and maximizing value in negotiation. By adopting an approach of mutual understanding and collaboration, it's more likely that satisfactory and lasting agreements will be reached.

Instead of competing, work together with the other party to address common challenges. Focus together on finding solutions that satisfy both parties and maximize the total value.

Collaboration in problem-solving is a key strategy for creating value in negotiation. Instead of adopting a competitive approach, it involves working together with the other party to find solutions that are beneficial for both parties and maximize the total value. Here are some guidelines on how to collaborate effectively in problem-solving during negotiation:

Begin the negotiation with a collaborative and friendly tone. Express your willingness to work together to find mutually beneficial solutions.

Identify the challenges or problems both parties face in the negotiation. This can include common obstacles such as budget constraints, tight deadlines, or technical requirements.

Encourage joint brainstorming. Encourage both parties to contribute their perspectives and suggestions for addressing the identified issues.

Don't limit yourself to a single solution. Explore multiple approaches and possible solutions to the identified problems. This increases the likelihood of finding an optimal solution.

Analyze the advantages and disadvantages of each proposed solution. This can help determine which ones are most viable and beneficial for both parties.

When making decisions, prioritize common interests and mutual benefits. This helps ensure that both parties benefit from the solution.

Collaboration may involve mutual concessions in areas where both parties can do so without sacrificing their fundamental interests. This promotes reciprocity and trust-building.

Open and effective communication is essential for successful collaboration. Ensure that ideas, concerns, and perspectives are shared clearly.

Trust is fundamental in collaboration. Keep your commitments and work to build a trusting relationship with the other party.

Creativity is an important element in collaborative problem-solving. Don't be afraid to consider innovative and unconventional solutions.

At the end of the negotiation, evaluate the overall outcome to ensure the solution is satisfactory and beneficial to both parties.

Collaboration in problem-solving is a constructive approach that can lead to stronger agreements and more solid business relationships. By working together to address common challenges, parties can maximize the total value and achieve more satisfactory and enduring solutions.

Try to expand the Zone of Possible Agreement (ZOPA) by identifying new options and opportunities. This could involve mutual concessions or the creation of value packages that satisfy both parties.

Expanding the Zone of Possible Agreement (ZOPA) is a fundamental strategy in negotiation to create value and increase the chances of reaching a mutually beneficial agreement. Here are some strategies for expanding the ZOPA:

Understand the preferences and priorities of both parties. The better you understand what is most important to each party, the easier it is to find options that expand the ZOPA.

Find shared interests and needs that may not necessarily be reflected in the initial positions. Often, these underlying interests can open up new opportunities.

Explore various alternatives and solutions that satisfy the interests of both parties. The more options you consider, the more likely you are to find an optimal solution.

Value packages combine various concessions and elements of the agreement into a set that benefits both parties. This may include agreements on prices, timelines, conditions, and other terms.

When making concessions, ensure that the value of what you receive in return is equal to or greater than the value of what you concede. This contributes to the expansion of the Zone of Possible Agreement (ZOPA).

Find a balance between what you offer and what you receive. Negotiation should be fair and equitable for both parties.

Offer reciprocal concessions. If you take a step towards the other party, they are more likely to reciprocate, thus expanding the ZOPA.

Seek solutions where both parties benefit. A win-win solution expands the ZOPA and fosters a strong business relationship.

During the negotiation, communicate openly and transparently about your goals, needs, and willingness to consider options that expand the ZOPA.

Consider how each element of the agreement contributes to the overall value. Sometimes, conceding on a particular aspect can lead to greater overall value.

Expanding the ZOPA requires creativity, flexibility, and a deep understanding of the needs and desires of both parties. By adopting a collaborative approach and seeking innovative solutions, you can increase the likelihood of reaching an agreement that benefits everyone involved.

Maintain open and transparent communication with the other party. This facilitates the identification of value-creating opportunities and builds trust in the negotiation.

Promoting open and transparent communication is essential in any negotiation process. Effective communication facilitates the identification of opportunities for value creation and contributes to the development of a trusting relationship between the parties. Here are some guidelines for promoting open communication in negotiation:

From the beginning, work to establish an environment of trust in which both parties feel comfortable sharing their perspectives and concerns.

Pay attention to what the other party is saying. Active listening involves not only hearing the words but also understanding the needs and desires behind those words.

Use open-ended questions to encourage a deeper conversation. Questions like "Can you tell me more about that?" or "What are your main concerns?" can generate a richer discussion.

Do not hesitate to share your own goals and interests. The more transparent your intentions, the easier it is to find areas of agreement.

Avoid ambiguity or lack of clarity in your communications. Use clear and direct language to prevent misunderstandings.

Observe the body language and facial expressions of the other party. Often, these signals can provide additional information about their emotions and perspectives.

Communicate any changes or new information in a timely manner. Last-minute surprises can undermine trust and hinder value creation.

Identify and build on areas where both parties agree or have common interests. This can be a starting point for collaboration.

If misunderstandings arise, address them immediately to clarify any confusion and prevent issues from accumulating.

Communication should be respectful at all times, even when disagreements arise. Keep calm and composed to maintain a constructive tone in the negotiation.

In some negotiations, it may be helpful to involve external experts or mediators to facilitate communication and the search for solutions.

Open and transparent communication is a crucial component of value creation in negotiation. By fostering an environment in which both parties feel free to share their ideas and needs, you increase the chances of finding solutions that benefit everyone involved.

Listen carefully to the concerns and needs of the other party. Ask about their goals and be willing to consider their perspectives.

Active listening is a fundamental skill in negotiation. It involves paying careful and genuine attention to what the other party is saying, understanding their concerns and needs, and demonstrating that you are willing to consider their perspectives. Here are some guidelines for practicing active listening in negotiation:

Ensure you are in a distraction-free environment and can fully focus on the conversation.

Eye contact is a sign of attention and shows the other party that you are engaged in the conversation.

Avoid interrupting the other party while they speak. Let them express their views before responding.

Nodding and using affirmative gestures, such as nodding or smiling, can show that you are listening and understanding what is being said.

Occasionally, restate what the other party has said in your own words to ensure you have understood correctly. This also shows that you are engaged in the conversation.

Ask open and clear questions to delve deeper into issues and better understand concerns and needs.

While the other party speaks, avoid planning your responses in your mind. Instead, focus on what is being said in that moment.

Maintain composure and self-control, even if the conversation becomes emotional. Active listening involves listening without judging or reacting immediately.

Try to understand and empathize with the emotions and perspectives of the other party. Empathy can help build a stronger relationship.

Don't feel like you have to solve all the issues immediately. Sometimes, it's necessary to listen fully before addressing concerns.

Don't let biases or prior assumptions influence your ability to actively listen. Keep an open mind.

Active listening not only allows you to better understand the needs and perspectives of the other party but also contributes to more effective communication and the building of a trust-based relationship. In negotiation, the ability to actively listen is essential for finding mutually beneficial solutions and reaching satisfactory agreements.

Instead of conceding on fundamental areas, consider making strategic concessions in less critical areas for you. This can foster reciprocity and value creation.

Offering strategic concessions is a smart tactic in negotiation as it allows you to maintain control over critical areas while fostering reciprocity and value creation. Here are some tips on how to effectively implement this strategy:

Before the negotiation, identify the areas where you are willing to make concessions. These areas should be less critical to your primary goals.

Maintain a clear understanding of your fundamental goals and needs in the negotiation. These are the elements you are not willing to compromise.

When making a concession, communicate it strategically and as part of a broader strategy. Explain how this concession can be beneficial for both parties and contribute to value creation.

Encourage the other party to make reciprocal concessions in areas that are less critical for them. Reciprocity is a key principle in negotiation and can lead to more effective collaboration.

Ensure that the value of what you receive in exchange for your concessions is equal to or greater than the value of what you concede. This way, you continue to progress toward your goals.

Avoid making significant concessions too early in the negotiation. Wait until you have gained a more complete understanding of the other party's needs and priorities.

As the negotiation progresses, maintain the flexibility to adjust your concessions based on changes in the dynamics or emerging needs.

Before making a concession, evaluate how it will impact your primary goals. Make sure your concessions do not compromise your fundamental interests.

Keep a record of the concessions you make and those received by the other party. This will help you assess fairness in the negotiation process.

Sometimes, concessions can lead to creative solutions that benefit both parties in ways you may not have anticipated.

Offering strategic concessions is an effective strategy for advancing in negotiation without compromising your key objectives. When done intelligently and thoughtfully, it can foster a collaborative environment and create value for both parties.

Focus your efforts on finding solutions that benefit both parties instead of trying to win at the expense of the other. A win-win solution is one in which both parties achieve a favorable outcome.

Seeking win-win solutions is a fundamental strategy in negotiation, as it focuses on finding outcomes that are beneficial for both you and the other party. A win-win solution does not imply that both parties get exactly what they initially wanted, but it strives to find a balance that is satisfactory and fair for both.

Before seeking a solution, ensure you fully understand the needs, goals, and concerns of both yourself and the other party.

Work with the other party to generate a variety of options and solutions. The more ideas considered, the more likely it is to find a win-win solution.

Evaluate the value of each proposed option for both parties. Consider how each solution will impact the interests and needs of both parties.

Focus your efforts on the interests and needs both parties share. These are ideal starting points for seeking mutually beneficial solutions.

Maintain a collaborative and friendly attitude during the negotiation. This encourages both parties' willingness to find an equitable solution.

Clearly and honestly explain your interests and concerns. This allows the other party to understand your needs and how they can be met.

Listen carefully to the perspectives and needs of the other party. Active listening is essential to finding solutions that benefit both parties.

Often, win-win solutions involve compromises by both parties. Be willing to concede on some points if it leads to a more equitable and beneficial outcome.

At the end of the negotiation, assess the overall outcome to ensure it is a win-win solution. Consider how the solution satisfies the interests and needs of both parties.

Win-win solutions contribute to building strong long-term relationships. Consider how your actions in the current negotiation can affect future interactions.

Focusing on the long term is an essential strategy in negotiation, recognizing that long-term relationships are fundamental in business. Here are some guidelines on how to maintain a long-term focus in your negotiations:

Trust is the foundation of long-term relationships. Work to build and maintain trust with the other party throughout the negotiation.

Be punctual and fulfill the commitments you make during the negotiation. This demonstrates your reliability and strengthens the other party's trust in you.

Instead of seeking short-term advantages, consider how your actions and agreements can have a positive impact on the long-term relationship. This may include considerations of service quality, customer loyalty, and reputation.

Avoid making impulsive decisions that could irreparably damage the relationship. Even if you cannot reach an agreement in a specific negotiation, maintaining respectful communication can allow for future opportunities.

As mentioned earlier, seek solutions that are beneficial for both parties. This promotes cooperation and the other party's willingness to do business with you in the future.

Conflicts can arise in any relationship. When they do, address them constructively and seek solutions that meet the needs of both parties.

Keep a record of past interactions and agreements with the other party. This can be useful for referencing previous agreements and maintaining consistency in business relationships.

If you intend to build a long-term relationship with the other party, communicate it openly and honestly. This can lay the foundation for a lasting collaboration.

Before making significant decisions, consider how they will affect the long-term relationship. Evaluate the balance between short-term benefits and potential long-term costs.

Reflect on past negotiations and learn from the experiences to improve your negotiation skills and build stronger relationships in the future.

By maintaining a focus on the long term in your negotiations, you can build strong and sustainable relationships that benefit both parties. Long-term business relationships are often more valuable and fruitful than short-term interactions and can lead to ongoing collaboration opportunities.

At the end of the negotiation, evaluate the total value created for both parties. This may involve analyzing financial benefits, improvements in the relationship, and the satisfaction of mutual goals.

Evaluating the total value at the end of a negotiation is an important practice to measure the success and effectiveness of the agreement reached. Here are some steps to conduct this evaluation:

Start by reviewing the goals you set at the beginning of the negotiation. Were these goals achieved? To what extent?

If the negotiation involved financial terms, such as prices, payment terms, or discounts, calculate the financial impact for both parties. Were favorable conditions obtained? Is the agreement profitable?

Analyze how the relationship between the parties has evolved as a result of the negotiation. Has trust been strengthened? Has a foundation been established for future collaborations?

Obtain feedback from both parties regarding their satisfaction with the agreement. Are they happy with the terms and conditions? Do they feel respected and valued?

Examine the concessions and commitments made by both parties. Were they fair? Were promises kept?

Integrate all these assessments to measure the total value of the agreement. This may include financial benefits, improvements in the relationship, and the satisfaction of mutual goals.

If the evaluation reveals areas where the agreement could have been more beneficial, use this information to identify opportunities for improvement in future negotiations.

Reflect on what worked well and what could have been done differently. Use the experience to enhance your negotiation skills and strategies in the future.

Keep a record of the total value assessments of each agreement for future reference in negotiations. This can help you make informed decisions and build stronger business relationships.

Total value evaluation is an important part of the negotiation process, as it allows both parties to understand the impact of the agreement and how it contributes to their respective goals. It also contributes to the building of long-lasting and mutually beneficial business relationships.

Do not be afraid to be creative in seeking solutions. Sometimes, innovative ideas can lead to greater value creation.

Creativity plays a crucial role in negotiation and can lead to innovative solutions that generate more value for both parties. Here are some ways to foster creativity in seeking solutions during a negotiation:

Create a negotiation environment that encourages the expression of creative ideas. Encourage parties to think outside the box and share their ideas freely.

Brainstorming is an effective technique for generating creative ideas. Invite both parties to participate in a brainstorming session to explore new solutions.

Creativity often arises when making unexpected connections between situations or concepts. Look for analogies and metaphors that can help you understand the situation differently.

Do not limit yourself to conventional solutions. Consider unconventional options that may satisfy the interests of both parties in unexpected ways.

In some negotiations, it can be helpful to consult with experts or people with experience in the subject. Their perspectives can provide valuable and creative ideas.

Lateral thinking techniques, such as role-playing or reverse thinking, can help you explore new perspectives and solutions.

Sometimes, creativity arises from combining elements of different proposals to create a unique solution.

Creative inspiration often comes from unexpected sources. Explore other fields or industries to find ideas that can be applied to your negotiation situation.

Creativity thrives when you have an open mind and are willing to consider ideas that may initially seem unconventional.

Examine proposed solutions from different perspectives to understand their viability and potential benefits.

Once you have identified a creative solution, test it and adjust it as needed. Creativity often involves an iterative process.

Creativity in negotiation can lead to surprising and valuable solutions that benefit both parties. Do not be afraid to think innovatively and explore new ways to create value in your negotiations.

Value creation in negotiation is a constructive approach that can lead to stronger agreements and business relationships. By focusing on mutual satisfaction of interests and needs, parties can achieve more satisfying and lasting results.

6.Concessions: When to Yield and How to Do It Effectively

Concessions are a crucial component of any negotiation. Knowing when to yield and how to do so effectively is essential for achieving mutually beneficial agreements. Ensure that any concession you make translates into a benefit or reciprocity from the other party. Avoid giving in without getting anything in return.

Ensuring that any concession you make translates into a benefit or reciprocity from the other party is essential in a negotiation. Here are some additional points to consider when applying this principle:

When making a concession, ensure that the value of what you receive in return is equal to or greater than the value of the concession you are offering. This ensures that the negotiation is fair and beneficial for both parties.

Before making a concession, ask the other party what they are willing to offer in return. This will help you understand if their offer is acceptable and if the concession you are considering is worthwhile.

Effectively communicate your expectations and needs. If the other party wants you to make a concession, make sure they understand your priorities and requirements.

Avoid giving in just because the other party is applying pressure. Ensure that the concession you make is fair and reasonable in the context of the negotiation.

Consider how concessions can affect the long-term relationship. Sometimes, making a small concession in the present can lead to stronger business relationships and more beneficial future agreements.

Promote a spirit of reciprocity in the negotiation. If you make a significant concession, expect the other party to make an effort to move towards an agreement.

The goal in a negotiation is to reach a mutually beneficial agreement. Making strategic concessions that result in fair and equitable benefits for both parties is essential to achieving that goal. Maintain a balance between flexibility and protecting your interests to maximize negotiation outcomes.

If the negotiation stalls and does not progress, consider making a strategic concession to break the deadlock and move forward.

Breaking a deadlock in a negotiation can be a challenge, but making strategic concessions can be an effective tool to rekindle discussions and progress towards an agreement. Here are some tips on how to do it effectively:

Before making a concession, try to understand why the negotiation has stalled. It can be helpful to ask the other party about their concerns or points of disagreement. The better you understand the cause, the more effective your concession will be.

Evaluate your goals and priorities. Identify what is most important to you and what is less critical. This will help you determine in which areas you are willing to make concessions.

Before making a concession, ensure you have clear limits. Decide how much you are willing to concede and how far you can go without compromising your core interests.

When making a concession, communicate it clearly and directly. Explain why you are willing to make it and how it benefits both parties. This can help build trust and encourage reciprocity.

You can ask the other party what concessions they are willing to make in exchange for yours. Reciprocity is an important part of overcoming a deadlock.

Instead of making a large concession right away, consider making gradual concessions. This allows the other party to make moves as well and creates a sense of progress.

Do not rigidly cling to your original position. Flexibility is key to overcoming deadlocks. Be willing to adjust your terms and conditions to move towards an agreement.

Explore alternative or creative solutions that can meet the needs of both parties. Sometimes, thinking outside the box can help overcome obstacles.

Look for areas where both parties can agree or that are less controversial. This can help rebuild trust and move towards more contentious areas.

As you make concessions and the negotiation progresses, evaluate whether progress is being made. If you see that the other party is also making efforts to overcome the deadlock, it is a positive sign of progress.

Overcoming a deadlock may require patience and effective communication skills. By being strategic in your concessions and focusing on finding mutually beneficial solutions, you can rekindle discussions and move towards a satisfactory agreement.

In some situations, it is important to make concessions to maintain a long-term working relationship or collaboration. This is especially relevant when negotiating with a business partner or regular customer.

Maintaining a positive relationship is crucial in many negotiations, especially when it comes to business agreements or long-term collaborations. Here are some tips on how to make concessions to preserve and strengthen positive relationships:

Before making a concession, reflect on the importance of the relationship with the other party. If this relationship is crucial for your business or holds significant value, you will be more inclined to make concessions to maintain it.

Let the other party know that you value the relationship and are willing to make concessions for the sake of a sustainable and mutually beneficial long-term collaboration.

Despite your desire to maintain a positive relationship, it is important to set clear boundaries. Decide how much you are willing to concede without compromising your fundamental interests or values.

Instead of viewing concessions as losses, look for solutions that are beneficial for both parties. This can help build a relationship based on cooperation and mutual benefit.

Trust is essential for maintaining positive relationships. Fulfill your commitments and be honest in your dealings. Mutual trust is crucial for long-term collaborations.

If you make significant concessions, consider including review clauses in the agreement. These clauses allow for a reevaluation and adjustment of terms if circumstances change.

Maintain open and honest communication with the other party. If issues or concerns arise, address them constructively and seek solutions.

Appreciate the effort and cooperation of the other party. Recognition and gratitude can further strengthen the relationship.

Instead of focusing on differences or disagreements, keep the focus on shared goals. This can help keep the collaboration on the right track.

Sometimes, short-term concessions can lead to significant long-term benefits in terms of successful business relationships or collaborations.

Maintaining a positive relationship is a valuable asset in the world of business and beyond. Making strategic concessions to preserve and strengthen these relationships can be a wise investment in long-term success. In certain cases, you may consider yielding on less critical aspects or those that do not significantly affect your primary objectives.

Making concessions on less critical aspects or those that do not significantly affect your primary objectives is an effective negotiation strategy. Here are some additional guidelines on how to apply this strategy effectively:

Before entering the negotiation, identify the aspects in which you are willing to make low-value concessions. These could be minor details, secondary terms, or issues that are not crucial to your primary objectives.

Classify your objectives in terms of essential and desirable. Essential elements are fundamental to your success in the negotiation, while desirable aspects may enhance the agreement but are not essential.

During the negotiation, communicate your priorities to the other party. Let them know which aspects are of utmost importance to you and in which you are willing to be more flexible.

You can use low-value concessions as bargaining chips. Offer to make a concession in a less critical area in exchange for advantages in an area that matters more to you.

When making concessions on low-value aspects, keep your long-term goals in mind. Sometimes, making tactical concessions in the short term can contribute to a positive working relationship and mutually beneficial agreements in the future.

Ensure that concessions on low-value aspects do not have an adverse impact on your primary objectives or the overall value of the agreement.

If an aspect is non-essential and does not add value to the negotiation, it may not be necessary to make any concessions. In such cases, maintaining your position may be the best strategy.

If you make a low-value concession, ensure that the compensation you receive is fair and equitable in relation to the value of the concession you are making.

Keep a record of the concessions you make during the negotiation to avoid misunderstandings and ensure that both parties are on the same page.

Making concessions on low-value aspects is a smart way to balance your interests and contribute to a successful negotiation. The key is to be strategic and attentive to how these concessions can influence the overall outcome of the negotiation.

If new circumstances or information arise that justify an adjustment to your terms, it is appropriate to consider a concession.

When circumstances change during a negotiation, it is essential to be willing to consider concessions to adapt to the new reality. Here are some guidelines on how to handle changes in circumstances and when to consider making concessions:

If a significant change in circumstances that could affect the negotiation occurs, communicate it to the other party honestly and promptly. Transparency is crucial.

Analyze how the changes affect your goals and priorities in the negotiation. Are the changes significant enough to justify a modification of your terms?

When circumstances change, consider different options to adapt to the new situation. This may include adjustments in timelines, terms, or prices.

If you believe a concession is necessary due to a change in circumstances, communicate your needs and explain why making adjustments is reasonable.

Ask the other party how they view the changes in circumstances and if they are willing to make concessions or adjustments accordingly.

Seek solutions that are beneficial for both parties. Changes in circumstances can open new opportunities to reach agreements that would not otherwise be possible.

Although it is appropriate to consider concessions due to changes in circumstances, do not yield excessively or compromise your core interests. Ensure that any concession is fair and equitable.

If a new agreement is reached based on the changing circumstances, make sure to clearly document the revised terms in writing. This prevents future misunderstandings.

As the negotiation progresses, continue to assess how changes in circumstances may affect your goals and strategies. Be willing to adjust your approach if necessary.

Flexibility is key in negotiation, especially when circumstances are dynamic. Be open to adaptation and seek creative solutions.

In a negotiation, the ability to adapt to changes in circumstances is essential for achieving successful agreements. Remaining open to strategic concessions when circumstances warrant it can be an effective way to navigate changing situations and achieve satisfactory outcomes.

When making a concession, communicate it clearly and directly. Explain why you are willing to make the concession and how it benefits both parties.

Effective communication of your concessions is essential in a negotiation, as it helps build trust and ensures that both parties understand the purpose and value of the concessions. Here are some tips on how to communicate your concessions clearly:

When communicating a concession, avoid beating around the bush or ambiguities. Explain your willingness to make the concession directly and straightforwardly.

Explain why you are willing to make the concession. Provide context about the reasons behind the concession and how it relates to the negotiation's objectives.

Show how the concession can be beneficial for both parties. This can help the other party understand that you are seeking a fair agreement.

Avoid jargon or complicated language that may lead to misunderstandings. Use clear and simple language to ensure that the other party fully understands your intentions.

After communicating your concession, listen carefully to the other party's response. Pay attention to their reaction and any comments they make about the concession.

Offer the other party the opportunity to ask questions or express concerns about the concession. This can help clarify any misunderstandings.

Encourage the other party to share their thoughts and opinions on the concession. Being open to dialogue can help reach an agreement that satisfies both parties.

If the other party makes counterproposals related to your concession, be receptive and consider these proposals seriously. It can be an opportunity to find mutually beneficial solutions.

Once both parties have agreed on the concession, make sure to document the terms in writing. This prevents future misunderstandings and provides a clear record of the agreements.

Honest and transparent communication is essential. Maintain trust and integrity in all your interactions to build a solid foundation in the negotiation.

Clear and effective communication of your concessions is a fundamental part of a successful negotiation. By explaining your intentions and benefits transparently, you can promote a collaborative atmosphere and move closer to an agreement that satisfies both parties.

Before making a concession, ensure that you are yielding on an aspect that is less critical to you or of lower value.

Prioritizing your concessions is a smart strategy in negotiation, as it allows you to manage your resources and concessions more effectively. Here are some steps to prioritize your concessions effectively:

Before entering the negotiation, conduct a detailed assessment of your goals and needs. Rank your goals based on their importance and impact on the final outcome.

Classify your goals in terms of essential and desirable. Essential goals are those that are fundamental to the negotiation's success, while desirable aspects would enhance the agreement but are not critical.

Determine in which areas you are willing to be more flexible. These are the areas where you can consider making concessions more easily.

Before the negotiation, set clear limits for your concessions. Decide how much you are willing to concede in each area and when you should hold your position.

During the negotiation, communicate your priorities to the other party. Let them know which aspects are most important to you and in which you are willing to be more flexible.

Instead of viewing concessions as losses, look for solutions that are beneficial for both parties. This can help build a cooperative relationship and achieve a mutually satisfactory agreement.

If the other party makes counterproposals related to your concessions, evaluate whether these proposals are reasonable and beneficial for both parties.

As the negotiation progresses, maintain flexibility to adjust your priorities and concessions based on the conversation's evolution.

Although you are willing to make concessions in less critical areas, do not yield on aspects that are fundamental to your goals or have a significant impact on the agreement.

Keep a record of the concessions you make during the negotiation to avoid misunderstandings and ensure that both parties are on the same page.

Prioritizing your concessions allows you to maintain control over the negotiation, ensure you are yielding in the right areas, and work toward an agreement that benefits you and the other party. This strategy helps you use your concessions effectively to achieve your goals.

Don't concede on all aspects indiscriminately. Instead, select the concessions that are truly necessary to move toward an agreement.

Being selective with your concessions is a smart strategy in negotiation, as it allows you to conserve and manage your resources more effectively. Here are some additional tips on how to be selective with your concessions:

Before the negotiation, identify your key goals and priorities. These are the aspects in which you are less willing to yield. Focus on protecting and advancing your most important priorities.

Classify your goals in terms of essential and negotiable. Essential goals are those that are fundamental to the negotiation's success, while negotiable aspects are areas in which you can be more flexible.

Before the negotiation, set clear limits for your concessions. Decide how much you are willing to concede in negotiable aspects and when you should hold your position in essential areas.

During the negotiation, communicate your limits to the other party clearly and respectfully. Let them know in which areas you are willing to be more flexible and in which you are not.

Maintain firmness in the essential aspects of your goals. Do not concede in areas that are crucial to your interests or have a significant impact on the desired outcome.

Before making a concession, consider the value it has for you and its importance in the context of the negotiation. Do not concede on aspects that hold high value for you without getting something in return.

If you are considering a concession, make sure that the other party is also willing to make concessions of similar value. Reciprocity is essential in fair negotiation.

Keep a record of the concessions you make during the negotiation to have a clear record of the agreed terms.

As the negotiation progresses, continually evaluate whether the concessions are necessary and if progress is being made in line with your goals.

Assessing the relative value of your concessions is crucial in negotiation to ensure that you are achieving a fair and beneficial agreement for both parties. Here are some steps you can follow to evaluate the relative value of your concessions:

Before making a concession, have a clear understanding of your interests and objectives. This will allow you to assess if the concession aligns with your overall goals.

Examine closely what the other party is willing to offer in exchange for your concession. Evaluate if what you are receiving is equal to or greater in value than the concession you are making.

Think about how the concession will impact the relationship and long-term outcomes. Sometimes, making a concession in the short term can lead to significant benefits in the future.

Recognize that the value of a concession can be subjective and may vary for each party. What is important to you may not be as important to the other party. Make sure to understand their perspectives.

Instead of viewing concessions as losses, look for solutions that are beneficial for both parties. This can help ensure that the relative value is equitable.

Consider what the cost of not making the concession would be and how it would affect your goals and the negotiation as a whole.

Before making a concession, ask the other party what they are willing to offer in return. This will help you understand if their offer is acceptable and if the concession you are considering is worthwhile.

Avoid making concessions simply because the other party is applying pressure. Ensure that the concession you make is fair and reasonable in the context of the negotiation.

Before making a concession, communicate your expectations to the other party. Let them know what you expect in return for your concession.

Flexibility is key in negotiation. Be willing to adjust your terms and conditions to ensure equitable relative value.

Measuring the relative value of your concessions helps you make informed decisions during the negotiation and ensures that agreements are fair and mutually beneficial. By doing so, you can maximize the value of the concessions you make and achieve successful results.

You can request reciprocity from the other party. This means that if you make a concession, you can ask what concessions the other party is willing to make in return.

Requesting reciprocity is a valid negotiation strategy that can help balance the relationship and ensure that concessions are mutually beneficial. Here are some guidelines on how to request reciprocity effectively:

When making a concession, clearly and directly communicate that you are seeking reciprocity from the other party. For example, you could say, "I am willing to make this concession, but I would like to know what concessions you would be willing to make in return."

Be clear about what you expect in return for your concession. This can include specific aspects you would like the other party to address or concessions in related areas.

When requesting reciprocity, emphasize how both parties can benefit from a fair negotiation. Emphasize that you are seeking an agreement that is beneficial for both parties.

After requesting reciprocity, remain open to dialogue and listen carefully to the other party's response. Encourage the other party to share their thoughts and proposals.

Once the other party has expressed their willingness to make concessions in return, negotiate constructively to reach a fair agreement. This may involve adjustments to both parties' concessions.

As agreements on concessions and reciprocity are reached, make sure to document them in writing. This provides a clear record of what has been agreed upon and prevents future misunderstandings.

Acknowledge that reciprocity may not always be symmetrical in all aspects. You may need to be flexible and willing to consider different forms of reciprocity

Remember that the primary goal is to reach an agreement that benefits both parties. Maintain a focus on shared objectives and seek win-win solutions.

Requesting reciprocity is a strategy that can contribute to balancing the negotiation and ensuring that both parties are willing to make fair concessions. By fostering open communication and mutual commitment, you can work toward a satisfactory agreement for all involved.

Once an agreement that includes your concessions has been reached, ensure that everything is documented in writing. This prevents future misunderstandings.

Securing a written agreement is an essential practice in any negotiation. It provides a solid foundation to avoid future misunderstandings and ensure that both parties adhere to the agreed-upon terms.

Ensure that the written agreement includes all the agreed terms and conditions. This should cover concessions made by both parties, timelines, responsibilities, and any other relevant aspects.

Use clear and straightforward language in the written agreement. Avoid unnecessary jargon and ambiguity to ensure that all involved parties can understand the terms.

Include specific details about the concessions made in the negotiation. This can be crucial to ensure that all parties are on the same page about what has been agreed upon.

Make sure that all involved parties sign and date the written agreement. This confirms their commitment and provides evidence that they agree with the terms.

Provide a copy of the written agreement to all involved parties. Each party should have their own record of the agreement.

In complex situations or when the agreement has significant legal implications, consider legal counsel before signing. A lawyer can help ensure that the agreement is sound and complies with all applicable laws and regulations.

Define how the enforcement of the agreement's terms will take place. This can include timelines, procedures, and specific responsibilities.

If the agreement has a long duration, plan for regular reviews and monitoring to ensure that both parties fulfill their commitments over time.

Keep a secure copy of the written agreement in an accessible and safe place. This allows you to refer to the terms in case of disputes or questions in the future.

Once the written agreement is secured, communicate it effectively to all involved parties and ensure they are aware of the terms and commitments.

Securing a written agreement is an essential part of the negotiation process and provides you with the assurance that the agreed-upon terms will be upheld. This practice also promotes transparency and clarity in the relationship between the involved parties.

When making a concession, do so calmly and confidently. Do not let the other party feel that you are giving in due to pressure or weakness.

Maintaining calm and confidence while making concessions is crucial for staying in control of the negotiation and ensuring that concessions are made strategically and effectively. Here are some tips on how to do it:

Before the negotiation, plan your concessions and consider which ones you are willing to make. This will help you make informed decisions at the right time.

Avoid yielding under pressure. Pressure may be a negotiation tactic, but it's important to stay calm and not make impulsive decisions.

When making a concession, communicate your decision with confidence. Explain your reasoning and how it fits into the pursuit of a mutually beneficial agreement.

Avoid giving the impression that you are making a concession out of weakness or desperation. Instead, frame the concession as a strategic step toward an agreement.

After making a concession, encourage open communication and dialogue with the other party. Listen to their feedback and respond constructively.

Although you are willing to make concessions, do not overcommit or compromise your fundamental interests. Ensure that the concessions are reasonable and fair.

If you make a concession, consider asking what concessions the other party is willing to make in return. This can balance the relationship and ensure that the agreement is fair.

Remember that a strategic concession in the short term can lead to a stronger relationship and positive long-term results.

Carefully listening to the other party's responses and concerns can help you understand their perspectives and adapt your concession strategies effectively.

Remember that the primary goal is to reach an agreement that benefits both parties. Maintain a focus on shared interests and seek mutually beneficial solutions.

Maintaining calm and confidence while making concessions allows you to negotiate effectively and work toward a satisfactory agreement. Confidence in your decisions and a strategic attitude can make a difference in the negotiation's outcome.

As the negotiation progresses, assess whether the other party is also making concessions and if they consider them fair.

Assessing reciprocity is a fundamental aspect of negotiation to ensure that the agreement is fair and beneficial for both parties. Here are some tips on how to assess reciprocity effectively throughout the negotiation:

Keep a record of the concessions made by both parties throughout the negotiation. This will help you have a clear view of what has been agreed upon.

Compare the magnitude of concessions made by both parties. Evaluate if the concessions are proportionate and equitable in relation to each party's goals and needs.

At appropriate times, you can ask the other party how they perceive reciprocity in the negotiation. This can open a dialogue about whether both parties are satisfied with the negotiation's progress.

Keep in mind that concessions can be of various natures. Some may be tangible, such as price reductions or deadlines, while others may be concessions in intangible aspects, like flexibility in terms of service. Evaluate the concessions in their context.

If you notice an imbalance in concessions, consider how you can balance it fairly. This might involve adjusting your concessions or finding ways to achieve a more equitable agreement.

Avoid making assumptions about what the other party values or expects in terms of reciprocity. Instead, ask and seek clarity.

As you assess reciprocity, be strategic with your own concessions. Consider how you can use your concessions to secure an agreement that benefits both parties.

If you feel that reciprocity is unbalanced, communicate your expectations constructively and seek solutions that are mutually beneficial.

Reciprocity may require adjustments throughout the negotiation. Maintain flexibility to adapt your strategies as the situation evolves.

Remember that the primary goal is to reach an agreement that benefits both parties. Maintain a focus on shared interests and seek win-win solutions.

Evaluating reciprocity is a key part of effective negotiation. Ensuring that concessions are fair and equitable contributes to a strong business relationship and agreements that are sustainable in the long term.

Making concessions is part of negotiation, and doing it effectively can be beneficial in reaching mutually satisfactory agreements. The key is to concede strategically and ensure that your concessions are supported by sound reasoning.

7.Negotiation Tactics: Win-Win Strategies

Win-win strategies, also known as "collaborative negotiation" or "mutually beneficial negotiation," are approaches aimed at maximizing positive outcomes for all parties involved in a negotiation. Instead of trying to gain an advantage at the expense of the other party, these tactics focus on cooperation and the creation of shared value.

Effective Communication: Open and honest communication is fundamental. Actively listen to the other party to understand their needs, interests, and concerns. Clearly explain your own goals and expectations.

Effective communication is a cornerstone of win-win negotiation. Here are more details on how to implement it efficiently:

Active Listening: Pay attention to what the other party is saying. Ask questions to clarify any unclear points and show a genuine interest in understanding their perspectives. Avoid interrupting or prematurely judging.

Empathy: Try to put yourself in the other person's shoes. Attempt to understand their emotions and underlying needs. Empathy can help build a bridge of understanding between both parties.

Clear and Concise Language: When expressing your own goals and expectations, use clear and direct language. Avoid ambiguity or vagueness, as this can lead to misunderstandings.

Nonverbal Communication: Remember that nonverbal communication, such as body language and facial expressions, also plays a significant role in negotiation. Maintain open and friendly body language to foster trust.

Open-Ended Questions: Use open-ended questions that encourage conversation instead of closed-ended questions that only require yes or no answers. This can open the door to deeper discussion and the expression of needs and desires.

Summarization and Confirmation: Occasionally, summarize what you have heard from the other party to ensure you have understood correctly. Ask the other person to confirm if your summary is accurate.

Avoid Confrontation: Instead of engaging in confrontation, seek common ground and areas of agreement. Try to minimize hostility and negativity in the conversation.

Constructive Feedback: Provide feedback in a constructive and respectful manner. If you have concerns or disagreements, express them in a way that does not harm the relationship.

Flexibility in Communication: Recognize that people may have different communication styles. Adapting to the other party's communication style can help establish a more effective connection.

Emotion Management: Control your emotions during the negotiation. If you feel frustrated or upset, take a moment to calm down before responding. Proper emotional management is essential for maintaining a positive negotiation environment.

Effective communication in negotiation will not only help you better understand the other party but also facilitate the building of a trusting relationship, which is crucial for achieving a win-win solution.

Identification of Interests: Instead of focusing on rigid positions, seek to understand the underlying interests of both parties. Why do they want what they want? This will help you find solutions that satisfy those needs.

Identifying the underlying interests of both parties is a crucial step in win-win negotiation. Here are some guidelines for effectively conducting this process:

Ask "why" instead of "what": Instead of directly asking about the other party's positions (what they want), try to discover why they want those things. Asking "Why is it important for you to get X?" can reveal the underlying interests.

Listen attentively: When the other party expresses their desires or positions, listen attentively and look for clues about the reasons behind those demands. Keywords or expressed emotions can provide valuable insights.

Use the "and" technique instead of "or": Instead of thinking in terms of "my interests or theirs," look for ways to satisfy both simultaneously. For example, instead of saying "I need to make more money," you could express, "I would like to make more money, and I also value my free time."

Seek interests that both parties share. These can serve as starting points for creating solutions that satisfy both parties. For example, if both parties value efficiency, you can look for ways to enhance efficiency in the negotiation.

Reflect on Your Own Interests: Engage in self-reflection to identify your own underlying interests. Why do you want what you're seeking in the negotiation? Understanding your motives will help you communicate more effectively and find solutions that satisfy you.

Do Not Assume the Other Party's Interests: Avoid making assumptions about the other party's interests. Instead of assuming you know what they want, ask open-ended questions to gain a clear understanding.

Once you've identified the underlying interests, work together with the other party to find creative solutions that efficiently satisfy those interests. This may involve thinking outside the box and exploring options that haven't been considered previously.

Help the other party identify their priorities. Some of their interests may be more important than others. Understanding these priorities can help focus on what truly matters.

Identifying underlying interests is essential for finding solutions that are beneficial to both parties. By understanding why people want what they want, you can work together to create an agreement that satisfies those needs fairly and effectively.

Look for opportunities to create additional value for both parties. This may include identifying innovative solutions or allocating resources more efficiently.

Creating joint value is one of the cornerstones of win-win negotiation. It involves finding ways to increase the overall value of the negotiation so that both parties gain additional benefits. Here are some strategies to achieve this:

Foster a collaborative environment where both parties are willing to work together to achieve an outcome that benefits everyone. Collaboration can lead to the identification of creative solutions.

Brainstorming: Invite both parties to participate in brainstorming sessions to generate ideas and solutions. This can help identify non-obvious opportunities and promote innovative thinking.

Search for shared interests or common goals between both parties. These can serve as a basis for creating value. If both parties wish to reduce costs, for example, you can explore ways to do so together.

Look for opportunities where the combined efforts of both parties can be more effective than working separately. This may include combining resources, knowledge, or skills.

Both parties should be committed to seeking solutions that generate additional value. This requires a willingness to give in some areas to gain benefits in others.

Identify the needs that both parties want to satisfy and find ways to address them together. This can lead to integrated solutions.

Think creatively to find solutions that go beyond traditional options. Creativity can open the door to more beneficial agreements.

Examine how resources can be distributed more efficiently to maximize joint value. This may include optimizing time, money, and other assets.

Sometimes, creating additional value may involve investing in the long-term relationship. If both parties expect to work together in the future, they are more likely to be willing to create value together.

As opportunities for creating joint value are identified, ensure that the agreement is equitable for both parties. There should be a balance in the benefits gained.

Creating joint value not only benefits both parties in the current negotiation but also lays the foundation for strong and collaborative long-term relationships. Actively seeking opportunities to increase value maximizes the chances of a mutually beneficial agreement.

Encourage both parties to generate ideas and solutions together. Joint thinking can lead to creative solutions that benefit everyone.

Brainstorming, or idea generation, is a highly effective technique for fostering creativity and generating innovative solutions during a win-win negotiation. Here are some tips on how to conduct a successful brainstorming session:

Create an environment where both parties feel comfortable sharing ideas without fear of premature criticism. Non-critical initial phases are key to effective brainstorming.

Encourage both parties to contribute their ideas and perspectives. Don't allow one party to dominate the conversation; ensure both have the opportunity to express themselves.

Start by clearly defining the problem or issue you're trying to solve. Ensure both parties agree on the problem description.

In the initial phase of brainstorming, focus on generating ideas without judgment. Encourage parties to think freely and not dismiss any idea, no matter how strange it may seem.

Record all ideas generated, whether on a whiteboard, on paper, or electronically. This helps maintain a record of all suggestions and facilitates later review.

After generating a series of ideas, encourage them to explore how they can be combined or improved upon. This can lead to more robust solutions.

Once several ideas have been generated, help them classify them by importance or feasibility. This can help identify the most promising solutions.

Reflect on implications: Before making a decision, discuss the implications of the proposed solutions. How will they affect both parties? What are the potential risks and benefits?

At the end of the brainstorming session, seek mutual commitment to implementing one or more solutions. Both parties must agree on the decisions made.

After the brainstorming session, make sure to communicate the agreed-upon solutions and next steps clearly and comprehensively.

Brainstorming can be a valuable tool for finding creative solutions in a win-win negotiation. It allows both parties to actively collaborate and participate in the creation of solutions that benefit everyone.

Adhere to ethical and fair principles in negotiation. Avoid deceptive or coercive tactics, as they can undermine trust and relationships.

Principled negotiation, also known as "ethical negotiation" or "fair negotiation," focuses on adhering to ethical and fair principles throughout the negotiation process. By following these guidelines, trust is promoted, and strong relationships are built. Here are some key practices in principled negotiation:

Honesty is fundamental. Provide accurate information and do not hide relevant facts. Lack of honesty can damage trust and undermine the relationship.

Act with integrity and keep your commitments. Integrity is essential for building a reputation of reliability in the business world.

Treat the other party with respect at all times. Avoid derogatory or personal comments and focus on issues rather than attacking the person.

Avoid deceptive negotiation tactics, such as the use of false information or manipulation. Honesty and transparency should be your guides.

Try to understand and respect the needs and perspectives of the other party. Empathy can help find solutions that satisfy both parties.

Focus on the issues at hand, not on the people. This helps keep the discussion centered on problem-solving and avoids emotional escalations.

Seek an agreement that is perceived as fair and equitable by both parties. Avoid imposing unfavorable or unjust conditions.

Make sure that the negotiation complies with the ethical and legal standards of both your organization and the other party. This may include issues of compliance and social responsibility.

Promote open communication and transparency. If there are issues or changes in the situation, share them in a timely and clear manner.

If conflicts arise during the negotiation, address the issues constructively. Seek solutions that satisfy both parties instead of trying to win at all costs.

Principled negotiation not only promotes strong and lasting relationships but also helps avoid legal and reputational problems in the future. By adhering to ethical and fair principles, you are laying the foundation for successful and respectful collaboration in any negotiation process.

Find areas where the interests of both parties overlap and focus on these areas to maximize mutual benefits.

Focusing on shared needs is essential to achieve a win-win negotiation, as it allows you to identify areas of convergence where both parties can obtain mutual benefits. Here are some strategies to apply this approach:

Before the negotiation, conduct a careful analysis of your own interests and the interests of the other party. Make sure you fully understand what each party seeks to achieve.

Identify areas where the interests of both parties overlap. These are the ideal starting points for creating joint value.

During the negotiation, ask open-ended questions to explore the interests and needs of the other party. Listen attentively to their responses to understand their perspectives.

Once you have identified shared needs, work together to find solutions that effectively satisfy those needs. This may involve creating specific agreements that address those shared interests.

Be willing to be flexible and adapt your own positions to accommodate shared needs. Flexibility is key to reaching mutually beneficial agreements.

Clearly communicate your intentions and expectations, and ensure that the other party does the same. Open communication is essential to avoid misunderstandings.

Remember to adhere to ethical and fair principles during the negotiation. This will help maintain an environment of trust and respect.

Avoid focusing on rigid positions and instead seek solutions that satisfy shared interests. This may require giving in some areas to gain benefits in others.

As the negotiation progresses, make sure that the final agreement is equitable for both parties. Both should feel they are getting fair value.

Attention to shared needs and the pursuit of mutually beneficial solutions contribute to the building of strong and lasting relationships. These relationships can be valuable for future collaborations.

Focusing on shared needs not only facilitates the creation of win-win agreements but also lays the foundation for strong and collaborative long-term business relationships. By finding common ground and working together to meet those needs, both parties can benefit from the negotiation.

Before the negotiation, make sure you have a clear understanding of your alternatives in case the negotiation does not reach an agreement. This will give you bargaining power and allow you to make informed decisions.

Having clear alternatives, also known as the "Best Alternative to a Negotiated Agreement" (BATNA), is essential for effective negotiation. Here are more details on how to develop and use clear alternatives in a negotiation:

Before entering a negotiation, identify what your best alternative would be if no agreement is reached with the other party. This could be an offer or agreement from another provider, an independent course of action, or any other available option.

Determine the quality and viability of your best alternative. How favorable is it compared to the agreement you are seeking in the current negotiation? This will help you understand how strong your position is.

Define your limits or thresholds for the negotiation. These are the points at which you are willing to withdraw from the negotiation and opt for your BATNA instead.

During the negotiation, compare the offers and proposals of the other party with your BATNA. If the current offer is not better, it may be wise to withdraw and opt for your alternative.

Do not disclose your BATNA to the other party unless necessary. Keeping this information confidential gives you an advantage in the negotiation.

Having a strong BATNA gives you confidence in the negotiation, as you know you have a solid option if a satisfactory agreement is not reached.

If you find that your BATNA is weak or unacceptable, consider strengthening it before returning to the negotiation table. This may include seeking more favorable alternatives.

Your knowledge of your BATNA allows you to make informed decisions during the negotiation. You can evaluate whether the proposed agreement is good enough to proceed or if it's better to opt for your best alternative.

Set a reasonable deadline for making a decision based on your BATNA. Don't unnecessarily prolong the negotiation if you have a strong alternative.

Be prepared to use it if necessary. Ensure that the agreements and conditions of your alternative are in place and ready to be implemented if you decide to withdraw from the current negotiation.

Building a trusting relationship is essential in a win-win negotiation. This facilitates future collaborations and conflict resolution.

Building strong and trusting relationships is essential in a win-win negotiation. It not only contributes to the success of the current negotiation but also lays the foundation for future collaborations and effective conflict resolution.

From the beginning, communicate your willingness to collaborate and find solutions that benefit both parties. This helps create a positive working environment.

Pay attention to the other party and demonstrate a genuine interest in their concerns and perspectives. Active listening shows respect and strengthens the relationship.

Be clear and honest in your communication. Avoid ambiguities and misunderstandings. Transparency is essential for building trust.

If you make promises or agreements during the negotiation, ensure that you fulfill them. Consistency and reliability reinforce trust.

Focus the negotiation on finding solutions that meet the needs and goals of both parties. This demonstrates your willingness to build a win-win relationship.

Research and learn more about the company or individual you are negotiating with. This shows respect and attention to detail.

If you are negotiating with people from different cultures, it's important to be aware of cultural differences and show respect for them.

Constructive conflict resolution: If disagreements or conflicts arise, address them in a constructive Avoid hostile confrontations and seek solutions instead of blame.

Instead of seeing the other party as an opponent, look for opportunities to build bridges and find areas of convergence. Collaboration rather than competition can improve the relationship.

Consider the negotiation as the beginning of a long-term business relationship. Investing in building strong relationships can lead to fruitful future collaborations.

After the negotiation, continue to maintain open communication with the other party. Regular follow-up and feedback can help sustain the relationship over time.

Building trust relationships is valuable both professionally and personally. A strong relationship can lead to future successful agreements, fruitful collaborations, and constructive conflict resolution, contributing to ongoing success in business and life.

Throughout the negotiation process, it may be necessary to adjust your proposals or solutions as the conversation unfolds. Being willing to be flexible can be key to achieving a beneficial agreement.

Flexibility and adaptability are essential qualities in the negotiation process, especially in the context of a win-win negotiation.

Pay attention to the other party and look for signals about their needs and desires as the conversation unfolds. Being willing to adjust your proposals based on what you hear is crucial.

Instead of rigidly sticking to a single solution, consider multiple alternatives. This gives you room to adapt if necessary.

If you find yourself at an impasse or facing resistance, refocus on shared needs. Look for solutions that satisfy those needs, even if it means changing your original approach.

Throughout the negotiation, you can make gradual concessions to reach an agreement. The ability to be flexible in the amount and timing of concessions is valuable.

Communicating your willingness to make adjustments demonstrates goodwill and can foster reciprocity from the other party.

Flexibility often involves seeking creative solutions. Don't be afraid to think outside the box and explore unconventional approaches.

Instead of solely focusing on your current position, consider the overall value of the agreement. You may need to adapt in certain areas to gain significant benefits in others.

While you should be flexible, don't lose sight of your core objectives. Make sure that any adjustments you make align with your long-term goals.

If you decide to make changes or adjustments in your approach, communicate them clearly and transparently to the other party. Open communication can help maintain trust.

While it's important to be flexible, it's also essential to establish boundaries. Determine when an adjustment would no longer be beneficial, and you'd be willing to walk away from the negotiation.

Flexibility and adaptability allow you to effectively navigate challenges and obstacles that may arise in a negotiation. These qualities help you find mutually beneficial solutions and build strong relationships with the other party.

Once an agreement has been reached, both parties must be committed to its implementation and fulfillment. Ongoing communication and continuous follow-up are important.

Commitment and effective execution of the agreement are crucial steps in the win-win negotiation process. Once an agreement has been reached, it's important to ensure that both parties are committed to fulfilling it. Here are some guidelines to ensure that the agreement is successfully implemented and fulfilled:

After reaching an agreement, communicate all the terms and conditions agreed upon clearly and comprehensively. Make sure both parties have a solid understanding of what is expected.

Develop a detailed plan for implementing the agreement, including timelines, responsibilities, and necessary resources. Establish a tracking system to ensure that commitments are met.

Define who is responsible for each aspect of the agreement. Make sure both parties know their roles and responsibilities.

While it's important to have a solid plan, be flexible to adapt to unexpected changes or challenges that may arise during implementation.

Maintain open and ongoing communication with the other party throughout the implementation process. Update on progress, discuss any issues that arise, and seek solutions together.

If challenges or conflicts arise during implementation, address them constructively and seek solutions instead of blaming each other.

Ensure that the agreed-upon deadlines are met. If necessary, mutually adjust the deadlines if difficulties arise.

Both parties should be accountable for their actions and for fulfilling their commitments. Accountability is essential for the successful execution of the agreement.

Results assessment: Periodically, evaluate the progress and outcomes of the agreement. Are the objectives being met? Are there areas that need adjustments?

Recognize and celebrate achievements as you progress in implementing the agreement. This can help maintain motivation and commitment from both parties.

If the implementation of the agreement is successful, consider the possibility of future collaborations or agreements. A strong business relationship can open doors to new opportunities.

Commitment and effective execution of the agreement are essential for a win-win negotiation to be truly successful. By maintaining open communication, planning effectively, and ensuring that both parties fulfill their commitments, a solid foundation is established for ongoing collaboration and long-term mutual benefits.

In a win-win negotiation, the goal is to achieve an outcome in which all parties feel they have received a fair and beneficial deal. This is not only beneficial for short-term relationships but also lays the groundwork for future successful collaborations.

8.Negotiation Tactics: Win-Lose Strategies

Although the ideal approach in most situations is to seek a win-win negotiation, there are occasions when one of the parties may adopt a win-lose strategy, which focuses on ensuring that one party gains benefits at the expense of the other. However, it is important to note that adopting a win-lose strategy can have negative long-term repercussions on business relationships and reputation. Here are some tactics that can be used in a win-lose strategy:

One common tactic in a win-lose strategy is to exert pressure on the other party to concede to your demands. This can include threats, intimidation, or coercion.

Confrontation and pressure are tactics that can be part of a win-lose strategy in a negotiation. However, it's important to consider that these tactics can have negative consequences for both the relationship with the other party and your own reputation. Here are more details on how these tactics are used and their potential impacts:

Confrontation involves a direct clash of positions and demands, often in an aggressive manner. It can include heated arguments, open challenges, and the vigorous expression of differences.

Pressure involves exerting influence or power over the other party to make them comply with your demands or yield to your interests. It can involve threats, coercion, or the application of sanctions.

The use of confrontation and pressure can damage the relationship with the other party, creating mistrust and hostility, making future collaborations difficult.

While these tactics may lead to short-term gains, they are likely to have negative long-term effects, such as the loss of business partners and a tarnished reputation.

The other party may respond to confrontation and pressure negatively, resisting further and turning the negotiation into a conflict.

By adopting a confrontational and pressure-based strategy, you may miss opportunities to find creative and mutually beneficial solutions.

Instead of resorting to confrontation and pressure, consider more collaborative and ethical approaches to negotiation, such as seeking win-win solutions, open communication, and mutual respect. These approaches are often more effective in maintaining strong and positive business relationships in the long term and foster an environment of trust and respect that facilitates conflict resolution and ongoing collaboration.

You can withhold information or provide false information to the disadvantage of the other party so that they make decisions based on incorrect information.

Withholding information or providing false information in a negotiation is a dishonest and unethical tactic. Although it can be used as part of a win-lose strategy, it's important to consider that this tactic can have serious consequences for the business relationship and reputation. Here are the possible impacts and issues associated with withholding information or providing false information:

Deception undermines trust in the relationship. If the other party discovers that they were given incorrect information or relevant information was withheld, they are likely to feel betrayed, and trust will erode.

Providing false or misleading information can have legal implications and harm your company's reputation. You may face legal actions if it's proven that you provided false information.

If your deception comes to light, the other party may be reluctant to engage in future negotiations with you, limiting collaboration opportunities.

The use of dishonest tactics can tarnish your own reputation and that of your company. In the business world, integrity and honesty are highly valued.

Withholding information can lead the other party to make decisions based on incorrect information, which could result in an agreement that is not beneficial for either party.

Instead of resorting to information withholding or deception, adhering to ethical principles in negotiation, such as honesty, transparency, and mutual respect, is encouraged. Building strong and trust-based business relationships is crucial for long-term success. Open communication and honest collaboration are often more effective in achieving mutually beneficial results and maintaining lasting business relationships.

Adopting a rigid stance and being unwilling to make concessions or compromises. This can force the other party to give in to your position.

Adopting inflexible positions in a negotiation is a strategy that, although sometimes used, can have negative consequences in the negotiation process and in long-term business relationships. Here are some issues associated with adopting inflexible positions:

When both parties adopt rigid positions and are unwilling to make concessions, the negotiation can deadlock. This can lead to a lack of agreement and the failure of the negotiation.

Inflexibility hinders the search for creative and mutually beneficial solutions. Solutions that satisfy both parties often require some degree of flexibility and compromise.

By refusing to make concessions, you may miss opportunities to gain additional benefits or advantages that could have been attainable through a more flexible approach.

Adopting inflexible positions can create frustration and resentment in the other party, which can damage the business relationship.

Inflexibility can lead to increased conflicts and a lack of mutual understanding, making long-term collaboration more difficult.

To avoid these issues and facilitate more effective negotiation, it is advisable to adopt a more flexible and open approach. Some strategies include:

Instead of focusing on rigid positions, seek to understand the underlying interests and needs of both parties. This can open the door to creative solutions.

Determine what the most important aspects of the agreement are and be willing to make concessions in less critical areas.

Focus on win-win solutions: Seek solutions that meet the needs and interests of both parties rather than aiming to win at the expense of the other party.

Open communication and a willingness to explore the perspectives and concerns of the other party are essential for finding common ground.

Once an agreement has been reached, be flexible in its implementation to address unexpected challenges or changes in circumstances. In summary, adopting inflexible positions can hinder the success of a negotiation. Being flexible and willing to make concessions when appropriate can be more effective in achieving beneficial agreements and maintaining healthy long-term business relationships.

Using tactics to manipulate the emotions of the other party, such as guilt or fear, in order to gain an advantage. Emotional manipulation in a negotiation is a dishonest and unethical tactic that can have negative consequences on business relationships and reputation. Manipulating the emotions of the other party, such as guilt or fear, to gain an advantage is not a fair practice and can undermine trust in the relationship. Here are some issues associated with emotional manipulation:

When emotional manipulation is discovered, trust in the relationship is undermined. The other party may feel betrayed and hurt.

Emotional manipulation can harm long-term business relationships. The other party may be reluctant to collaborate or do business with you in the future.

Emotional manipulation can have a negative impact on your team's morale and your own reputation. It can lead to a negative perception of your business ethics.

Emotional manipulation goes against ethical principles in negotiation and in business in general. Acting with integrity and honesty is crucial for maintaining strong and healthy relationships.

Instead of resorting to emotional manipulation, adhering to ethical practices and open, respectful communication in negotiation is encouraged. Seek solutions that meet the needs and interests of both parties and promote the building of trust-based business relationships. Honesty and integrity are highly valued in the business world and can lead to more positive long-term outcomes.

Setting deadlines or ultimatums that pressure the other party into making hasty decisions or accepting unfavorable terms. The use of ultimatums in a negotiation is a tactic often associated with a win-lose strategy. An ultimatum involves setting a deadline or condition that pressures the other party into making a hasty decision or accepting unfavorable terms. However, it's important to consider that excessive use of ultimatums can have negative consequences on business relationships and the quality of the agreement reached. Here are some issues related to the use of ultimatums in negotiation:

Ultimatums can undermine trust and damage the relationship with the other party. The sense of pressure and coercion is not conducive to building a strong and lasting business relationship.

When faced with an ultimatum, the other party may feel pressured to make a quick decision, which can lead to agreements that are not thoroughly considered or beneficial.

If the other party deems the ultimatum unfair or unacceptable, they may decide to walk away from the negotiation altogether, which can lead to a lack of agreement.

Ultimatums can increase hostility and conflict in the negotiation, making collaboration and the search for mutually beneficial solutions more difficult.

Instead of using ultimatums, it is more advisable to seek more collaborative and ethical approaches to negotiation. Some effective strategies include:

Foster open and respectful communication with the other party to understand their needs and interests.

Rather than imposing inflexible deadlines, seek creative solutions that can meet the needs of both parties.

If it is necessary to set deadlines, be flexible in their management and consider the possibility of extending or adjusting them if reasonable.

Try to identify shared needs and work together to find solutions that satisfy them.

In summary, the use of ultimatums should be limited and applied carefully in situations where it is absolutely necessary. In general, a more collaborative and respectful approach is recommended to achieve beneficial outcomes and maintain healthy business relationships.

Focus on achieving your goals at any price, without consideration for the well-being or interests of the other party. The "win-at-all-costs" strategy is an approach in which one party focuses on achieving their goals at any price, without considering the well-being or interests of the other party. This strategy can be detrimental in a negotiation and in business relationships in general. Here are some reasons why the win-at-all-costs strategy is problematic:

The focus on winning at all costs can lead the other party to feel exploited and betrayed, undermining trust in the relationship.

The constant use of this strategy can lead to the breakdown of the relationship with the other party, limiting opportunities for future collaboration.

Adopting a win-at-all-costs strategy can damage your own and your company's reputation in the market. Ethical business practices are highly valued.

By focusing solely on short-term victories, opportunities to build strong and collaborative relationships that generate long-term value can be overlooked.

The win-at-all-costs strategy often leads to increased conflicts and can result in prolonged and costly disputes.

Instead of adopting a win-at-all-costs strategy, a more equitable and collaborative approach to negotiation is recommended. Some effective strategies include:

Focus the negotiation on finding solutions that meet the needs and interests of both parties.

Foster open and respectful communication with the other party to understand their perspectives and concerns.

Consider the negotiation as the beginning of a long-term business relationship and look for opportunities for future collaborations.

Act ethically and with integrity in all business interactions is crucial for maintaining strong and healthy relationships.

If disagreements arise, seek constructive solutions rather than imposing your will. In summary, the win-at-all-costs strategy can have serious repercussions on business relationships and reputation. Adopting a more collaborative, ethical, and solution-oriented approach is often more effective in achieving successful outcomes and maintaining healthy business relationships.

It is important to note that a win-lose strategy can have negative consequences, such as a loss of trust and degradation of business relationships. In many situations, seeking a win-win approach is often more effective and sustainable in the long term as it promotes stronger and collaborative business relationships. Most parties prefer to work with partners who are fair and ethical rather than adopting aggressive and selfish tactics. Therefore, it is important to carefully consider the negotiation strategy you adopt and its long-term impact on your business relationships.

9.Competitive Negotiation vs. Collaborative Negotiation

Competitive negotiation and collaborative negotiation are two different approaches to resolving conflicts or reaching agreements between parties. Each has its own characteristics, goals, and strategies:

Competitive negotiation is based on competition and conflicting interests among the involved parties. The primary goal in this type of negotiation is to maximize one's own interests, often at the expense of the other party's interests. Typical strategies include withholding information, timing plays, making threats, and using power tactics to gain advantages.

In competitive negotiation, one party "wins" while the other "loses," and the outcome tends to be an agreement where one party gains more than the other. Competitive negotiation focuses on the competition and conflict of interests among the involved parties. In this approach, it is assumed that the goals and interests of the parties are incompatible or in disagreement, and the negotiation process becomes a struggle for limited resources or competitive advantages.

The parties involved often view the negotiation as a game in which winning means one party gains more than the other. In competitive negotiation, a dynamic is established in which the parties compete directly for limited resources, advantages, or concessions.

Unlike collaborative negotiation, where parties seek to maximize joint value and work together to find mutually beneficial solutions, competitive negotiation often involves conflicting interests among the parties.

 In competitive negotiation, it is assumed that there is a zero-sum game, meaning what one party gains, the other party loses. In this context, the success of one party is often measured in terms of how much they can obtain compared to the other party. This win-at-the-expense-of-the-other mentality can lead to a more adversarial approach to negotiation.

In competitive negotiation, each party has specific goals they seek to achieve, and these goals may be in direct conflict with each other. For example, in a salary negotiation between an employee and an employer, the employee may be trying to secure the highest possible salary, while the employer aims to keep labor costs low.

These goals compete directly. In competitive negotiation, parties often employ strategies and tactics aimed at maximizing their own interests and minimizing the interests of the other party. This can include persuasion techniques, withholding information, threats, and pressure to gain an advantage in negotiation. In contrast to collaborative negotiation, where the goal is to reach an agreement that benefits all parties involved, competitive negotiation tends to be more limited in its scope. In collaborative negotiation, parties seek to create value together, while in competitive negotiation, existing value is distributed, and there is competition for one's share.

In competitive negotiation, parties often focus on gaining concessions from the other party. This means that one party is willing to concede in certain aspects to gain advantages in others. Concessions are seen as a bargaining chip in the quest to gain more from the other party. Given that one of the premises of competitive negotiation is the idea that one party wins and the other loses, the outcome tends to be unequal in terms of what each party gains.

The party that secures an advantage in the negotiation is considered the winner, while the party that concedes or doesn't obtain what they were seeking is seen as the loser. In competitive negotiation, parties compete for limited resources or advantages, and the dynamic is based on the premise that one party's success comes at the expense of the other. This can lead to a more adversarial relationship and unequal agreements where one party gains more benefits than the other.

In contrast, collaborative negotiation is based on the idea that the interests of the parties can be compatible, or that creative solutions can satisfy the needs of both parties. Instead of competing, the parties work together to find mutually beneficial solutions. The outcome tends to be an agreement in which both parties win.

The choice between a competitive or collaborative approach to negotiation depends on the situation and the goals of the parties involved. In some cases, competition may be necessary, while in others, collaboration may be more effective in achieving satisfactory results for all parties. The choice between a competitive or collaborative negotiation approach largely depends on the nature of the situation, the goals of the parties involved, and the existing relationships between them.

Competitive negotiation can be appropriate in situations where parties have opposing goals or when they are competing for scarce resources. It can also be useful when it's necessary to protect one's own interests, and complete cooperation isn't possible. However, overusing this approach can damage long-term relationships.

Collaborative negotiation is often effective when parties share common interests or when a creative solution that maximizes joint value is sought. This approach is based on open communication, trust, and the pursuit of mutually beneficial solutions. It can strengthen relationships and create a cooperative environment.

In many situations, a mixed approach that combines elements of competitive and collaborative negotiation can be most effective. Parties may compete in some aspects while collaborating in others, allowing them to protect their own interests without completely undermining their relationship with the other party.

Ultimately, the choice of negotiation approach depends on the specific situation, the balance between competition and collaboration needed, and short- and long-term goals. An effective negotiator can adapt to different negotiation styles based on the circumstances. Collaborative negotiation is based on cooperation and the pursuit of mutually beneficial solutions.

The primary goal in this type of negotiation is to find solutions that satisfy the interests of both parties and maximize joint value. Strategy: Typical strategies include open communication, information sharing, seeking common interests, and jointly generating options. In collaborative negotiation, both parties work together to find a solution that is beneficial for both. The outcome tends to be an agreement where both parties win.

Competitive negotiation focuses on individual gain, often at the expense of the other party, while collaborative negotiation centers on finding mutually beneficial solutions and building a long-term relationship. The approach to use depends on the situation, the relationships between the parties, and the specific goals of the negotiation. In many cases, a mixed or integrative approach can be more effective, utilizing elements of both strategies as needed.

Collaborative negotiation, often referred to as interest-based or win-win negotiation, is distinguished by its focus on cooperation and the pursuit of solutions that benefit both parties, rather than focusing on competition and confrontation. Here is an elaboration of the key concepts related to collaborative negotiation:

In collaborative negotiation, it starts with the premise that the interests of the involved parties are not necessarily incompatible or mutually exclusive. While there may be differences of opinion or specific needs, it is believed that ultimately, it is possible to find areas of overlap or common interests that allow for mutually beneficial solutions.

Instead of solely focusing on rigid positions or demands, collaborative negotiation centers on understanding the underlying needs, desires, and concerns of each party. This involves exploring the reasons behind the demands and seeking solutions that effectively address those needs.

In collaborative negotiation, creativity and the pursuit of innovative solutions are encouraged. Parties work together to find agreements that maximize joint value and allow both parties to gain additional benefits compared to what they could have achieved in a competitive negotiation.

Open communication and the building of trust are essential elements in collaborative negotiation. Parties share information honestly and transparently, which helps create an environment in which both parties feel secure in exploring joint solutions.

Collaborative negotiation often takes a long-term perspective on the relationships between the parties involved. It seeks to not only resolve the immediate issue but also to maintain and strengthen the relationship in the future. By seeking mutually beneficial solutions, it promotes the construction of a solid foundation for continued collaboration.

In this approach, both parties play an active role in creating solutions. Joint decision-making is promoted, which means that parties have greater control and participation in the negotiation process and in defining the terms of the agreement.

In summary, collaborative negotiation is based on the premise that, often, the interests of the parties can be compatible, and actively seeks the development of solutions that satisfy the needs and desires of both parties. Instead of competing and winning at the expense of the other party, collaborative negotiation encourages cooperation and the creation of joint value, which can result in more lasting and mutually beneficial agreements.

10.Types of Power in Negotiation

In a negotiation, power refers to the ability to influence the other party to achieve desired objectives. There are various types of power that can influence the outcome of a negotiation. Here are some of the most common types of power in negotiation:

This type of power is based on one party's ability to influence the negotiation outcome due to their position or resources. For example, a company that is the sole provider of a product is likely to have high bargaining power.

Bargaining power is directly related to a party's capacity to influence the negotiation outcome due to their specific position, resources, or advantages. Bargaining power can be an important tool for achieving beneficial agreements. Some additional examples of how this type of power can manifest in a negotiation include:

A company that controls a significant portion of the market or is the sole provider of a product or service can dictate its terms and prices to buyers, giving it high bargaining power.

If a party has access to scarce or valuable resources that are essential to the other party, such as key raw materials, land, exclusive technology, etc., they hold significant power in the negotiation.

A large organization that can make bulk purchases or has a substantial customer base may have bargaining power in obtaining discounts or preferential terms from suppliers.

A company with a strong brand or a solid reputation can influence consumer preferences and, therefore, has bargaining power in licensing agreements, franchises, or marketing deals.

The current market conditions, such as supply and demand, can also influence bargaining power. In a market with high demand and low supply, sellers may have more bargaining power.

It's important to remember that bargaining power is not static and can change over time. Furthermore, in a negotiation, parties can employ strategies to enhance their own power or weaken the power of the other party. The ability to assess and manage power effectively is a key skill in successful negotiation.

It involves one party's ability to exert pressure or coercion on the other party. This can include threats of economic, legal, or reputational harm. However, excessive use of this power can damage long-term relationships.

Coercive power in negotiation is based on one party's ability to exert pressure or coercion on the other party, often through threats of economic, legal, or reputational harm. This type of power can take various forms, such as:

It can involve the threat to withdraw a business deal, cancel an existing contract, or take actions that financially harm the other party.

A party may threaten legal action, filing a lawsuit, or resorting to legal processes to gain advantages in the negotiation.

It refers to the threat of harming the other party's reputation through the disclosure of negative information, negative advertising, or creating a public scandal.

While coercive power can be effective in specific situations, its excessive or inappropriate use can harm long-term relationships and generate resistance from the other party. Additionally, it can lead to negative consequences, such as legal disputes or reputational damage for both parties.

In general, the prudent and limited use of coercive power in negotiation is recommended. It is important to consider the long-term implications and seek mutually beneficial solutions rather than resorting to coercive tactics that can result in a hostile and unproductive environment. Open communication and a focus on collaboration are often more effective in building long-term relationships in negotiation.

It is based on one party's ability to grant rewards to the other party. For example, a company can offer financial incentives to an employee during a salary negotiation.

Reward power in negotiation is based on one party's ability to grant rewards, incentives, or benefits to the other party. This type of power can be an effective tool for influencing the negotiation outcome. Some additional examples of how reward power can manifest in a negotiation include:

As you mentioned, a company can offer a salary increase, bonuses, stock options, or other financial incentives to an employee during a salary negotiation.

In a buying or selling negotiation, one party can offer additional benefits, such as extended warranties, free maintenance services, or future discounts as part of the agreement.

In the workplace context, a party can offer professional development opportunities, promotions, or career advancement as rewards to influence the other party's decision.

In the context of business agreements, one party can offer opportunities for future collaboration, such as strategic alliances, to motivate the other party to reach an agreement.

Public recognition or prestige can be significant rewards in certain negotiations. For example, an artist seeking a renowned gallery to exhibit their work may value the associated prestige.

It is important to remember that reward power can be an effective tool for influencing the other party, but it should also be used ethically and transparently. Additionally, it is crucial for both parties in the negotiation to be willing to accept the proposed rewards. In some cases, reward power can lead to mutually beneficial agreements that satisfy both parties.

It refers to the authority or legitimacy of one party to make decisions or demand certain conditions in the negotiation. This may be supported by laws, regulations, or industry standards.

Legitimate power in negotiation is based on one party's authority or legitimacy to make decisions or impose certain conditions. This type of power derives from a legal, regulatory, or normative basis and can be an effective tool for influencing a negotiation. Some examples of how legitimate power can manifest in a negotiation include:

A party may argue that certain conditions or requirements are necessary due to laws, government regulations, or previous contractual agreements.

Norms and accepted practices in a specific industry can support one party's demands. This is common in highly regulated areas such as health, safety, and quality. Contracts or prior agreements between the parties can establish conditions and obligations that must be met, giving legitimacy to the party insisting on their fulfillment. Position within an organization, such as a manager, director, or president, can confer legitimacy to make decisions on behalf of the organization.

In cases of intellectual property, such as patents or copyrights, the party holding legal rights can exercise legitimacy to control the use of those rights in a negotiation. However, it's important to remember that legitimacy does not always guarantee that a party will get what it seeks in the negotiation.

The other party may question the validity of the authority or there may be legal nuances requiring interpretation. Additionally, in negotiation situations, it is crucial that both parties are treated fairly and respectfully. Effective negotiation often involves finding solutions that are legal and fair for both parties, even if there are differences in legitimacy power.

Norms and accepted practices in a specific industry can support one party's demands. This is common in highly regulated areas such as health, safety, and quality.

Contracts or prior agreements between the parties can establish conditions and obligations that must be met, giving legitimacy to the party insisting on their fulfillment.

Position within an organization, such as a manager, director, or president, can confer legitimacy to make decisions on behalf of the organization.

In cases of intellectual property, such as patents or copyrights, the party holding legal rights can exercise legitimacy to control the use of those rights in a negotiation.

However, it's important to remember that legitimacy does not always guarantee that a party will get what it seeks in the negotiation. The other party may question the validity of the authority or there may be legal nuances requiring interpretation. Additionally, in negotiation situations, it is crucial that both parties are treated fairly and respectfully. Effective negotiation often involves finding solutions that are legal and fair for both parties, even if there are differences in legitimacy power.

It is based on one party's knowledge, experience, or specialization in a topic relevant to the negotiation. Those with deep knowledge of a subject often have expertise power.

Expertise power is one of the sources of power in the context of negotiation and is based on one party's knowledge, experience, or specialization in a topic relevant to the negotiation. Those with deep and specialized knowledge in a specific area often have expertise power that can significantly influence the negotiation outcome. This power can manifest in various ways:

The party with expertise has access to information crucial to the negotiation that is not readily available to the other parties. This information can include technical data, statistics, research, patents, or other specialized information that can support their position in the negotiation.

Experience and in-depth knowledge of a subject increase the credibility of the party with expertise. This can make the other parties trust their arguments and proposals, leading to more favorable agreements.

Problem-solving ability: Parties with expertise are often better equipped to address and resolve complex problems related to the negotiation topic. This can be valuable for finding practical and effective solutions that benefit all parties involved.

Influence on perception: Expertise power can also influence how one party is perceived in the negotiation. Others may view the party with expertise as an authority on the subject and, therefore, be more willing to follow their recommendations.

Strategic negotiation: The party with expertise can use their specialized knowledge to design more effective negotiation strategies. This includes the ability to identify the strengths and weaknesses of the other parties' positions and adapt their approach accordingly.

It's important to note that expertise power can be a source of advantage in negotiation, but it should also be used ethically and with consideration for the needs and goals of all parties involved. In effective negotiation, expertise power is often combined with other sources of power, such as bargaining power, coercive power, reward power, and legitimacy power, to achieve a mutually beneficial agreement.

This power is derived from the identification or admiration that the other party has for a particular person or entity. For example, a celebrity endorsing a product can influence purchasing decisions.

Referent power is a source of influence in negotiation and other social interactions. It is based on the identification or admiration that one person or entity holds over the other party. Essentially, this type of power implies that one party is influenced by the presence, support, or approval of a referent figure, be it a celebrity, an authority, an opinion leader, or any individual or entity with prestige or status.

Some important characteristics of referent power include:

The party with referent power can influence through identification. The other party identifies or feels connected with the referent figure and is therefore more willing to follow their recommendations or adopt their viewpoint.

Admiration for the referent figure is a key component of this power. The party admiring the referent figure tends to value their opinion and may be more inclined to accept their ideas or suggestions.

Referent power can influence a wide range of decisions, from purchasing decisions, as mentioned in your example, to political decisions, workplace decisions, and other decision-making contexts.

Common examples of referent power include:

The endorsement of products or causes by celebrities can significantly influence public perception and purchasing decisions.

Experts in a field or those with a large following on social media can exert referent power in their respective areas.

Politicians with a high degree of popularity can influence public opinion and electoral decisions.

In matters of faith and beliefs, religious figures can wield significant referent power.

Referent power is based on persuasion and the ability to influence people's attitudes and behaviors through association with admired or respected figures. It's important to note that this type of power is not always used ethically and can be exploited for manipulative purposes. Therefore, it is crucial to wield it responsibly and with consideration for the needs and desires of the other party.

It is based on one party's network of contacts and relationships. Connections can provide access to valuable information or other key parties in the negotiation.

Connection power, also known as "network power," is a significant source of influence in negotiation and various aspects of life. It is derived from a person's or entity's network of contacts and relationships. This type of power is based on the idea that connections and relationships can provide access to valuable information, resources, and other key parties in a negotiation or in everyday situations.

11.Psychology of Negotiation: Emotions and Decision-Making

Psychology plays a fundamental role in negotiation, especially concerning emotions and decision-making. Here are some key aspects of how emotions affect decision-making in the context of negotiation:

Emotions can lead to irrational decision-making. In a negotiation, people can be influenced by emotions such as anger, frustration, fear, or euphoria, leading to impulsive or suboptimal decisions. Therefore, it is essential to recognize and manage emotions during a negotiation to prevent them from negatively affecting decisions.

Indeed, emotions can have a significant impact on decision-making, sometimes leading to irrational decisions.

People often seek immediate emotional gratification rather than making decisions based on a logical, long-term evaluation of options. For example, impatience or emotional urgency in a negotiation can lead to accepting a suboptimal agreement instead of waiting for a more favorable offer.

Emotions like fear and risk aversion can lead to irrationally conservative decision-making. People may avoid taking risks, even when they could be rational from an objective perspective, simply because they feel afraid.

Emotions can give rise to cognitive biases that distort perception and evaluation of information. For example, loss aversion can make people overvalue what they might lose in a decision, leading to suboptimal decision-making.

In emotional situations, people can overreact to emotional stimuli, clouding their judgment and leading to impulsive decisions. For example, in a negotiation, anger or frustration can lead to an excessive emotional response that hinders rational decision-making.

Emotions and the desire for social acceptance can lead to conformity with group or societal expectations, even if it is irrational from an individual perspective. This can influence a person's decisions in a group negotiation, for instance.

Recognize and manage one's own emotions.

Take emotional distance to evaluate options objectively.

Consider data and facts rather than relying solely on emotional reactions.

Use rational decision-making techniques such as cost-benefit analysis, risk analysis, and consideration of alternatives.

Take time to reflect and not succumb to the pressure of making hasty decisions.

Making rational decisions in emotional situations can be a challenge, but it is essential to achieve optimal results in negotiation and other areas of life.

Emotional anchoring is a phenomenon in which the first offer or proposal made in a negotiation can significantly influence subsequent ones. If an initial offer triggers an emotional response, such as surprise or frustration, it can set an anchor that affects later concessions. Negotiators should be aware of this effect and strive to establish rational anchors based on solid data and arguments.

Emotional anchoring is a cognitive phenomenon that refers to the influence of an initial offer or early proposal on the negotiation process. In particular, this influence is manifested through the establishment of an "anchor" that tends to affect subsequent concessions and terms in the negotiation. While it is commonly associated with financial offers, emotional anchoring can be applied to any aspect of negotiation, including terms, conditions, or even expectations.

The first offer or proposal tends to influence the perception of both parties in the negotiation. The party making the initial offer often seeks to establish a reference point (anchor) that will influence the other party's perceived value.

Emotional anchoring can lead to parties feeling influenced by the initial offer, even if it is not necessarily the most reasonable or fair. This can lead to concessions closer to the emotional anchor than to what might be an equitable distribution.

The initial offer can vary depending on the negotiation strategy. The offeror may set it aggressively to gain an advantage or moderately to encourage a collaborative relationship. The other party can react to the emotional anchor with counterproposals or by rejecting the offer.

Throughout the negotiation, parties may attempt to adjust or negotiate the original emotional anchor. This can lead to a process of mutual concessions as the parties move closer to an agreement.

Negotiators should be aware of the emotional anchoring phenomenon and consider it in their negotiation strategy. This includes not being swayed by emotional reactions to an unexpected initial offer and, instead, carefully considering objective terms and conditions. It also involves the ability to recognize when emotional anchoring is influencing decisions and being able to adjust proposals and concessions rationally and strategically.

Emotional anchoring is a powerful tool in negotiation and can significantly affect the negotiation outcome. Therefore, understanding how it works and how to manage it effectively is essential for negotiators.

Empathy is the ability to understand and share another person's feelings. Showing empathy toward the other party in negotiation can help build stronger relationships and foster a spirit of cooperation. However, it is essential to balance empathy with the need to achieve negotiation goals.

Empathy is a fundamental skill in negotiation and social interaction in general. As you mentioned, empathy is defined as the ability to understand and share another person's feelings. In the context of negotiation, empathy plays an essential role in building trust and respect. Here are some key points about how empathy influences negotiation:

Displaying empathy toward the other party helps build relationships based on trust and respect. When people feel understood and valued, they are more willing to collaborate and work together effectively.

Empathy enhances communication in negotiation. When one strives to understand the feelings and perspectives of the other party, they are more likely to communicate clearly and receptively, facilitating conflict resolution and joint decision-making.

Empathy can help reduce conflicts and tensions in negotiation. By showing understanding of the concerns and needs of the other party, it is more likely to find mutually acceptable solutions.

Empathy acts as a bridge between the parties, facilitating the overcoming of differences and obstacles. It helps the parties find common ground and work together to achieve shared goals.

Empathy is also valuable in problem-solving. When one party shows empathy toward the other, they can more effectively identify underlying issues and collaborate in finding solutions.

It's important to note that empathy does not necessarily imply agreeing with the other party or giving in excessively in the negotiation. Instead, it's about understanding the emotions and perspectives of the other party to effectively address their concerns and needs while progressing toward a mutually beneficial agreement.

Empathy is a skill that can be developed and improved over time. In negotiation, the ability to be empathetic can make a difference in building strong relationships and achieving successful outcomes.

Loss aversion is a concept from behavioral economics suggesting that people value losses more than equivalent gains. In negotiation, this can lead to reluctance to make concessions or demands due to fear of losing something. Negotiators should be aware of this bias and strive to make decisions based on objective value, not just loss aversion.

Loss aversion is a fundamental concept in the field of behavioral economics and decision-making. It was popularized by psychologists and economists Daniel Kahneman and Amos Tversky in their prospect theory. Loss aversion refers to people's tendency to weigh losses more heavily than equivalent gains, meaning they are willing to take more risks to avoid losses than to secure gains.

Loss aversion suggests that, in decision-making, people tend to consider losses as more important than gains of equivalent magnitude. For example, losing $100 may generate more distress than gaining $100 in satisfaction.

Prospect theory argues that people have an asymmetric utility function in which losses and gains are weighted differently. This asymmetry is manifested in an "S"-shaped utility curve, where loss aversion is represented by a steeper slope in the loss region than in the gain region.

Loss aversion can influence a wide range of decisions, from financial choices to consumption decisions and personal choices. People may be more cautious with their investments, more hesitant to take financial risks, and more prone to avoid situations they perceive as loss threats.

Loss aversion can lead to cognitive biases in decision-making, such as confirmation bias, the endowment effect (assigning higher value to what one already possesses), and the disposition effect (holding on to losing investments rather than selling them).

Understanding loss aversion is crucial for decision-makers, as it can help explain why people make seemingly irrational decisions and why they may be reluctant to take risks even when significant gains are possible. In negotiation, this concept can influence how parties evaluate offers and risks, which can be relevant when seeking mutually beneficial agreements.

In some cases, emotions can be strategically used in negotiation. For example, showing genuine enthusiasm for an agreement or expressing appreciation for the other party can contribute to a more positive negotiation atmosphere and facilitate conflict resolution.

Emotional negotiation is a strategy in which emotions are consciously used as a tool to influence the outcome of a negotiation. While negotiation typically relies on rational arguments, emotional negotiation acknowledges that emotions play a significant role in decision-making and can be strategically leveraged to achieve objectives.

Fostering a positive negotiation atmosphere can make parties feel more comfortable and open to collaboration. This can involve using friendly language, acknowledging past achievements, and establishing a cordial working relationship.

Showing empathy toward the other party can help build an emotional connection. When parties feel understood and respected, they are more likely to be flexible and find mutually beneficial solutions.

Emotional negotiation can involve effectively managing emotions in conflict situations. By addressing the emotions of the parties in a positive and collaborative manner, you can work to resolve differences and prevent conflicts from obstructing the negotiation process.

Displaying genuine enthusiasm for an agreement or expressing appreciation for the other party can contribute to a more positive negotiation atmosphere. This can make parties more willing to compromise and commit to reaching an agreement.

Emotional persuasion involves appealing to the emotions of the other party to support an argument or proposal. This can include telling compelling stories, using powerful metaphors, or highlighting the emotional benefits of an agreement.

It's important to note that emotional negotiation should be used ethically and with respect for the needs and desires of the other party. The goal is not to manipulate emotions negatively but to create an environment in which both parties feel valued and can work together effectively.

The ability to understand and manage emotions, as well as the skill to use them strategically in negotiation, are important components of emotional intelligence and effective negotiation.

Emotional negotiation can be a valuable tool for achieving mutually beneficial agreements, especially when combined with effective communication and a solid strategy.

Emotional regulation is the ability to manage and control one's emotions in a negotiation. Effective negotiators can recognize their own emotions and maintain emotional balance to make rational and strategic decisions.

Emotional regulation is a fundamental skill in negotiation and in life in general. It refers to the ability to effectively manage and control one's own emotions, especially in situations of tension or conflict, as often encountered in the negotiation process. Emotional regulation is essential for making rational decisions, maintaining mental clarity, and building constructive relationships.

Emotional regulation starts with self-awareness. It's important for negotiators to be aware of their own emotions and how they can influence their behavior and decision-making.

In negotiation situations, it's common to experience intense emotions like frustration, anger, or stress. Emotional regulation involves the ability to control these emotions to avoid impulsive reactions that could harm the negotiation.

The ability to stay calm under pressure is an essential component of emotional regulation. This means not allowing emotions to dominate the decision-making process and communication.

Emotional regulation is also related to active listening, which is the skill of paying attention to the concerns and perspectives of the other party without reacting emotionally in a negative way.

Emotional regulation helps negotiators stay focused on their goals and desired outcomes rather than being swept away by momentary emotions.

When negotiators can effectively regulate their emotions, they are better able to communicate constructively, resolve conflicts, and reach mutually beneficial agreements.

Emotional regulation doesn't mean suppressing emotions but managing them in a healthy way. Strategies for emotional regulation can include deep breathing, positive visualization, self-control, and effective communication. It can also be helpful to take a short break if needed to calm down before continuing with the negotiation.

Emotional regulation is a skill that can be developed over time through practice and awareness. It is essential for negotiators looking to achieve successful outcomes in emotional and high-pressure situations, such as those often encountered in negotiation.

In summary, psychology plays an essential role in negotiation because emotions can significantly influence decision-making. Effective negotiators are aware of these emotional influences and develop skills to manage and use emotions constructively in the negotiation process.

12. Intercultural Negotiation: Key Aspects

Intercultural negotiation involves the interaction between individuals from different cultures with the aim of reaching mutually beneficial agreements. To succeed in such negotiations, it is important to understand and address several key aspects. Before entering an intercultural negotiation, it is crucial for the involved parties to have a solid understanding of cultural differences. This includes aspects such as values, beliefs, social norms, and communication.

Cultural awareness is an essential element in intercultural negotiation. Here is a more detailed explanation of what cultural awareness entails before a negotiation:

Different cultures have distinct systems of values and beliefs. Some values may be related to hierarchy, individualism versus collectivism, the importance of tradition or innovation, and many other aspects. Understanding these values can help anticipate how the negotiating parties will react to certain proposals or situations.

Social norms dictate how people should behave in a given society or cultural group. These norms can encompass everything from how to greet and shake hands to how to treat older individuals or express gratitude. Knowing these norms is crucial to avoid offending the other party during the negotiation.

Communication can be a sensitive point in intercultural negotiation. Each culture may have different communication styles, both in terms of verbal language and body language. Some cultures may be more direct and explicit, while others may be more indirect and reliant on nuances. Misinterpretation of communication can lead to misunderstandings and conflicts.

Having a solid understanding of these cultural aspects allows you to adapt your approach and communication more effectively during the negotiation. It also helps demonstrate respect for the other party's culture, contributing to building a solid foundation for the relationship and future negotiations.

Communication is fundamental in any negotiation but is especially crucial in an intercultural context. Differences in communication styles, such as language use, physical proximity, eye contact, and gestures, can lead to misunderstandings. It is important to be aware of these differences and adjust communication accordingly.

Effective communication is one of the most critical aspects of intercultural negotiation. Here are some key considerations:

Language is a fundamental component of communication. Ensure that both parties understand each other in the language in which you are negotiating. If there are language barriers, consider using professional interpreters to avoid misunderstandings.

Different cultures have distinct communication styles. Some cultures may be very direct and express their opinions bluntly, while others may be more indirect or use circumlocutions in their communication. It is important to be aware of these styles and adapt as necessary.

Body language and gestures are also part of communication. Some cultures may give a firm handshake as a sign of trust, while in others, it may be perceived as aggressive. Gestures and facial expressions can vary significantly between cultures, so it is essential to consider these differences.

Active listening to the other party is essential. Ensure that you understand their viewpoints and concerns and show genuine interest in what they are saying. This not only facilitates communication but also builds trust.

Do not take anything for granted. Do not assume that what is evident or common in your culture is also so in the other party's culture. Ask and verify if you have doubts instead of making assumptions that can lead to misunderstandings.

Adaptability in communication is key. If you perceive that the other party is not understanding your message or is responding unexpectedly, be willing to adjust your communication to address those differences.

Request and provide feedback regularly during the negotiation. This helps confirm that both parties are on the same page and avoids misunderstandings.

Effective communication in intercultural negotiation requires cultural sensitivity, patience, and a willingness to learn and adapt. By paying attention to these aspects, you can increase your chances of achieving successful agreements in an intercultural context.

Flexibility and adaptability: Flexibility is essential in intercultural negotiation. Parties must be willing to adapt their approaches and strategies to accommodate cultural differences and reach a middle ground that works for both parties.

Flexibility and adaptability are key qualities in intercultural negotiation as they allow parties to overcome cultural differences and reach mutually beneficial agreements. Here are some additional considerations regarding the importance of flexibility and adaptability:

Flexibility involves respecting and accepting cultural diversity. Recognize that there is no single "correct" approach in negotiation, and different cultures may have different methods and priorities.

Adaptability means being willing to learn and adjust your strategies as you progress in the negotiation. As you gain experience in intercultural negotiation, you can improve your skills and better understand cultural nuances.

Being flexible means being empathetic and understanding the perspectives and needs of the other party. Sometimes, this involves putting yourself in their shoes and considering how they feel and what they expect.

Adaptability is also related to seeking creative solutions that can meet the needs of both parties. Instead of clinging to a single strategy, consider different approaches and alternatives that may be acceptable from a cultural perspective.

Encourage open and candid communication where both parties can express their concerns and expectations. This allows for constructive addressing of cultural differences and working together to overcome obstacles.

Intercultural negotiations may sometimes take longer due to the need to build relationships and understand the other party's perspectives. Be flexible regarding timelines and avoid pushing too quickly, as it may be perceived as disrespectful in some cultures.

Adaptability also involves learning from your mistakes. If you make a cultural error, do not give up, but use the experience as a learning opportunity to improve your skills in future intercultural negotiations.

Before any intercultural negotiation, it is essential to understand cultural differences in values, beliefs, social norms, and communication. This will help you anticipate the other party's reactions and avoid misunderstandings.

Communication is a fundamental pillar in any negotiation, but in intercultural contexts, it is even more critical. Ensure that you speak the same language, adapt your communication style, consider body language and gestures, actively listen, and avoid making assumptions.

Being flexible and adaptable is crucial in intercultural negotiation. Recognize cultural diversity, learn from your mistakes, and seek creative solutions that satisfy both parties. Do not rush in negotiations and promote open communication.

Try to understand the perspectives and needs of the other party. Show respect for their culture and demonstrate genuine interest in their viewpoint.

Intercultural negotiation is a continuous learning process. The more experience you gain, the better you will become at adapting to cultural nuances and achieving successful agreements.

Intercultural negotiation demands an open mindset, a willingness to learn and adapt, and effective communication. Handling these aspects with cultural sensitivity significantly increases the chances of reaching mutually beneficial agreements in an intercultural context.

Flexibility and adaptability are essential skills for any intercultural negotiator. By demonstrating these qualities, you can build strong relationships, effectively solve problems, and achieve mutually beneficial agreements in diverse cultural contexts.

Showing respect for the other party's culture is an effective way to establish a solid foundation for the relationship. When parties feel that their values and ways of life are respected, they are more likely to trust the negotiation process and the intentions of the other party.

Mutual respect can help reduce conflicts during negotiation. When cultural diversity is recognized and respected, parties are less likely to make impulsive decisions or react negatively to unexpected cultural differences.

Mutual respect fosters open and candid communication. Parties feel more comfortable sharing their perspectives and concerns when they know they are respected, which, in turn, facilitates problem-solving and decision-making.

Mutual respect creates a positive environment where parties feel valued and heard. This can have a significant impact on the attitude and willingness of parties to collaborate and find mutually beneficial solutions.

To show respect for the culture and customs of the other party in an intercultural negotiation, consider the following actions:

Research and learn about the culture of the other party before the negotiation.

Ask about the cultural expectations and preferences of the other party.

Avoid hasty judgments or cultural stereotypes.

Show genuine interest in the culture and background of the other party.

Seek feedback on how you are performing in terms of cultural respect and willingness to adapt.

In general, mutual respect is essential for fostering a collaborative and mutually understanding environment in an intercultural negotiation. This, in turn, increases the likelihood of achieving successful and lasting agreements.

Each culture has its own etiquette and social protocols. It is important to know and respect these rules to avoid offending the other party.

Knowledge and respect for etiquette are essential in intercultural negotiation. Etiquette rules vary from one culture to another and can cover a wide range of aspects, from how to greet and dress to how to behave in formal or informal meetings. Here are some guidelines to consider:

The way you greet the other party may vary depending on the culture. Some cultures use firm handshakes, while others may prefer a hug, a cheek kiss, or even a bow. Research the greeting norms of the culture you are dealing with.

Appropriate attire can be important in some cultures. Make sure to dress appropriately for the occasion and respect any specific dress code that may exist.

Dining etiquette varies widely. For example, in some cultures, it is common to eat with your hands, while in others, precise table manners are expected. Know the specific etiquette of the culture you are in.

Punctuality is valued differently in various cultures. Some cultures are very strict about punctuality, while in others, some flexibility is allowed. Make sure to understand the culture's attitude toward punctuality.

Some cultures have specific rituals and protocols for the start and progression of meetings and negotiations. This may include who speaks first, how proposals are presented, and how decisions are made. Familiarize yourself with these protocols to avoid misunderstandings.

Gestures and signals can have different meanings in different cultures. For example, a gesture that is considered friendly in one culture might be offensive in another. Avoid making gestures that can be misinterpreted.

Courtesy norms, such as saying "please" and "thank you," may vary in their usage and meaning. Familiarize yourself with common courtesy expressions in the culture you are dealing with.

Some cultures value hierarchy and authority more than others. It is important to show respect for hierarchy and follow authority-respecting rules in professional interactions.

Research and knowledge of these specific etiquette rules of the culture will help you avoid misunderstandings and show respect for the other party. Additionally, show a willingness to learn and correct your actions if you make mistakes, as most people will appreciate your effort to understand and respect their culture.

Actively listening and demonstrating interest in the concerns and perspectives of the other party is essential. This shows empathy and a willingness to find mutually beneficial solutions.

Active listening skills are fundamental in any negotiation process, but they are especially important in an intercultural context. Active listening involves carefully paying attention to what the other party is saying and showing genuine interest in their concerns and perspectives. Here are some key points on why active listening is essential in intercultural negotiation:

Active listening allows you to better understand the needs and perspectives of the other party. This promotes empathy, meaning that you can put yourself in the other person's shoes and understand their viewpoint from their cultural and personal framework.

When you demonstrate that you are willing to listen and value the opinions of the other party, you create a trusting atmosphere in the negotiation. People tend to feel more comfortable sharing their thoughts and concerns in an environment where they feel heard and respected.

The lack of active listening can lead to cultural misunderstandings. People may perceive that their views and concerns are not taken into account, which can lead to conflicts and hinder the negotiation process.

Active listening enables you to identify common interests and areas of agreement. By fully understanding both parties' perspectives, you can seek solutions that benefit both parties and take cultural differences into account.

Active listening promotes more effective communication. By being truly present in the conversation and paying attention to the nuances of language and non-verbal communication, you can avoid misunderstandings and respond more appropriately.

To practice active listening in an intercultural negotiation, consider the following tips:

Ask open-ended questions to encourage conversation and gather more information.

Confirm and repeat what you have heard to ensure you understand correctly.

Pay attention to non-verbal communication, such as gestures and facial expressions.

Avoid interrupting and allow the other party to finish speaking before responding.

Show genuine interest in the concerns and perspectives of the other party.

Active listening is a valuable skill that can significantly contribute to the success of intercultural negotiations as it promotes mutual understanding and the search for mutually beneficial solutions.

Conflict resolution can be different in different cultures. Some cultures may avoid conflict, while others may address it more directly. Understanding how to manage conflicts effectively in an intercultural context is important.

Conflict management in an intercultural context is a crucial aspect of negotiations. Different cultures have distinct approaches to dealing with conflict, and understanding these differences can help prevent misunderstandings and effectively resolve disputes. Here are some key guidelines:

Some cultures tend to avoid conflict and may perceive it as a lack of harmony or a sign of disrespect. Others may address conflict more directly and view it as a way to clarify differences. It's important to understand the cultural attitude toward conflict in the context of your negotiation.

Regardless of the cultural attitude toward conflict, it is essential to remain calm and respectful toward the other party during a dispute. Avoid emotional or confrontational responses, as they can exacerbate the conflict and harm the relationship.

Actively listening to the concerns and perspectives of the other party is fundamental in the management of intercultural conflicts. This can help you understand the root of the conflict and seek mutually beneficial solutions.

In many cases, finding compromise solutions may be the key to resolving intercultural conflicts. Solutions should be acceptable to both parties, and often this involves making concessions in certain aspects.

In situations where the conflict is complex or highly emotional, consider using a neutral mediator who can help facilitate communication and conflict resolution.

In some cultures, it is essential to maintain privacy and avoid embarrassing the other party during a conflict. The concept of "face" is relevant in many cultures and may be essential to avoiding situations in which the other party may lose face.

If you are negotiating with a culture that addresses conflict differently from your own, be adaptable and willing to adjust your approach to meet the cultural expectations of the other party.

Managing intercultural conflicts requires a deep understanding of cultural differences and the ability to find effective solutions that respect the perspectives and values of both parties. By demonstrating respect and empathy, you can resolve disputes in a way that strengthens relationships rather than damages them.

Time and patience: In some cultures, negotiations may take more time and be more relationship-oriented than in others. It is important to have patience and be willing to invest time in building strong relationships.

Consideration of time and patience is essential in intercultural negotiations due to differences in cultural perceptions of time management and relationship building. Here are some reasons why time and patience are important:

In many cultures, building strong relationships is a priority before entering actual negotiations. This involves spending time with the other party, getting to know people on a personal level, and developing trust. Investment in strong relationships can take time, but it is crucial for success in many intercultural negotiations.

Patience in relationship building contributes to the development of trust. People tend to trust those with whom they have had positive relationships over time. Trust is crucial in negotiations because people are more likely to make concessions and reach agreements when they trust the other party.

In some cultures, negotiations may progress at a slower and more methodical pace than in others. Respecting and adapting to the cultural pace is essential to avoid impatience or perceived pressure from damaging the relationship and hindering negotiation.

Patience is also key to overcoming cultural obstacles that may arise during negotiations. Cultural misunderstandings or unexpected challenges may require time to be resolved.

In many cultures, the value of long-term relationship building is emphasized. Patience and investment in strong relationships can benefit not only the current negotiation but also future ones.

It's important to remember that patience should not be interpreted as inaction. While building strong relationships may take time in some cultures, it doesn't mean you should indefinitely postpone the negotiation. The key is to find a balance between relationship building and achieving negotiation goals.

Patience and respect for the cultural pace of the other party are signals of consideration and adaptability, which can significantly contribute to success in intercultural negotiations.

Concessions and Compromises: The way concessions and compromises are made can also vary depending on the culture. It is essential to understand how these aspects are addressed and be willing to find compromise solutions that are acceptable to both parties.

The way concessions and compromises are made in intercultural negotiations is a critical aspect of achieving mutually beneficial agreements. Different cultures have different approaches and expectations in this regard. Here are some key considerations:

Some cultures may take a more collaborative approach with reciprocal concessions, while others may be more competitive and focused on gaining advantages. Understanding the predominant negotiation style in the other party's culture will help you adapt your approach.

In many cultures, the preservation of personal relationships is essential. This can affect how concessions are made. Parties may be more willing to compromise on certain aspects to maintain a harmonious relationship.

In some cultures, hierarchy and respect for authority are important. This can influence how concessions are made, as it may require the party with less authority to make concessions rather than the one with more authority.

Some cultures may prefer a slower and gradual negotiation pace, while others may be willing to reach agreements quickly. Patience and adaptability are key to handling these differences.

The way concessions and compromises are expressed can vary. Some cultures may use direct and clear communication, while others may express themselves more indirectly or subtly. Pay attention to cultural cues and signals in communication.

Seeking compromise solutions that are acceptable to both parties is essential in intercultural negotiation. This may require a willingness to adjust the terms and consider different approaches to reach a fair agreement.

The concept of "face" (maintaining dignity and reputation) is important in many cultures. Avoiding putting the other party in a situation where they lose face is crucial for maintaining harmony and trust.

Ensure that agreements are clear and detailed, especially if there are cultural differences in the interpretation of terms. This will help prevent misunderstandings in the future.

The key to managing concessions and compromises in intercultural negotiation is open communication and a willingness to adapt to the other party's culture's expectations and practices. Empathy and respect are essential to reach mutually beneficial solutions that are acceptable to both parties.

Proper Preparation: Before entering into an intercultural negotiation, it is important to research and prepare in terms of both the other party's culture and the negotiation topic itself.

Proper preparation is a crucial step before engaging in an intercultural negotiation. This involves researching and understanding both the other party's culture and the negotiation topic itself. Here are some reasons why proper preparation is essential:

Researching and understanding the other party's culture is crucial to avoid unnecessary misunderstandings and conflicts. You should be familiar with social norms, values, beliefs, and common practices in the culture you are dealing with.

Proper preparation will help you avoid behaviors or comments that may be considered offensive in the other party's culture. This will contribute to building a more positive relationship from the outset.

Understanding cultural differences in communication will allow you to adapt your communication style to be more effective in the intercultural context. This includes aspects such as language, tone of voice, the use of gestures, and non-verbal communication.

In addition to cultural understanding, you should be well-prepared on the negotiation topic itself. This includes having a solid knowledge of the details, statistics, and relevant data related to the subject under discussion.

Preparation allows you to identify common interests and areas of agreement that can be used as starting points for negotiation. This can facilitate the search for mutually beneficial solutions.

Before entering the negotiation, you should set clear and realistic goals for what you expect to achieve. This helps you stay focused during the negotiation.

Preparing strong negotiation strategies will give you an advantage at the negotiation table. You should have a plan in mind and be prepared to adjust it as needed.

If an agreement cannot be reached, you should have alternatives in mind. Proper preparation includes considering what your options are if the negotiation is unsuccessful.

Proper preparation demonstrates respect for the other party and their culture, and provides you with the confidence and tools necessary to address the negotiation successfully. Through research and preparation, you are better equipped to deal with cultural differences and find mutually beneficial solutions.

Intercultural negotiation involves not only attempting to reach an agreement but also understanding and respecting cultural differences. The key lies in cultural awareness, adaptability, and the ability to build trust in a multicultural environment.

13.Negotiation in the Business Environment

Business negotiation is a key process that involves interaction between two or more parties with the aim of reaching agreements that benefit all parties involved. Here are some fundamental aspects related to business negotiation:

Preparation is essential. Before entering into a negotiation, you must thoroughly research the other party, understand their needs, goals, and constraints, and prepare regarding the negotiation topic.

Preparation is one of the most crucial aspects in any negotiation, as it provides you with a solid foundation to achieve your goals and maximize results. Here are some additional guidelines on the importance of preparation and how to carry it out in the context of a negotiation:

Begin by conducting thorough research on the other party. Find out about their history, background, values, organizational culture, and any relevant public information about their business activities. Also, research the individuals involved in the negotiation, such as their roles and personalities.

Understand the needs, goals, and limitations of both your own party and the other party. Identify what is essential and what is negotiable. The better you understand the goals of all parties, the easier it will be to find mutually beneficial solutions.

Define your own objectives and limits before the negotiation. Have a clear idea of what you are trying to achieve and what your priorities are.

Identify your BATNA, which stands for your Best Alternative to a Negotiated Agreement. This provides you with a reference point to evaluate any proposed agreement.

Think about what you are willing to concede and in which areas you are less willing to make concessions. This will prepare you for concession discussions.

Before the negotiation, visualize how the discussion could unfold. Consider different scenarios and how you might respond to each one.

Prepare your arguments and key messages. Think about how you will effectively present your views during the negotiation. Consider possible questions and objections that may arise.

Conduct simulations or practice with colleagues or advisors to refine your communication skills and practice presenting your arguments.

Do not underestimate the importance of building strong relationships before and during the negotiation. Trust and goodwill can be valuable assets at the negotiation table.

Consider different scenarios and develop a contingency plan to deal with unexpected situations or crises during the negotiation.

Proper preparation gives you confidence, helps you make informed decisions, and allows you to navigate the complexities of a negotiation more effectively. The more you prepare, the more likely you are to reach mutually beneficial agreements for all parties.

You should have clear objectives and limits before the negotiation. Define what is essential and what concessions you are willing to make.

Establishing goals before a negotiation is a fundamental step that helps guide your actions and decisions throughout the process. Here are some guidelines on how to set clear objectives in a negotiation:

Start by clearly defining what your objectives are. What are you trying to achieve in this negotiation? Set specific goals and ensure they are clear and measurable.

Prioritize your objectives. Identify the core objectives that you are not willing to compromise on and those in which you can be more flexible. This will help you maintain a clear focus during the negotiation.

It is essential to set boundaries and define what you are willing to concede. Before the negotiation, determine your potential concessions in case you need to make compromises to achieve your core objectives.

Make sure your objectives are realistic and achievable. Do not set goals that are unreasonable, as this can jeopardize the possibility of reaching an agreement.

During the negotiation, communicate your objectives and limits clearly and directly. This avoids misunderstandings and allows the other party to understand your expectations.

While it is important to maintain a focus on your core objectives, you should also be flexible in certain areas. Controlled flexibility allows you to adapt to circumstances and seek mutually beneficial solutions.

Consider your Best Alternative to a Negotiated Agreement (BATNA). This provides you with a solid reference point for evaluating any proposed agreement. If an agreement does not satisfy your core objectives and your BATNA is more attractive, it may be better to withdraw from the negotiation.

If you have multiple objectives, establish a hierarchy for them. This will help you make informed decisions if you need to make concessions.

Consider the time factor when setting your objectives. Are there deadlines or time constraints in the negotiation that you must consider?

Consider documenting your objectives and limits in writing before the negotiation. This can serve as a guide during the discussion.

Remember that setting clear objectives helps you stay on track and make informed decisions during the negotiation. Additionally, being transparent and communicative about your objectives can help create an environment of trust and mutual understanding among the parties involved.

Effective communication is key. Actively listening to the other party, asking questions, expressing your views clearly, and being aware of non-verbal communication are important aspects.

Effective communication is crucial in any negotiation process. Here are more details on how you can improve your communication in the context of a negotiation:

Pay careful attention to what the other party is saying. Don't just listen to their words, but also their tone of voice and body language. Ask questions to clarify any points that are not clear and show genuine interest in their concerns and perspectives.

Express your views and objectives clearly and concisely. Avoid ambiguity and confusion. Use simple and direct language to ensure that your messages are understood.

Nonverbal communication, such as body language, gestures, and facial expressions, can convey important information. Be aware of your own nonverbal cues and observe those of the other party to pick up additional signals about what they are feeling or thinking. Try to understand the emotions and perspectives of the other party. Empathy allows you to establish a stronger connection and better understand their needs and desires. Open-ended questions encourage conversation and allow the other party to share more information. This can help you gain a more complete view of their concerns and goals. Let the other party finish speaking before responding. Interrupting can be perceived as disrespectful and hinder effective communication. Maintain a positive attitude during the negotiation. Negativity and unnecessary conflict can impede the process. If you are negotiating with people from different cultures, be aware of cultural differences in communication. Some cultures may use a more direct style, while others may be more indirect. If necessary, document key points and agreements in writing. This helps prevent misunderstandings and provides a clear record of what was discussed. If conflicts arise, try to resolve them effectively through communication. Listen to the concerns of the other party and seek solutions that satisfy both sides. Effective communication is essential for building trusting relationships and reaching mutually beneficial agreements. Practicing active listening, being clear and direct in your communication, and being aware of nonverbal communication are skills that can make a difference in the success of a negotiation.

In the business environment, building strong relationships can be fundamental. Trust and goodwill are valuable assets in negotiations. Building strong relationships is a fundamental aspect in the business environment and in negotiations. Here are some tips on how to build effective relationships:

Recognize that building a strong relationship takes time and effort. Take the time to get to know the people you are negotiating with and show interest in their perspectives and needs. Promote open and honest communication. Be transparent about your goals and expectations and encourage the other party to do the same. Trust is essential in a business relationship. Keep your commitments and agreements and demonstrate that you are trustworthy. Trust is developed over time through consistent actions. Actively listen to the other party, showing genuine interest in their concerns and perspectives. Active listening is essential for understanding the needs and desires of the other party. Try to understand the emotions and perspectives of the other party. Empathy helps you establish a stronger connection and adapt to their needs. If conflicts arise, try to resolve them effectively. Facing problems openly and constructively can strengthen the relationship. Share relevant and useful information with the other party. Transparency in communication can build an atmosphere of trust. Seek solutions that are mutually beneficial. The focus on creating shared value can strengthen the relationship and generate long-term benefits. Celebrate shared successes and achievements. Recognizing each other's efforts and contributions strengthens the relationship. While you are building strong relationships, maintain professionalism at all times. Respecting boundaries and agreements is essential. After reaching an agreement, make sure to stay in touch and follow up. This demonstrates that you value the long-term relationship.

If you are negotiating in an intercultural context, be aware of cultural differences in relationship building. Understanding and respecting cultural practices and expectations is essential.

Strong relationships in the business environment are not only valuable in a specific negotiation but can also lead to future collaborations and strengthen your company's brand and reputation. Building effective relationships is a long-term investment that can provide significant benefits in the business world.

Seeking solutions that benefit all parties is the goal. Avoid a competitive approach that can lead to a winner and a loser. The focus on mutually beneficial solutions is a key philosophy in successful negotiations. By seeking solutions that benefit all parties involved, a collaborative environment is created, and the value created is maximized. Here is more information on how to apply this approach:

Start by identifying shared interests and goals among the parties. These are the points on which mutually beneficial agreements can be built.

Rather than viewing the negotiation as a competition for a fixed pie, approach the negotiation as an opportunity to create value together. Consider how you can increase the size of the pie so that everyone gets more.

Use open-ended questions to explore the needs and desires of the other party. You may discover areas where they are willing to make concessions that benefit them in other aspects.

Ensure that the proposed solutions satisfy the needs and concerns of all parties involved. The satisfaction of all parties is essential for a mutually beneficial solution.

Focus on building long-term relationships. The ongoing pursuit of mutually beneficial solutions is not only advantageous in the current negotiation but also lays the groundwork for future successful collaborations.

Be creative in seeking solutions. Sometimes, innovative solutions can lead to results that satisfy all parties more effectively.

Make sure all parties fully understand the terms of the agreement. Clear communication is essential to avoid future misunderstandings.

Be flexible in seeking solutions but keep a focus on the essential goals. Concessions should be carefully considered to ensure they are mutually beneficial. Seek the commitment of all parties to the agreement. An agreement in which all parties are actively involved tends to be more solid and enduring. Document the agreement in writing to avoid later misunderstandings. This also provides a clear record of what was agreed upon.

An emphasis on mutually beneficial solutions not only promotes effective conflict resolution but also creates a more positive and constructive negotiating environment. Instead of a competitive approach that can result in winners and losers, this approach seeks to create winners on all sides, often leading to more sustainable and satisfying agreements.

Adaptability is important. As the negotiation progresses, you may need to adjust your strategies and concessions based on the circumstances and signals from the other party. Flexibility is a crucial skill in any negotiation process since circumstances and dynamics can change over time. Here are some guidelines on how to apply flexibility effectively in a negotiation:

During the negotiation, make an ongoing assessment of the situation. Monitor the responses and signals from the other party to adapt your strategies as needed. Be strategic when making concessions. Don't concede on critical aspects right away, but consider making concessions in less crucial areas to maintain momentum and foster a collaborative atmosphere. Pay attention to what the other party is saying.

Their comments and concerns can give you clues on how to adjust your approach and find mutually beneficial solutions. If new priorities or concerns arise during the negotiation, be open to addressing them. It may be necessary to reevaluate your goals and strategies as circumstances change. If you find yourself at an impasse or face an unexpected obstacle, seek creative solutions. Sometimes, flexibility in seeking alternative approaches can unlock progress. Maintain constant communication with the other party. Open communication allows you to address changes in circumstances constructively. Maintain a positive and goodwill attitude, even when facing challenges. A negative attitude can hinder flexibility and problem-solving.

As the negotiation evolves, consider how the current offer compares to your Best Alternative to a Negotiated Agreement (BATNA). This can help you make informed decisions about whether to continue negotiating or withdraw. If you reach agreements or make significant changes during the negotiation, be sure to document them in writing to avoid later misunderstandings. If you are negotiating across cultures, be aware of cultural signals that may require adjustments in your approach and strategy.

Flexibility is a valuable skill in negotiation as it allows you to adapt to changing circumstances and find effective solutions as challenges arise. Being rigid or inflexible can hinder progress and make it difficult to build strong relationships in negotiation.

Ethics: Ethical practices are fundamental in the business environment. Maintain high standards of integrity and adhere to agreements. Ethics play a fundamental role in all business interactions, including negotiations. Maintaining high standards of integrity is essential for building strong relationships, maintaining trust, and ensuring long-term success. Here are some considerations on ethics in the business environment and negotiations:

Personal integrity is the foundation of business ethics. You should keep your commitments and be honest in all your interactions. Lack of integrity undermines trust and can damage your reputation. Fulfill the agreements and contracts you make. Do not promise what you cannot deliver. Breaching agreements can have legal consequences and harm your reputation. Be transparent in your communications and transactions.

Hiding information or acting deceptively can lead to distrust and the loss of business relationships. Avoid situations where you may have a conflict of interest. Objectivity and impartiality are essential for making ethical decisions in the business world. Comply with all applicable laws and regulations.

Ethical business practices also include respect for the law. Consider corporate social responsibility (CSR) when making business decisions. This involves considering broader impacts, such as the environmental and social impact of your operations. Maintain professional conduct in all your business interactions. Courtesy, respect, and politeness are essential in negotiations. Avoid exaggeration, defamation, and deceptive advertising in your communications. Advertising and promotion should be honest and truthful. When making significant business decisions, consider not only the economic benefit but also the ethical and social impact. Ethical decisions can bring long-term benefits.

Promote an ethical culture in your organization. This involves setting ethical standards, providing training, and promoting ethics at all levels of the company.

Ethics in business is not only a moral obligation but can also be a valuable asset for the company. Businesses and individuals who adhere to high ethical standards tend to gain the trust of customers, business partners, and employees, which often translates into long-term success. Furthermore, companies that follow ethical practices are often viewed more positively by society at large.

It's important to consider your Best Alternative to a Negotiated Agreement (BATNA) in case the negotiation is unsuccessful. Knowing your alternatives gives you a stronger position. Having clarity about your Best Alternative to a Negotiated Agreement (BATNA) is a fundamental part of preparing for a negotiation.

BATNA is an acronym that stands for "Best Alternative to a Negotiated Agreement." In the context of the art of negotiation, BATNA refers to the evaluation and consideration of the best alternative that a person or party in a negotiation has available if an agreement is not reached with the other party.

Identifying and understanding your BATNA is essential in the negotiation process, as it provides you with a benchmark for assessing whether the proposed agreement is favorable or if it would be more beneficial not to reach an agreement and seek a more attractive alternative. If your BATNA is strong and preferable to the terms proposed in the negotiation, you will have a stronger position and can negotiate more effectively.

Knowing your BATNA helps you make informed decisions during a negotiation since it allows you to determine whether you should accept the proposed agreement or seek better options outside of the negotiation. Knowing it enables you to evaluate the risks associated with the negotiation. If the other party is unwilling to reach a satisfactory agreement, having a solid BATNA provides you with an alternative, giving you a stronger position at the negotiating table. Knowing that you can walk away and turn to a viable alternative gives you more bargaining power and allows you to maintain your essential goals.

If you lack a good understanding of it, you may feel pressured to accept an unfavorable agreement out of fear of not having another option. Knowing it gives you the confidence to reject agreements that do not meet your needs.

Considering it allows you to make informed decisions. You can compare any proposed agreement with your BATNA and determine if it is a significant improvement or if you should continue negotiating.

When both parties have strong BATNAs, negotiation tends to be more effective and based on the search for mutually beneficial solutions rather than pressure.

With your BATNA in mind, you are better prepared to adapt to changes in the negotiation. If circumstances change, you can adjust your strategies accordingly.

If you decide to withdraw from the negotiation, have a strategy in place to implement your BATNA. Make sure your alternative is viable and well-documented.

Having a solid BATNA allows you to maintain a long-term perspective. If an agreement is not feasible at the moment, you can return to the negotiation in the future with a stronger position.

In some cases, you can use it as a bargaining tool. For example, you can mention that you have other options and are willing to explore them if a mutually beneficial agreement is not reached.

Considering your BATNA is part of solid strategic planning before negotiation. Evaluate your alternatives carefully and prepare to make decisions based on them.

Knowing and understanding it is an essential part of negotiation preparation. It provides you with a safety net and a stronger position at the negotiating table, allowing you to make more informed decisions and negotiate more effectively.

Conflicts can arise in any negotiation. Learning to manage them effectively is crucial. Active listening and empathy can help resolve disputes.

Conflict management is an important skill in any negotiation process. Conflicts are inevitable, but how they are handled can make a difference in the success of the negotiation.

Active listening is essential in conflict management. Pay attention to the concerns and perspectives of the other party. Make sure you fully understand their point of view before responding.

Try to understand the emotions and perspectives of the other party. Empathy helps you build a stronger connection and find solutions that address their concerns.

Stay calm and composed, even in conflict situations. Anger or frustration can worsen the situation. Instead, try to maintain a respectful and professional attitude.

Express your views clearly and concisely. Avoid ambiguity and misinterpretation. Clear communication can help avoid misunderstandings and unnecessary conflicts.

Look for common ground and shared goals. Identifying mutual interests can help find solutions that benefit both parties.

Invite both parties to contribute ideas and solutions to resolve the conflict. Collaborating on generating options can lead to creative solutions.

Evaluate whether the conflict is better suited for hard or soft negotiation. In some cases, a tougher negotiation may be necessary to defend your interests, while in others, a more flexible and conciliatory approach may be preferable.

Instead of focusing on the past or assigning blame, concentrate on how to move forward together. Focus on solutions and the future rather than getting stuck in past problems.

In particularly difficult situations, consider mediation by an impartial third party. A mediator can help facilitate communication and find equitable solutions.

Ensure that the conflict resolution is ethical and complies with the ethical standards of your industry and company.

If an agreement is reached to resolve the conflict, be sure to document it in writing. This provides a clear record and avoids future misunderstandings.

Effective conflict management is essential for keeping a negotiation on track and for building strong relationships. Instead of viewing conflicts as obstacles, you can see them as opportunities to find mutually beneficial solutions and strengthen the relationship with the other party.

It is recommended that agreements be documented in writing to avoid future misunderstandings.

Documenting agreements in writing is a crucial practice in any negotiation process.

Written documentation provides clarity about the terms and conditions of the agreement. It prevents misunderstandings and ambiguities by accurately setting the expectations of both parties.

A written document serves as a reference record. You can refer back to it in case questions or disputes arise in the future. This is especially useful if the negotiation takes place over time, and circumstances may change.

Ensure that the agreed-upon deadlines are met. If necessary, mutually adjust the deadlines if difficulties arise.

Both parties should be accountable for their actions and for fulfilling their commitments. Accountability is essential for the successful execution of the agreement.

Results assessment: Periodically, evaluate the progress and outcomes of the agreement. Are the objectives being met? Are there areas that need adjustments?

Recognize and celebrate achievements as you progress in implementing the agreement. This can help maintain motivation and commitment from both parties.

If the implementation of the agreement is successful, consider the possibility of future collaborations or agreements. A strong business relationship can open doors to new opportunities.

Commitment and effective execution of the agreement are essential for a win-win negotiation to be truly successful. By maintaining open communication, planning effectively, and ensuring that both parties fulfill their commitments, a solid foundation is established for ongoing collaboration and long-term mutual benefits.

In a win-win negotiation, the goal is to achieve an outcome in which all parties feel they have received a fair and beneficial deal. This is not only beneficial for short-term relationships but also lays the groundwork for future successful collaborations.

14. Negotiation in the Workplace

Negotiating in the workplace is an integral part of human resource management and the development of effective professional relationships. Here are some key considerations for workplace negotiation:

One of the most common labor negotiations is salary negotiation. Employees can negotiate initial salaries, salary increases, bonuses, and other incentives. Employers should be willing to consider employee requests and reach fair agreements.

Salary negotiation is a crucial part of the relationship between employers and employees. Employees often seek salary agreements that reflect their value, experience, and contribution to the company. Here are some guidelines for salary negotiation:

Before negotiating, research the typical salary range for the position and industry in your area. This will provide a solid basis for your arguments and expectations.

Create a list of your achievements, relevant experience, and skills that support your request for a specific salary. Be prepared to effectively communicate why you deserve the salary you are seeking.

Define your salary goals and set clear limits on what you are willing to accept. This will help you negotiate with confidence and avoid accepting a lower salary than you are willing to accept.

Clearly and directly communicate your salary expectations during the negotiation. Don't let the topic of salary remain a mystery, as this can lead to misunderstandings.

Listen to what the other party has to say about the salary offer. Ask about the details and reasons behind the offer. Understanding their perspective can help find mutually beneficial solutions.

Be willing to be flexible in the negotiation. You can consider aspects of the compensation package, such as benefits, bonuses, time off, or a salary increase plan.

Maintain a respectful and professional tone during the negotiation. Courtesy and respect are important for maintaining a positive work relationship.

Accept that you may not get everything you want in salary negotiation. Prepare for rejection and consider when it's appropriate to withdraw and seek other opportunities.

If you can't achieve the desired salary, consider other valuable benefits such as professional development plans, flexible work arrangements, remote work options, or performance-based bonuses.

Once you reach an agreement, ensure that the salary terms are documented in writing. This provides a clear record and prevents future misunderstandings.

After closing the salary agreement, follow up and reevaluate your salary goals over time. Regular performance reviews and salary increase negotiations are common practices in most companies.

Salary negotiation is an important skill for both employees and employers. Both parties should strive to reach fair and equitable agreements that reflect the employee's value and contribution while maintaining a healthy and positive work relationship.

In addition to salary, employees can negotiate benefits and compensation such as health insurance, retirement plans, time off, and other incentives. Employers should offer competitive packages and be willing to adapt to employees' needs.

Negotiating additional benefits and compensation is an important part of labor negotiation, as these elements can be equally valuable as the base salary in terms of satisfaction and quality of life. Here are some guidelines for negotiating benefits and compensation:

Before entering into negotiations on benefits, identify your personal needs and priorities. Which benefits matter most to you? For example, some may value comprehensive health insurance more, while others may prioritize time off or work-life balance.

Research the benefits and compensation offered by the company. Understand which benefits are standard and which may be negotiable. This will allow you to focus on specific areas during the negotiation.

During the negotiation, communicate your needs and desires in terms of benefits and compensation. Ensure that the other party understands your priorities and expectations.

Consider flexible options. For example, if an employer cannot offer health insurance, they may be willing to provide a salary increase that allows you to purchase your own insurance.

Time off, such as paid vacations and sick days, is a negotiable benefit. Discuss the possibility of additional days or flexibility in work schedules.

Inquire about retirement and savings plans offered by the company. Some companies match contributions to retirement plans, which can be a significant advantage.

If you have a family, consider family-related benefits, such as health insurance for spouses and children, childcare, or education support.

Performance-based bonuses and recognition of achievements can be important. Discuss the possibility of annual bonuses or incentives for specific accomplishments.

Ensure that agreements regarding benefits and compensation are documented in writing to avoid misunderstandings. This may include changes to the employment contract or separate agreements.

Recognize that in benefit negotiations, fairness is important. Not all demands can be met, so it's essential to reach an agreement that benefits both employees and the company.

Once an agreement on benefits and compensation is reached, regularly follow up and assess your satisfaction with them. Changes in your circumstances or needs may require adjustments in the future.

Negotiating benefits and compensation can be an integral part of the work relationship and can significantly contribute to your satisfaction and well-being at work. Open communication and flexibility in negotiation are key to achieving mutually beneficial agreements.

In some cases, employees may be covered by employment contracts or union agreements. Negotiating employment contracts can be an important part of the relationship between employers and employees.

Contractual negotiations are an important aspect of the workplace when employees are covered by employment contracts or union agreements. These contracts establish the terms and conditions of employment and can address a variety of issues, from salaries and benefits to working hours and terms of employment. Here are some key guidelines related to contractual negotiations:

The first thing you should do is fully understand the employment contract or union agreement that applies to your situation. Read and analyze the document carefully to have a clear understanding of what is stipulated in it. Identify the areas that are of particular interest to you and your colleagues. It can be salary, benefits, working conditions, or any other relevant aspect.

If you are a member of a union, seek guidance and support from the union. Unions have experience in negotiating labor contracts and can represent you in the negotiations. If you are part of a negotiating team (as in a union agreement), make sure the team is well-coordinated and represents the interests of employees effectively.

Define your priorities and goals before entering into negotiations. This will help you focus on what is most important to you and your colleagues. Open and effective communication with the company's or union's representatives is essential. Express your needs and concerns clearly and respectfully.

In contractual negotiations, it is important to build consensus both within the negotiation team and with the other party. Seek mutually beneficial solutions whenever possible. Once an agreement is reached, ensure that both parties are committed to the implementation of the employment contract.

This involves following the agreed-upon terms and conditions. Make sure the employment contract is properly documented, and maintain a clear record of the agreements. This prevents future misunderstandings.

Educate employees about the terms of the employment contract and how they relate to their rights and responsibilities. Awareness of the contract terms is crucial for effective implementation. Continuously monitor and evaluate the employment contract to ensure that the terms are being met and that changes in working conditions are addressed appropriately.

Contractual negotiations can be a complex process and often involve multiple parties. Effective communication, union representation (if applicable), and commitment to implementation are key factors in ensuring that employment contracts reflect the interests and needs of employees fairly and equitably.

Employees can negotiate professional development opportunities, such as training, continuous education, promotions, and transfers. Employers can promote the training and growth of their employees. Professional development is a fundamental aspect of an employee's career, and negotiating professional development opportunities can help advance in one's career and acquire new skills. Here are some key considerations for negotiating professional development opportunities:

Before negotiating development opportunities, identify your professional development goals and needs. What skills or certifications do you want to acquire? Do you want to advance in your career in a specific direction? Having clarity about your goals is essential.

During the negotiation, effectively communicate your professional development goals to your employer or supervisor. Explain why these goals are relevant and how they can benefit the company.

If you are interested in training or continuous education, discuss the available options. This could include courses, workshops, seminars, conferences, or training programs. Inquire if the company can fund or support your development.

Mentorship and guidance are valuable tools for professional development. You can negotiate the possibility of having a mentor or advisor within the company.

If your goal is to advance within the company's hierarchy, discuss promotion opportunities. Inquire about the promotion criteria and how you can work towards those goals.

Transferring to different departments or locations can provide valuable work experience. If this is relevant to your development, explore the possibility of transfers within the company.

On-the-job training can be an effective way to acquire new skills and experience. Discuss the possibility of taking on additional responsibilities or working on projects that provide learning opportunities.

Ensure that your development is recognized and documented. This may include regular performance reviews and feedback on your progress.

Once an agreement on professional development opportunities is reached, demonstrate a commitment to your professional growth. Actively participate in training opportunities and apply what you learn in your work.

Monitor your professional development over time. Regularly evaluate your progress toward your goals and make adjustments as necessary.

Negotiating professional development opportunities is beneficial for both employees and companies. Employees gain new skills and advance in their careers, which can benefit the company by improving the quality of its workforce and talent retention. Open communication and aligning your development goals with the company's objectives are essential for successful professional development.

Conflict management is essential in the workplace. Employees and employers must be willing to address and resolve conflicts effectively to maintain a healthy work environment.

Conflict management is crucial in the workplace, as conflicts can arise for a variety of reasons, such as differences of opinion, misunderstandings, communication issues, or disagreements on policies and procedures. Here are some strategies for addressing and resolving conflicts effectively in the workplace:

Encourage open and honest communication in the workplace. Encourage employees to express their concerns and opinions respectfully.

Actively listen to all parties involved in the conflict. Ensure you understand their perspectives and concerns before responding.

Try to identify the underlying causes of the conflict. There may be deeper factors at play that need to be addressed."

"It is important to remain calm during discussions and avoid excessive emotional responses. Empathy and self-control are crucial. Instead of seeking a winner and a loser, look for solutions that are mutually beneficial.

This may require compromises and concessions from both parties. In situations where the parties involved cannot resolve the conflict on their own, consider mediation. An impartial mediator can help facilitate the conversation and find solutions. Establish workplace behavior norms that promote respect and peaceful conflict resolution.

If the conflict is severe or persistent, document the conversations and incidents related to the conflict. This can be helpful in case further action is needed. Ensure that your company has clear human resources policies and processes for addressing conflicts appropriately. Provide conflict management training to employees and supervisors so they are better prepared to address and resolve disputes. Once a conflict has been resolved, follow up to ensure that the implemented solutions work and that there are no relapses in the conflict.

In addition to conflict management, focus on prevention. Promote a culture of respect and open communication to reduce the occurrence of conflicts. Effective conflict management can greatly contribute to maintaining a healthy and productive work environment. Instead of avoiding conflicts, it is important to proactively address them and find solutions that benefit all parties involved.

Open and effective communication is essential in the workplace. Employees should feel free to express their concerns and needs, and employers should actively listen and respond to those concerns.

Effective internal communication is a fundamental pillar for building healthy relationships and successful management in the workplace. Both employees and employers play a crucial role in fostering a work environment where open communication is valued. Here are some key considerations:

Promote a culture of open communication in the company. It should be a norm for employees to feel free to express their concerns and opinions.

Employers should practice active listening. This means paying attention to what employees say, asking follow-up questions, and demonstrating empathy toward their concerns.

Establish effective communication channels, both formal and informal. This can include regular meetings, feedback from supervisors, employee satisfaction surveys, and feedback systems.

Ensure that employees feel comfortable expressing their concerns, and that these concerns are handled confidentially when necessary.

Promote transparency in communication. Provide information about policies, procedures, and decisions that affect employees.

Encourage constructive feedback in both directions. Employers should provide feedback to employees, and vice versa.

Proactively and efficiently address concerns and issues. Do not ignore concerns but seek solutions and take action to resolve problems.

In situations of crisis or significant changes in the company, communicate effectively and empathetically. Ensure that employees are informed and reassured.

Provide communication skills training to employees and supervisors to improve the quality of interactions and conflict resolution.

Company leaders should be role models for communication. If leaders demonstrate a commitment to open communication, employees tend to follow their example.

Adjust the pace and style of communication to make it clear and understandable for all employees, regardless of their level of technical knowledge or experience.

Recognize and appreciate employees for their contributions. Positive recognition is a powerful way to reinforce communication and morale.

Effective internal communication improves employee satisfaction, morale, talent retention, and productivity. By fostering an environment where employees feel valued and heard, companies can build stronger and healthier working relationships.

Human resources policies should be fair and transparent. Labor policies and procedures should be clearly defined and communicated and should be followed consistently.

Human resources policies (HR) are essential to establish a fair and effective framework in a company. These policies define the rules and expectations governing employee relationships and conduct. Here are some key considerations related to HR policies:

HR policies should be fair and equitable for all employees, regardless of their position, race, gender, age, or other personal characteristics. This helps promote an inclusive and diverse work environment.

Policies should be clearly defined and transparently communicated to all employees. This includes having employee handbooks and policy guides that are easily accessible.

Policies should be applied consistently throughout the organization. Decisions and actions based on policies should follow a uniform process.

HR policies should be updated and reviewed periodically to reflect changes in labor laws, best practices, and changing company needs.

It is helpful to involve employees in policy review and development, as this can increase acceptance and understanding.

Policies should include procedures for conflict resolution. This can include steps for filing complaints or disputes and how they will be handled.

HR policies should respect employee privacy and rights, especially in matters related to data protection and confidentiality.

Ensure that HR policies comply with labor laws and other applicable regulations in your area."

"Provide guidance to new employees on the company's policies and procedures, which helps them understand the expectations and responsibilities.

Maintain ongoing communication with employees regarding any changes in labor policies or procedures. Ensure that they are aware of updates and how to access updated information.

HR policies should include provisions related to employee training and development. This can address topics such as skills training, professional development, and learning opportunities.

When policies include penalties for violations, ensure that they are applied fairly and proportionally to the infringement.

Well-designed and properly applied HR policies can contribute to a positive work environment, compliance with labor laws, and employee well-being. Justice, fairness, transparency, and communication are fundamental elements in the successful development and implementation of human resources policies.

Negotiation in the workplace may also include discussions about the work-life balance. Employees may seek flexibility in schedules or remote work options.

Work-life balance is crucial for employee satisfaction and well-being. Negotiating agreements that allow for a better work-life balance can be beneficial for both parties. Here are some guidelines for addressing this issue:

Before negotiating, identify your specific needs regarding work-life balance. Do you need more flexible hours, the option to work from home, or additional time for personal commitments?

Communicate your needs and desires clearly and respectfully to your employer or supervisor. Explain how a better work-life balance can be beneficial for both you and the company.

Demonstrate your commitment to work and the company. Often, employers are more receptive to flexibility requests when employees show that they will remain productive and fulfill their responsibilities.

Explore flexible options such as compressed work schedules, remote workdays, or a flexible work plan. Provide examples of how these options can work in your situation.

Show how a better work-life balance can benefit the company, such as increased employee satisfaction, higher talent retention, and greater productivity.

Investigate if the company has existing policies or programs related to flexible work arrangements. There may be established rules and procedures.

If you reach an agreement with your employer, make sure the terms of any work-life balance agreement are documented in writing to avoid future misunderstandings.

Recognize that, in negotiating work-life balance, mutual commitment may be required. Ensure that both parties are willing to abide by the agreement.

Once a work-life balance agreement has been implemented, periodically review its effectiveness and make adjustments as needed.

Work-life balance is important for employee health and well-being, and many companies recognize its value. By addressing this issue with open and respectful communication, you are more likely to find solutions that allow you to achieve a satisfactory work-life balance.

Performance reviews and salary evaluations are key moments for negotiation. Employees can discuss their performance and corresponding compensation.

Performance reviews and salary evaluations are critical moments for negotiation in the workplace. During these instances, employees can discuss their performance and the compensation they receive. Here are some guidelines for addressing these situations effectively:

Before the review, prepare by reviewing your achievements and contributions to the company. Set clear goals for the conversation.

During the review, encourage open communication and feedback. Actively listen to your supervisor's feedback and provide examples of your performance.

If you have concerns about working conditions, expectations, or development opportunities, address them constructively.

Inquire about professional development opportunities, such as additional training, challenging projects, or promotions. Express your interest in growth and advancement within the company.

Research salaries and benefits in your industry and geographic area to understand if your compensation is in line with the market.

Highlight your achievements and contributions to the company during the salary evaluation. Show how your performance has benefited the organization.

If you believe your current compensation is not competitive, professionally and data-supportedly communicate your concern.

If you feel your salary is inadequate, request a salary review. Present arguments and evidence for why you deserve an increase.

Show flexibility in the negotiation. If an immediate salary increase is not possible, consider other options, such as performance-based raises or a development plan.

In addition to salary, consider other benefits, such as bonuses, stock options, health benefits, and paid time off.

Inquire about additional benefits, such as access to a retirement plan or family benefits.

If you reach an agreement on a salary review, ensure that the terms are documented in writing to avoid misunderstandings.

Performance reviews and salary evaluations are opportunities to discuss your progress and development within the company. Open communication and preparation are key to ensuring your needs and achievements are considered during these evaluations.

Diversity and inclusion policies are important in the workplace. Employers should promote diversity and equality and be willing to address issues related to discrimination and equity."

"Diversity and inclusion policies are fundamental in the workplace and play a significant role in promoting an equitable work environment and respecting employee diversity. Here are some guidelines on how to address and promote diversity and inclusion in the workplace:

Establish clear diversity and inclusion policies that indicate the company's commitment to equal opportunities and non-discrimination. These policies should be communicated and accessible to all employees.

Provide education and awareness about diversity and inclusion. Employees should understand the importance of respecting and valuing differences.

Offer training on implicit and conscious biases to help employees recognize and overcome prejudices and stereotypes.

Involve employees from diverse backgrounds in decision-making and strategic planning for the company. This may include affinity groups or diversity committees.

Establish a clear and accessible process for filing complaints related to discrimination or lack of inclusion, and ensure that complaints are handled fairly and efficiently.

Ensure that all employees have equal access to development, promotion, and training opportunities.

Proactively work to promote diversity in hiring and promotion, seeking candidates from diverse backgrounds and fostering an inclusive work environment.

Use inclusive language and communication in the company, avoiding terms and actions that may be exclusionary.

Track progress toward diversity and inclusion goals and measure the impact of implemented initiatives.

Celebrate and recognize the diversity of your workforce through events and activities that highlight different cultures and backgrounds.

Company leaders should be role models for diversity and inclusion. Their commitment and behavior in this regard can influence the company's culture.

Ensure that information about diversity and inclusion is handled with confidentiality and respect for employee privacy.

Promoting diversity and inclusion in the workplace is not only an ethical act but can also have significant benefits, such as enhancing creativity, innovation, and talent retention. By following these guidelines and fostering an inclusive work environment, companies can create healthier and more diverse work cultures.

In the workplace, negotiation is not limited to employees requesting salary increases. It encompasses a wide range of interactions in which the involved parties seek mutually beneficial agreements. Effective communication, empathy, and conflict management are key skills for addressing and resolving these negotiations effectively. Additionally, a work environment based on trust and respect promotes strong and healthy working relationships."

Negotiating is like weaving a tapestry—it's not just about haggling over terms, but creating a collaborative masterpiece. Effective communication means articulating your needs clearly and really listening to the other side. It's not just about words; it's about understanding the underlying message and decoding the unsaid.

Then there's empathy, the secret sauce. It's about stepping into the other person's shoes, understanding their motivations, fears, and aspirations. It's like having a backstage pass to their thoughts and feelings. When you lead with empathy, negotiations become less of a battlefield and more of a shared journey towards a common goal. But let's not forget conflict management.

It's the art of turning sparks into a well-contained flame. Conflicts are inevitable, but how you handle them defines the course of the negotiation. It's about finding common ground, exploring compromises, and turning potential roadblocks into stepping stones. Now, sprinkle in a healthy dose of trust and respect. They're the pillars holding up the entire structure.

A work environment built on trust is like a sturdy bridge—you can confidently walk across it, knowing it won't collapse beneath you. Respect, on the other hand, is the currency of effective collaboration.

It creates a positive atmosphere where ideas can flourish, and people feel valued. So, in the grand gallery of negotiation, these skills and values are your brushes and colors. Each stroke contributes to a masterpiece of collaboration, understanding, and success. How do you navigate the delicate dance of negotiations?

15.Negotiation in Sales

Negotiation in the field of sales is a fundamental part of any business transaction. Here are some key tips for conducting effective sales negotiations:

Before starting a negotiation, thoroughly research your potential customer. Understand their needs, their industry, their budget, and any other relevant information. The more you know, the better you can tailor your approach.

Preparation before a sales negotiation is essential for success. Here are some specific steps you can take to thoroughly research your potential customer:

Gather detailed information about the potential customer's company. This includes their history, mission, vision, values, and corporate culture. Understanding these aspects will help you tailor your approach and align your offer with their values and objectives.

Research your potential customer's specific needs. What problems or challenges are they facing? What solutions have they tried in the past? The better you understand their needs, the more effectively you can present your product or service as the ideal solution.

Try to determine the customer's available budget or at least an approximate estimate. This will help you adjust your offer to be financially viable for them. It will also allow you to present options that fit their spending capacity.

Research the competition. Understand who the customer's competitors are and what makes them stand out. This will help you differentiate your offer and highlight your competitive advantages.

If possible, review the potential customer's past purchase history. This will give you an idea of what products or services they have acquired in the past and what kind of relationship they have with previous suppliers.

Identify the key decision-makers within the customer's company. This includes decision-makers, influencers, and potential obstacles in the sales process.

Stay updated on trends and developments in the customer's industry. This information will enable you to speak knowledgeably about how your offer relates to the customer's business environment.

Understand the customer's short and long-term business goals and challenges. What are they trying to achieve in the next year or more? With this information, you can demonstrate how your product or service will contribute to achieving those goals.

If you have had previous communication with the customer, review any previous correspondence or conversations to understand their concerns and expectations.

Once you have gathered this information, you will be in a stronger position to adapt your sales approach and present an offer that addresses the specific needs and desires of your potential customer. This preparation can make a difference in the effectiveness of your sales negotiation.

Define your negotiation goals in advance. What is the minimum price you would accept? What are the terms you are not willing to change? Having clear goals will help you stay focused during the negotiation.

Establishing clear goals is essential for conducting effective sales negotiations.

Determine the minimum price you are willing to accept for your product or service. This should be realistic and based on your costs, profit margins, and value to the customer. Having a minimum price in mind will help you avoid selling below your costs and maintain profitability.

Identify the terms and conditions you are not willing to change in the negotiation. This could include delivery times, warranties, return policies, payment methods, among others. These elements are fundamental to the integrity of your business and should be held firm unless there is a compelling reason to change them.

Define specific sales goals. How many units of the product or how many service contracts do you expect to sell in this negotiation? Setting quantitative goals will give you a clear measure of negotiation success.

Consider additional elements you can offer to add value to the offer. This may include complementary services, training, technical support, long-term discounts, or any other benefit that can make your offer more attractive.

Think about the alternatives you would be willing to offer if the customer does not accept your initial terms. These concessions can be an important part of the negotiation and allow you to maintain some flexibility without compromising your key objectives.

Set time limits for the negotiation. This will help prevent the negotiation from dragging on indefinitely and give you a sense of urgency. However, make sure the deadline is reasonable to allow for effective negotiation.

Visualize different closing scenarios. This will help you be prepared for different outcomes. What will you do if the customer accepts your terms? What if they reject the initial offer but are willing to negotiate? Having plans for different results will help you stay in control of the situation.

Make sure your entire sales team and other relevant departments are aligned with your negotiation goals. Internal communication is essential to ensure that everyone is working toward the same objectives.

Once you have defined your negotiation goals, it is important to communicate them effectively during the negotiation. Keep your goals in mind but be flexible and willing to adapt if the situation requires it. Clarity in your goals will help you stay focused and achieve a successful sales negotiation.

Effective communication is essential. Listen to what your potential customer has to say and seek to understand their needs and concerns. Ask open-ended questions to encourage conversation.

The ability to listen actively is fundamental in sales negotiation. Here are some guidelines for applying active listening effectively:

Show that you are interested in what your potential customer has to say. This creates an atmosphere of trust and openness in the conversation.

Avoid monopolizing the conversation. Let the customer speak and express their needs, desires, and concerns. Listening attentively will provide valuable information that you can use to tailor your offer.

Open-ended questions promote conversation and allow the customer to express themselves in more detail. You can ask things like "Can you tell me more about the challenges your company is facing?" or "What aspects do you consider most important in a service provider?"

Repeating or paraphrasing what the customer has said shows that you are paying attention and care about what they are saying. You can say something like, "I understand that your main concern is X, is that correct?"

Avoid interrupting the customer while they are speaking, even if you have the answer or a solution in mind. Wait for them to finish to respond appropriately.

The customer's body language also provides valuable information. Observe their gestures, facial expressions, and posture to better understand their level of interest and comfort.

Try to put yourself in the customer's shoes and understand their emotions and perspectives. Empathy can help establish a stronger connection.

Keeping a record of what the customer is saying will help you remember important details and follow up effectively after the conversation.

When appropriate, show understanding and empathy towards the concerns or issues the customer has raised. This can help build a stronger relationship.

After actively listening, ask follow-up questions that clarify details or request more information about specific points the customer has mentioned.

Active listening not only helps you better understand the customer's needs and concerns but also creates a solid foundation for effective communication and successful sales negotiation. When customers feel heard and understood, they are more likely to be willing to collaborate and reach an agreement.

Instead of focusing solely on price, emphasize the value of your product or service. Demonstrate how what you are selling can solve the customer's problems or meet their needs.

Highlighting the value of your product or service is a key strategy in sales negotiation. As mentioned earlier, active listening is fundamental. Before you can highlight the value, you need to understand the specific needs of your customer. Ask and listen carefully to identify the issues they are facing and what they are looking for.

Once you understand the customer's needs, tailor your message to highlight how your product or service addresses those needs specifically. Make the customer see how their life or business will improve with what you are offering.

Don't just list the features of your product; explain to the customer how those features translate into benefits for them. How does it make their life or business easier? What problems does it solve?

Provide specific examples of how your product or service has benefited other customers. Success stories and testimonials are powerful evidence of the value you offer.

If relevant, compare your product or service to the competition and highlight how it is superior in terms of value. This can include price, quality, unique features, and more.

If possible, demonstrate how the investment in your product or service will generate a positive return for the customer. This is particularly effective in business-to-business sales.

Provide additional information that helps the customer make an informed decision. The more information they have, the easier it will be for them to see the value of what you are offering.

Show empathy towards the customer's concerns and objections and demonstrate how your product or service can help overcome those concerns.

If possible, tailor your offer to the customer's specific needs. It could be a customized solution or a special offer that fits their unique circumstances.

If your product or service allows for long-term savings, highlight it. Often, customers are willing to pay a little more upfront if they can see a long-term benefit.

Emphasizing value over price can make a big difference in the customer's perception and the effectiveness of your sales negotiation. The customer should feel that they are getting more than what they are paying for, making the price secondary in their decision-making.

Instead of sticking to a single offer, present multiple options to give the customer some flexibility. This can include different packages, delivery times, or payment methods.

Presenting options is an effective strategy in sales negotiation, as it provides flexibility to the customer and can increase the chances of reaching a satisfactory agreement. Here are some guidelines for presenting options effectively:

Before presenting options, make sure you understand the customer's needs and preferences. This will allow you to tailor the options to be relevant and appealing.

Present a limited number of options. Offering too many alternatives can be overwhelming and make it difficult for the customer to make decisions. Typically, three options are a good starting point.

Ensure that each option is clearly different from the others in terms of price, features, or benefits. This helps the customer see the distinctions and make an informed decision.

Along with the price, highlight the key benefits and features of each option. Show how each alternative can meet the specific needs of the customer.

Provide a comparison table or summary that clearly shows the differences between the options. This makes decision-making easier by allowing the customer to see the advantages and disadvantages of each alternative.

After presenting the options, ask the customer which one they prefer or which one best fits their needs. This gives them the opportunity to express their preferences and provides you with additional information to guide the negotiation.

Be willing to adjust the options if the customer has specific requirements or requests changes. Flexibility is crucial to adapting to the customer's changing needs.

Consider including value-added offers, such as discounts, flexible payment terms, or additional services, to make the options even more attractive.

If relevant, show how the options can scale as the customer grows or evolves. This can help establish a long-term relationship with the customer.

Once the customer has chosen an option, ensure that you close the sale effectively. Confirm the details, clarify any doubts, and guide the customer through the purchasing process.

Presenting options in a sales negotiation can increase the chances of success by allowing the customer to choose the solution that best fits their needs. Additionally, it demonstrates flexibility and a willingness to collaborate, which can strengthen the customer relationship.

At times, you will need to make concessions in certain aspects of the negotiation. However, ensure that these concessions align with your goals and that you receive something in return.

Making strategic concessions in a sales negotiation is an important skill that can help you achieve a satisfactory agreement while keeping your goals and limits in mind.

Before the negotiation, determine which aspects you might be willing to concede on. This could include prices, deadlines, payment terms, additional features, or discounts.

Despite being willing to make concessions in certain aspects, set clear limits for these concessions. For example, you can decide what the minimum price you are willing to reach is or what the maximum discount you can offer.

Before making concessions, make sure you understand the value of what you are offering. What are you getting in return? How will it impact the customer relationship and the profitability of the sale?

When making a concession, look to get something in return. It could be a commitment to long-term purchasing, a reference or testimonial, an agreement on a favorable term or condition for your company, or any other mutual benefit.

When you make a concession, communicate it clearly and transparently. Ensure that the customer understands the value of what you are offering.

Making a concession often creates a sense of reciprocity in the customer. This can lead them to be willing to make concessions in turn, which can be beneficial for both parties.

Don't make concessions on all aspects at once. Manage your concessions strategically and sequentially to maintain control of the negotiation.

Even though you are willing to make concessions in certain aspects, do not concede on elements that are essential for the profitability or integrity of the sale. Keep your key objectives in mind.

As you make concessions, pay attention to the concessions the customer is willing to make. This will help balance the negotiation and ensure that both parties are committed.

If you reach a point where the concessions you are making are unsustainable or not beneficial for your company, do not hesitate to withdraw from the negotiation. Sometimes, walking away is the most strategic decision.

Making concessions strategically in a sales negotiation involves balancing the pursuit of a successful agreement with the protection of your interests and objectives. Maintain flexibility, but do not lose sight of what is essential for your business.

Negotiation should not be a battle. Maintain a positive and professional attitude at all times, even if the negotiation becomes challenging. Maintaining a positive attitude is crucial in the field of sales and negotiation. A positive attitude not only creates a collaborative and trust-based environment but also helps you address challenges effectively.

A positive attitude makes you more approachable and creates an atmosphere of trust. Customers are more likely to do business with people who convey confidence and assurance.

Negotiations often involve disagreements and moments of tension. A positive attitude can help reduce this tension and keep the conversation in a constructive tone.

A positive attitude fosters more effective communication. You will listen more attentively and be more understanding of the customer's needs and concerns.

When you maintain a positive attitude, you are more open to exploring creative and flexible solutions that can meet the customer's needs and your objectives.

Long-term business relationships are essential in sales. A positive attitude helps you build strong relationships with customers, which can lead to repeat sales and referrals.

Emotions can play a significant role in negotiation. A positive attitude helps you maintain emotional control, which is crucial for making rational and strategic decisions.

In sales, you will inevitably encounter obstacles and objections. A positive attitude allows you to proactively address these obstacles and find solutions rather than getting caught up in negativity.

Customers often prefer to work with salespeople who are positive and pleasant. A positive attitude can be a differentiating factor that attracts customers to you rather than the competition.

Maintaining a positive attitude not only benefits your interactions with customers but is also important for your own emotional and mental well-being. Negotiating positively can reduce stress and increase job satisfaction.

Remember that maintaining a positive attitude does not mean giving in on your goals or being weak in negotiation. You can be positive while also being a firm and strategic negotiator. A positive attitude helps you create an environment in which both parties feel comfortable and open to finding mutually beneficial solutions.

Negotiation can take time. Do not rush to close the deal. Sometimes, it is necessary to allow the customer to reflect and return with a decision.

Patience is an important virtue in the field of sales and negotiation. Here are some reasons why it is essential to be patient during the negotiation process:

Patience shows respect for the customer and their decision-making process. Understanding that customers may need time to consider your offer is crucial.

Excessive pressure or the feeling that you are rushing the customer can be counterproductive. Patience allows you to avoid uncomfortable situations and ensures that the customer feels more at ease in the negotiation.

Customers often need time to reflect on the offer and evaluate how it fits their needs and budget. Patience enables customers to make more informed decisions.

Patience helps you build strong, long-term relationships with customers. Not all customers will be ready to buy at the time of the initial presentation, but if you maintain a good relationship, they may return in the future.

When you are patient, you demonstrate confidence in your product or service. This can positively influence the customer's perception of your offer.

Patience creates a more relaxed negotiating environment in which the customer feels less pressured and more willing to engage in an open and honest conversation.

To apply patience effectively in negotiation, consider the following strategies:

Set appropriate expectations with the customer regarding the negotiation process and the time it might take.

Provide support and answers to the customer's questions during their reflection period.

Follow up after the initial negotiation to stay in touch and provide additional information if necessary.

Establish a follow-up schedule to reconnect with the customer at a time when they may be more prepared to make a decision.

Remember that, while patience is essential, it is also important to remain proactive and available to answer customer questions and provide necessary assistance. The combination of patience and strategic follow-up can be effective in closing sales and maintaining positive customer relationships.

Although it's important to be flexible, it's also essential to know your limits and be willing to withdraw if the offer is not beneficial for your company.

Knowing your limits is a critical part of sales negotiation. While it's important to be flexible and adapt to customer needs, you must also be clear about your limits to protect your company's interests. Here are some guidelines for knowing and managing your limits in a sales negotiation:

Before starting the negotiation, define your limits in terms of the minimum acceptable price, non-negotiable terms, and other critical aspects. This will provide you with clear guidance during the negotiation.

Having a solid understanding of your costs and margins will help you determine your financial limits. You should not sell below your costs without a strategic reason.

Recognize the aspects in which you are willing to be flexible and those that you cannot change. For example, you can be flexible on the delivery time but not on the product's quality.

As the negotiation progresses, constantly evaluate whether the proposed offer is worthwhile based on your limits and objectives. Do not feel pressured to accept a deal that is not beneficial for your company.

Maintain your limits, but also consider if there are creative ways to find common ground that is beneficial for both you and the customer. Flexibility is important, but within certain limits.

It's important that the customer understands what your limits are and the reasons for maintaining them. Communicating these limits transparently can help prevent misunderstandings.

If you reach a point where the offer does not meet your limits and is not beneficial for your company, do not hesitate to withdraw from the negotiation. Sometimes, it's better not to close a deal than to accept an agreement that results in losses.

Even if you withdraw from a negotiation, it's important to maintain a good relationship with the customer. Making it clear that you're willing to explore future opportunities or available to answer questions can be valuable.

After each negotiation, reflect on what worked and what didn't. Use that feedback to adjust your limits and approaches in future negotiations.

Knowing your limits and firmly maintaining them when necessary is essential to protect your company's financial health and integrity. However, it's important to balance this with the ability to be flexible and find mutually beneficial solutions in sales negotiations.

Once you've reached an agreement, close the sale with confidence. Ensure that both parties clearly understand the agreed terms and conditions.

Successfully closing a sale is a crucial step in the negotiation process. Here are some tips to ensure that the closing is successful:

Before closing the sale, review key details with the customer to ensure that both parties are on the same page. Make sure that all conditions, prices, deadlines, and terms are clear and understood.

Provide a summary of the key benefits and features of your product or service to reinforce the value of the offer. This can help solidify the customer's decision.

Ensure that the customer has no lingering doubts or questions before closing the sale. Be available to answer any inquiries and provide additional information if necessary.

Directly ask the customer if they are ready to move forward and if they agree with the agreed terms. Obtain their confirmation before proceeding.

If possible, document the agreement in a written contract or agreement. This provides clarity and legal protection for both parties. Ensure that the customer understands and signs the document if necessary.

If the sale involves a payment, offer clear and flexible payment options. Ensure that the customer understands how the payment process will be carried out.

Express your gratitude to the customer for their decision to do business with you. A simple thank you can strengthen the relationship and show appreciation.

Offer a post-sale follow-up plan or after-sales service to ensure customer satisfaction and address any future needs they may have.

If it's a product or service that requires delivery or implementation, confirm the timelines and related details to ensure a seamless experience.

Maintain a professional and confident attitude at all times. The confidence you display can influence the customer's confidence in their decision.

A successful sale closure means not only that the customer has agreed to purchase but also that they understand and are satisfied with the terms of the agreement. Clear communication and a professional approach are essential for closing with confidence and establishing a strong foundation for future business relationships.

After closing the sale, stay in touch with the customer to ensure satisfaction and maintain a long-term relationship.

Follow-up after closing a sale is an essential practice in the field of sales. It not only demonstrates your commitment to customer satisfaction but also lays the groundwork for future sales and long-term business relationships. Here are some steps and tips for effective follow-up:

Sending a thank-you message after closing the sale is a courteous way to express your gratitude for the opportunity to do business with the customer. It can be an email, a phone call, or even a handwritten note.

If the sale involves product delivery or service implementation, ensure that everything is proceeding as agreed. Ask if the customer is satisfied with the product or service and if they have any questions or concerns.

Ask the customer about their experience and if they have any feedback on the sales process. Their feedback can provide valuable information for improving your sales approach.

Provide ongoing assistance to the customer for any questions or issues that may arise after the sale. Ensure that they have a point of contact for help if needed.

If the customer is satisfied with your product or service, consider asking them for a reference or testimonial. These can be helpful for future sales by endorsing the quality of your offering.

Create a long-term follow-up plan to stay in touch with the customer. This could include periodic communications, product or service updates, special offers, and more.

Ensure that follow-up communications are tailored to the customer's needs and interests. The more personalized the approach, the more effective it will be.

Keep a record of all interactions and relevant details with the customer in your Customer Relationship Management (CRM) system. This will allow for more effective follow-up and maintain a complete history of the relationship.

Don't wait for the customer to have a problem to contact them. Proactive follow-up ensures that they are satisfied and offers solutions before issues arise.

Maintain open communication and respond promptly to any customer questions or requests. Timely responsiveness is key to maintaining a good relationship.

Post-sale follow-up is an opportunity to strengthen the customer relationship, gain valuable feedback, and ultimately foster customer loyalty. Additionally, a satisfied customer is more likely to provide referrals and recommendations to others, which can further drive your business.

Remember that sales negotiation is an ongoing process, and each situation is unique. Practice and experience will help you refine your negotiation skills over time.

16.Negotiation in Legal Context

Legal negotiation refers to the resolution of legal disputes or conflicts through conversations and agreements among the involved parties, instead of resorting to litigation or a court trial. Negotiation is a fundamental tool within the legal system and can be applied to a wide range of situations, from business agreements and contracts to civil and criminal disputes.

Many legal cases commence with an attempt at negotiation before reaching a court. The involved parties, along with their attorneys, can convene and attempt to reach an agreement acceptable to both sides.

Prior to filing a formal lawsuit or initiating a legal process, the involved parties or their attorneys often engage in initial communication to discuss the conflict and the possibility of reaching an agreement. This represents an initial effort to resolve the dispute in a more amicable and cost-effective manner.

If the initial communication does not result in an agreement, one of the parties may file a formal legal complaint, and the other party will respond. Nonetheless, even after filing a complaint, the parties can continue to negotiate in pursuit of an agreement before the case proceeds to trial.

Some advantages of pre-trial negotiation include time and cost savings, preserving privacy, and the potential to reach an agreement more favorable to both parties compared to a judicial decision.

At this stage, the parties may also opt for mediation or arbitration as alternative methods of dispute resolution, involving the intervention of a neutral third party to facilitate negotiation or render a binding decision.

If the parties reach an agreement, it is important to document the terms and conditions in an extrajudicial contract or agreement. This ensures the agreement's legal enforceability and prevents future misunderstandings.

Although pre-trial negotiation can be beneficial, it is not always possible to reach an agreement, especially when the parties have significantly different demands. In such cases, the legal process may proceed to trial.

Pre-trial negotiation offers an opportunity to efficiently and effectively resolve disputes and is often encouraged within the legal system as a means to reduce the burden on the courts and minimize litigation-associated costs.

In mediation, a neutral third party, known as a mediator, facilitates communication between the parties and assists them in reaching a mutually acceptable agreement. Mediation is voluntary and can be a quicker and less costly alternative to a trial.

In mediation, the mediator is an impartial individual without an interest in the dispute's outcome. Their primary role is to facilitate communication and negotiation between the conflicting parties. The mediator does not take sides or issue a judgment, in contrast to a judge in a court.

Discussions and communications in mediation are typically confidential. This allows the parties to openly and freely share their concerns and positions without the fear of their statements being used against them in a subsequent trial.

Mediation is generally a voluntary process. Parties must be willing to participate and make an honest effort to resolve the dispute. In some cases, a court or contract may require parties to attempt mediation before proceeding to a trial.

Mediation is a flexible process in which the parties have greater control over the final resolution. They can explore a wide range of options and agreements that may not be feasible in traditional litigation.

The primary goal of mediation is for the parties to reach an agreement they deem fair and acceptable. The mediator helps the parties identify their interests, explore solutions, and reach a compromise that resolves the dispute.

Mediation tends to be quicker and less costly than litigation in a court. Parties save on legal fees and court expenses, and the mediation process can be tailored to a schedule that works for all involved.

Mediation is employed in a wide array of legal contexts, including family disputes, employment conflicts, business disputes, neighborhood disputes, and more.

If the parties reach an agreement during mediation, that agreement is typically documented in an extrajudicial contract or agreement and is legally binding.

Mediation is an effective tool for peacefully and cooperatively resolving disputes. It helps parties maintain control over the outcome and preserve relationships, which is especially valuable in situations where parties wish to maintain an ongoing relationship, such as in the family or business sphere.

In arbitration, the parties agree that a third party (the arbitrator) will make a binding decision on the dispute. Arbitration is more formal than mediation and is generally used when the parties have previously agreed to this process.

Arbitration is a method of dispute resolution in which the involved parties agree that a neutral third party, known as an arbitrator, will make a binding decision on the dispute instead of taking the case to court.

The arbitrator is an impartial and neutral person appointed by the parties or an arbitration organization. The arbitrator possesses expertise in the relevant area of the dispute and is authorized to make a decision on the matter.

Unlike mediation, where the mediator facilitates negotiation but does not impose a decision, arbitration results in a binding decision. The arbitral award issued by the arbitrator is legally obligatory for both parties and is akin to a court judgment.

Similar to mediation, discussions and proceedings in arbitration are often confidential, allowing the parties to maintain the privacy of the dispute.

Parties often agree to arbitration before a dispute arises, through an arbitration clause in a contract. In other cases, parties may agree to arbitration after a dispute arises as an alternative to traditional litigation.

Parties have some control over the arbitration process, meaning they can agree on specific procedures, timelines, and rules that are appropriate for their dispute.

Arbitration is often considered faster and less expensive than court litigation, although costs can vary depending on the complexity of the case and the number of hearings.

The arbitral award carries the same legal weight as a court judgment and, in most countries, can be enforced by a court if one of the parties fails to comply with the award.

Arbitration is common in commercial and contractual disputes, as well as in other contexts where parties seek a faster and more efficient resolution than traditional litigation. It is especially useful in situations where parties desire the privacy and confidentiality of the dispute or when they require an arbitrator with specific expertise in the field related to the dispute.

Alternative dispute resolution methods, such as negotiation, mediation, and arbitration, provide an alternative to traditional court proceedings.

The arbitral award holds the same legal validity as a judicial judgment, and in most countries, it can be enforced by a court if one of the parties fails to comply with the decision. Arbitration is common in commercial and contractual disputes, as well as in other contexts where parties seek a quicker and more efficient resolution than traditional litigation. It is especially useful in situations where parties wish to maintain privacy and confidentiality in the dispute or when they require an arbitrator with specific expertise in the relevant field of the dispute. Alternative dispute resolution methods, such as negotiation, mediation, and arbitration, provide an alternative to traditional court proceedings.

Alternative dispute resolution methods (ADR) are a way to address legal conflicts outside of traditional court processes.

As mentioned earlier, negotiation is the process in which parties involved in a dispute attempt to reach a mutually acceptable agreement without resorting to a court. They may be assisted by lawyers, but the outcome depends on their ability to reach a consensus.

Mediation involves the participation of a neutral third party, the mediator, to facilitate communication and negotiation between the parties. The mediator does not make decisions but helps the parties find solutions. Mediation is voluntary and confidential.

Arbitration, as previously mentioned, involves the parties agreeing that an arbitrator will make a binding decision on the dispute. Unlike mediation, the arbitrator issues an award that is legally binding on both parties.

Conciliation is a process similar to mediation, where a neutral third party, the conciliator, assists the parties in reaching an agreement. However, unlike mediation, the conciliator may offer specific recommendations or solutions to resolve the dispute.

In the digital age, online platforms have been developed that allow dispute resolution through alternative methods, including online negotiation and mediation. These platforms can be useful for online disputes, such as e-commerce disputes.

In some cases, parties may choose to submit their disputes to specialized arbitration tribunals instead of litigating in state courts. These arbitration tribunals are designed to address specific cases and often have faster and simplified procedures.

In certain industries, such as medicine and architecture, there are professional ethics and arbitration committees that address disputes between professionals in those fields and their clients.

Collaborative resolution is an approach in which parties and their lawyers commit to resolving the dispute through a collaborative process, avoiding the threat of litigation. If an agreement is not reached, the parties must hire new lawyers and proceed to trial.

These alternative dispute resolution methods offer parties flexibility and control over the process and are often faster and less costly than traditional litigation. The choice of method depends on the nature of the dispute, the parties' preferences, and applicable legal regulations.

An extrajudicial agreement is an agreement between the parties involved in a dispute that resolves the issue without the need for a trial. These agreements are legally binding and are typically documented in a contract or agreement.

Extrajudicial agreements, also known as out-of-court agreements or extrajudicial settlements, result from the parties' willingness to resolve the dispute. No one can be forced to accept an extrajudicial agreement against their will.

In many cases, extrajudicial agreements include confidentiality provisions that prevent the parties from disclosing details of the agreement to third parties. This can be important in sensitive or commercial disputes.

Extrajudicial agreements can apply to a wide range of legal disputes, from contractual and civil disputes to negligence cases, family disputes, and more.

For an extrajudicial agreement to be legally binding, it is typically documented in a written contract or agreement. This ensures that all parties understand and accept the terms and conditions.

Extrajudicial agreements offer several benefits, such as a faster and more cost-effective resolution of disputes, privacy, and flexibility in defining the agreement's terms.

Once an extrajudicial agreement has been reached and properly documented, it becomes a legally binding contract. If one of the parties fails to adhere to the agreed-upon terms, the other party can seek legal remedies.

Extrajudicial agreements can be an effective way to reduce the uncertainty associated with a trial, as parties have greater control over the outcome and are not dependent on a court's decision.

It's important to note that, while extrajudicial agreements are an effective way to resolve disputes, they may not be suitable for all cases. In some situations, parties may fail to reach an agreement and may need to resort to litigation in court. In many legal situations, parties involved are represented by lawyers who negotiate on their behalf. Lawyers play a crucial role in legal negotiation and provide legal expertise and specific skills to ensure their clients' interests are protected.

Lawyers offer legal counsel to their clients, which includes explaining their rights and obligations as well as the legal implications of different courses of action. This allows clients to make informed decisions during the negotiation.

Lawyers work closely with their clients to develop effective negotiation strategies. This involves assessing the strength of their client's legal position, as well as the other party's position, and determining the best way to achieve a favorable agreement.

Lawyers act as intermediaries in communication with the other party and their legal representatives. They help maintain a professional and constructive tone in conversations and prevent misunderstandings.

Lawyers draft and present proposals and counteroffers on behalf of their clients. This involves drafting legal documents, contracts, and other documents related to the agreement.

In some situations, lawyers may directly participate in negotiations on behalf of their clients. They can discuss the details of the agreement with the other party and attempt to reach a consensus.

Lawyers have the responsibility of protecting the legal and financial interests of their clients. This includes ensuring that the proposed agreement does not unfairly harm their client and that all applicable laws and regulations are followed.

Lawyers thoroughly review the documentation related to the agreement, such as contracts and agreements, to ensure they align with their client's needs and goals and comply with the law.

Lawyers advise their clients on when to accept a proposed agreement or when to continue negotiating. They consider legal, financial, and strategic factors to help their clients make informed decisions.

In some cases, despite negotiation efforts, the parties do not reach an agreement. In such situations, lawyers are prepared to take the case to court and provide legal representation in court.

In summary, lawyers are essential in legal negotiation as they provide legal guidance, protect interests, and offer expertise in strategy formulation. Their primary goal is to help their clients achieve fair and favorable agreements, and when necessary, resort to legal proceedings to resolve disputes.

Confidentiality is an important aspect of many legal negotiations, especially in sensitive cases. Parties often agree to keep the details of the negotiation and the agreement confidential.

Confidentiality is a fundamental aspect of many legal negotiations, especially in sensitive or commercial cases. Maintaining the confidentiality of negotiation and agreement details can be crucial for several reasons:

In many negotiations, parties must share confidential and strategic information to discuss the dispute or reach an agreement. Confidentiality ensures that this information is not publicly disclosed or shared with third parties not directly involved in the dispute.

Confidentiality protects the privacy of the parties involved. In family cases, labor disputes, or personal conflicts, maintaining confidentiality may be essential to avoid damaging the reputation or privacy of the parties.

When parties know that conversations and negotiation details will remain confidential, they are more likely to be sincere and open in their discussions. This can facilitate finding mutually acceptable solutions.

In many cases, parties are more willing to resolve their disputes outside of court if they have the assurance that the details of the negotiation and the agreement will remain confidential. This can encourage out-of-court dispute resolution.

In certain cases, laws and regulations may require parties to maintain the confidentiality of certain legal matters. Failure to comply with these regulations can have legal consequences.

Confidentiality is especially important in cases where the publicity of the dispute could harm the reputation of the parties involved. Avoiding public disclosure may be essential to preserve the image and integrity of the parties.

In the business context, confidentiality can be crucial when negotiating mergers and acquisitions, nondisclosure agreements, and other commercial agreements involving sensitive and strategic information.

Confidentiality is often established in a confidentiality agreement or in a confidentiality clause within the resolution agreement. These clauses specify the conditions under which information related to the negotiation and the agreement can be shared and with whom. It is important for parties to understand and comply with these clauses to effectively maintain confidentiality.

Negotiation can be beneficial because it is often faster, more cost-effective, and flexible compared to litigation. Parties have greater control over the outcome and can reach solutions that more effectively satisfy their interests.

Given that the parties have greater control over the solution, they are more likely to be satisfied with the outcome. This can lead to a more enduring agreement and higher overall satisfaction.

Negotiation can eliminate the uncertainty associated with litigation. Parties are not reliant on a judge or jury's decision and instead determine the outcome themselves.

In summary, negotiation offers many advantages, including speed, cost-effectiveness, flexibility, and greater control over the outcome. It is a valuable tool in the resolution of legal disputes and can be especially beneficial when parties want to find effective solutions, preserve privacy, and maintain positive relationships.

Not all disputes can be resolved through negotiation, and it can be challenging to reach an agreement when parties have significantly divergent positions. In such cases, resorting to litigation may be necessary.

Negotiation has several advantages but also comes with disadvantages and limitations.

Not all disputes can be resolved through negotiation. Some legal issues or extremely complex disputes may be difficult to resolve without the intervention of a neutral third party, such as a judge or arbitrator. In such cases, litigation may be necessary.

When parties have extremely distant or inflexible positions, negotiation can be ineffective. If parties are unwilling to compromise or if their demands are incompatible, reaching a mutually acceptable agreement can be challenging.

In some disputes, there may be a significant power imbalance between the parties, making it difficult for one party to negotiate on equal terms. In such cases, the weaker party may feel disadvantaged and may be reluctant to engage in negotiations.

Lack of effective communication between the parties or the presence of personal conflicts can hinder negotiation. If parties cannot communicate constructively or if emotions dominate the conversation, negotiation may be unproductive.

Unlike a trial where a court issues a binding judgment, a negotiation agreement is not always enforced. If one of the parties does not adhere to the agreement, the other party may be forced to take legal action to enforce the agreement, which can be costly and time-consuming.

Distrust between the parties can hinder negotiation. If one or both parties feel that the other is not honest or will not comply with the terms of the agreement, negotiation can be problematic.

If negotiation is unsuccessful, and the parties ultimately opt for litigation, time and resources will have been wasted on a negotiation process that did not lead to a resolution. This can be frustrating and costly.

Negotiation is not suitable for all disputes and may face challenges when parties have extremely distant positions, there is a power imbalance, or there are communication issues. In such cases, litigation may be the only viable option for resolving the dispute. The choice between negotiation and litigation depends on the nature of the dispute and the specific circumstances of the parties involved.

Legal negotiation is an important tool for dispute resolution and conflict resolution. It helps parties find mutually acceptable solutions and avoid the costly and lengthy litigation process in a courtroom.

17.Negotiation in Crisis or Conflict Situations

Negotiating in crisis or conflict situations can be especially challenging, but it is also crucial for resolving disputes and finding peaceful solutions.

In crisis situations, maintaining calm and composure is fundamental. Emotions may run high, but effective negotiation requires the ability to manage stress and anxiety.

Staying calm in crisis situations is a fundamental piece of advice for effective negotiation. Emotions can be on edge during times of conflict or crisis, and the ability to manage stress and anxiety is essential for achieving positive outcomes.

When you are emotionally upset, it's more challenging to make rational and logical decisions. Staying calm allows you to think clearly and make informed decisions.

Calmness helps you communicate more effectively. You can express your thoughts and needs more coherently and listen to the other party with empathy.

Strong emotions can lead to an escalation of the conflict. Maintaining calm can help prevent the dispute from intensifying and promote a more constructive negotiation environment.

Calmness contributes to building trust in negotiation. Parties are more likely to trust someone who remains calm and respectful, rather than someone who acts impulsively or aggressively.

Calmness enables you to be more creative and flexible in seeking solutions. You can explore options that you wouldn't consider in an emotionally charged state.

In many negotiation situations, especially in the family or business context, preserving relationships is important. Staying calm helps avoid irreparable damage to personal or business relationships.

To maintain calm in a negotiation situation, it is helpful to practice stress management techniques such as deep breathing, mindfulness, and emotional self-control. It can also be useful to take some time to cool off if emotions are running too high before returning to the negotiation table.

Remember that effective negotiation requires patience, empathy, and the ability to stay calm, even in conflict or crisis situations. These skills are essential for reaching mutually acceptable agreements and resolving disputes effectively.

Communication is key in any negotiation, but it is especially important in crisis situations. Actively listen to the other party to understand their concerns and needs, and communicate your own views clearly and respectfully.

Effective communication is crucial in any negotiation, but its importance is amplified in crisis situations. In such contexts, the ability to communicate clearly, openly, and respectfully can make a difference in conflict resolution.

Effective communication is essential to ensure that both parties understand each other's concerns and needs. This allows addressing the root causes of the conflict and finding solutions that satisfy both parties.

Respectful and empathetic communication can help reduce hostility and antagonism between parties. A confrontational or accusatory tone can worsen the situation, while calm and respectful communication can reduce tension.

Effective communication can foster empathy, meaning that parties can put themselves in each other's shoes and understand their perspectives and emotions. This can lead to greater understanding and the possibility of finding mutually acceptable solutions.

Effective communication is essential for identifying and discussing potential solutions. Through constructive dialogue, parties can explore options and assess their viability.

Communication allows parties to express their desires and limitations. This is essential for reaching compromises and agreements that take into account the needs of both parties.

Lack of communication or poor communication can lead to misunderstandings that exacerbate the conflict. Effective communication helps prevent misunderstandings and clarify any ambiguities.

Respectful, transparent, and sincere communication contributes to building trust between parties. Trust is essential for successful conflict resolution.

Effective communication creates a safe environment in which parties feel comfortable expressing their concerns and needs. Confidentiality and respect are essential for this safe environment.

Instead of avoiding conflict, effective communication allows parties to face conflict productively and seek solutions.

To achieve effective communication in crisis situations, it is important to actively listen, ask questions to clarify any unclear points, and express your thoughts and needs clearly and respectfully. It is also helpful to avoid confrontation and maintain a calm tone of voice and body language.

In summary, effective communication is essential for addressing crisis situations and conflicts constructively, fostering mutual understanding, and finding solutions that satisfy both parties.

Rather than focusing on the parties' initial positions, try to identify the underlying interests. What motivates each party? Understanding these interests can help find solutions that satisfy both parties.

Identifying underlying interests is a fundamental aspect of effective negotiation. Often, parties in a dispute have initial positions that are incompatible, but by exploring and understanding their underlying interests, it is possible to find solutions that satisfy both parties.

Positions are the specific demands that parties present in the negotiation, while interests are the broader needs, desires, and concerns that motivate those positions. It's important to distinguish between the two to understand why parties want what they want.

For example, in a salary negotiation, an employee may demand a 10% raise (position), but their underlying interest may be the need to feel valued at work and to maintain an adequate standard of living.

To identify underlying interests, you can ask open-ended questions of the parties. Asking, "What are you really looking for in this negotiation?" or "What is your biggest concern in this matter?" can reveal valuable information.

Active listening is essential. Pay attention to the responses of the parties and show empathy. Sometimes, underlying interests can be emotional or personal, so it's important to provide space for people to express themselves.

Once you've identified the underlying interests of both parties, look for areas of overlap or common interests. These are points where both parties can find solutions that meet their needs.

Based on the underlying interests, work on generating creative options to resolve the conflict. These options can be solutions that address the concerns of both parties fairly.

Negotiating based on underlying interests promotes a more collaborative approach in which parties work together to find mutually beneficial solutions instead of fighting for fixed positions.

By addressing underlying interests, it's more likely to reach lasting and sustainable agreements since the solutions address the true needs of the parties.

Being flexible in seeking solutions can be essential. If parties are willing to adapt to their underlying interests rather than their initial positions, it's more likely to find acceptable solutions.

Identifying underlying interests is a powerful strategy for addressing disputes and conflicts more constructively and finding solutions that satisfy both parties. By focusing on what truly motivates the parties, initial differences can be overcome, leading to more satisfactory agreements.

In a crisis situation, conventional solutions may not be sufficient. Creativity in seeking solutions can be crucial. Explore different approaches and options to resolve the dispute.

Seeking creative solutions is essential in crisis situations, as conventional solutions often may not effectively address the issues. Creativity in negotiation can help find innovative and mutually acceptable solutions.

Instead of sticking to traditional or conventional solutions, adopt a creative thinking approach. Open your mind to new ideas and solutions that may not have been considered before.

Hold brainstorming sessions with all parties involved in the negotiation. Encourage people to freely share ideas without initial criticism. Often, the best solutions emerge from collaboration and diverse perspectives.

Identifying common interests or shared goals among the parties can be a starting point for finding creative solutions. Solutions that address these common goals may be more acceptable to all parties.

Don't limit yourself to a single solution. Instead, seek a variety of options. The more alternatives you consider, the greater the chances of finding a solution that works for everyone.

Consider how the proposed solutions may affect all parties in the future. A solution may seem acceptable in the short term, but it's important to evaluate its long-term impact.

Creativity often involves being flexible and willing to embrace new ideas. Being open to change and experimentation can lead to more innovative solutions.

In technical or complex situations, consider consulting experts in the field or individuals with relevant experience. They can provide specialized knowledge to help find creative solutions.

Reflect on past conflict or crisis resolution experiences and consider what worked and what didn't. These insights can provide ideas for more effective solutions in the present.

When considering creative solutions, evaluate the associated risks and the feasibility of implementing them. Ensure that the solutions are practical and realistic.

Keep the negotiation's goal in mind. Resolving the crisis or conflict is the primary objective, and solutions should align with this goal.

Creativity in seeking solutions can not only help overcome crisis situations but can also lead to innovative and satisfactory agreements. Through creative thinking and collaboration, it's possible to find solutions that address the needs and concerns of all parties involved.

Create a safe negotiation environment where parties feel comfortable expressing their concerns and needs. Confidentiality and privacy can be especially important in delicate situations.

Establishing a safe negotiation environment is essential, especially in delicate or crisis situations. A safe environment promotes open communication and trust among the parties, which can be crucial for resolving the conflict effectively.

Make it clear that the conversations and negotiation details will remain confidential. This can alleviate concerns about the disclosure of sensitive or compromising information.

Provide a suitable physical space for negotiation where parties can speak without worrying about interference or intrusion from third parties. If the negotiation takes place online, use secure and private platforms.

Ensure that the negotiation location or online platform is perceived as neutral by both parties. This can help prevent one party from feeling disadvantaged or uncomfortable.

Practice active listening and show empathy toward the concerns and needs of the parties. Make them feel heard and understood, even if you don't agree with their views.

Establish rules for respectful behavior and communication for all parties involved. You can agree on rules, such as not interrupting, avoiding offensive language, or respecting speaking turns.

Encourage an environment where mutual respect is expected. Having parties treat each other with respect and courtesy can help maintain a safe environment.

Encourage parties to express their emotions in a controlled and constructive manner. This can help release tension and clarify the feelings that may be at play.

Offer time for parties to reflect on proposals and decisions. This can be especially useful in emotional situations or complex conflicts.

In some cases, it can be beneficial to have a neutral mediator or facilitator who helps maintain a safe environment and prevents the escalation of the conflict.

Ensure that the parties feel comfortable expressing their needs and preferences regarding the negotiation process. Flexibility can help tailor the process to the unique circumstances of the situation.

A safe negotiation environment is fundamental for parties to feel willing to openly share their concerns and needs. This, in turn, can help find mutually acceptable solutions and effectively resolve the conflict.

In a crisis situation, it's important to avoid conflict escalation. Instead of increasing confrontation, look for ways to reduce tension and antagonism.

Avoiding conflict escalation is a crucial principle in negotiation, especially in crisis situations. When tensions are high, and emotions are heightened, conflict escalation can worsen the situation and make it challenging to find effective solutions.

As mentioned earlier, maintaining calm is fundamental. Your own attitude and behavior can influence the reactions of the other parties. Avoid impulsive or aggressive reactions.

Listen empathetically to the parties involved. Allow them to express their views and concerns. Feeling heard can decrease hostility.

Avoid accusations, offensive language, or direct confrontation. Instead, use respectful language and focus on the issue.

Instead of focusing on differences, look for areas where the parties can agree. Finding common ground can be a starting point for conflict resolution.

Promote a common goal that all parties can support. This can help align interests and reduce opposition.

Recognize and validate the emotions of the parties. You can say something like, "I understand that this is a stressful situation" or "I know this has been frustrating." Validating emotions can help relieve tension.

If the situation becomes too tense, suggest taking a short break so that all parties can cool down and regain composure.

Instead of striving for control or superiority, seek constructive collaboration. Work together to resolve the conflict rather than compete.

Your body language, tone of voice, and facial expression can send important messages. Maintain a relaxed body language and a calm tone of voice to avoid escalation.

Collaborate to find solutions that satisfy both parties. Collaboration can reduce confrontation and promote a more productive negotiation environment.

Instead of rehashing past disputes, focus on how to move forward and build a more positive future relationship.

Avoiding conflict escalation is essential to maintaining a constructive negotiation environment and finding mutually acceptable solutions. By reducing tension and promoting collaboration, parties are more likely to effectively resolve the crisis.

In particularly complex or highly emotional situations, it can be helpful to involve a neutral mediator. The mediator can help facilitate communication and negotiation and work to find common ground.

Mediation is a valuable strategy in particularly complex or highly emotional situations. A neutral mediator can play a crucial role in facilitating communication and negotiation between parties in conflict. Here is more information on how mediation works and when it can be useful:

A mediator is a neutral and trained person who acts as an impartial facilitator in negotiation. Their primary goal is to help parties communicate effectively, identify common interests, and find mutually acceptable solutions.

The mediator works to improve communication between the parties. They can establish an environment that encourages active listening and discourages confrontation.

The mediator helps parties explore their underlying interests and generate solution options. This may involve questions and exercises that promote creativity and collaboration.

The mediator's neutrality is critical. They do not take sides and do not pass judgment on who is right or wrong. Their aim is to help both parties reach an agreement that works for them.

Most mediation processes are confidential. This means that what is discussed in mediation generally cannot be used in court if mediation is unsuccessful. Confidentiality can encourage parties to be more open.

Mediation is usually a voluntary process. Parties must be willing to participate. However, in some jurisdictions and certain types of cases, mediation may be mandated by a court or agency.

Mediation is often used in family disputes, such as divorces, child custody disputes, and conflicts among family members.

In the workplace, mediation can be used to resolve disputes between employers and employees, as well as conflicts among coworkers.

Neighbor disputes, such as noisy disturbances or property issues, are common situations where mediation is sought.

Commercial disputes, such as contract conflicts or disputes between business partners, are often resolved through mediation.

In situations where a community or group faces conflict, mediation can help find solutions that satisfy all parties.

In emotionally charged crisis situations, like the loss of a loved one, mediation can help manage tensions and issues that arise in a highly emotional context.

Mediation is a powerful tool for effectively addressing conflicts and reaching mutually acceptable solutions. It can be especially useful when tensions are high, emotions are heightened, or parties have difficulty communicating effectively.

Identify the most important priorities for all parties involved. This can help focus the negotiation on areas that are fundamental and find solutions that address those priorities.

Establishing priorities in negotiation is a fundamental strategy to ensure that the most important needs of all parties are effectively addressed. Identifying and understanding these priorities allows you to concentrate efforts on finding solutions that are critical and mutually acceptable.

Encourage all parties to express their concerns and needs. Actively and empathetically listening is essential for identifying what is most crucial for each party.

Ask the parties involved what their priorities are in the conflict. You can ask, for example, "What are the most critical aspects for you in this situation?"

Once you've gathered information from all parties, rank priorities in order of importance. This will help you understand which concerns are most critical.

Identify priorities that are shared by all or most parties. These are the points where you are more likely to find acceptable solutions for everyone.

Evaluate how satisfying one priority may affect other parties and the overall negotiation outcome in the long run. Balancing immediate needs with future considerations is essential.

By focusing the negotiation on the identified priorities, you can work on options that effectively address those priorities. This may require creativity and collaboration.

Be flexible in seeking solutions. Priorities may change as the negotiation progresses or more information is obtained. Being willing to adapt is crucial.

Once priorities are identified, define a clear goal that summarizes what you expect to achieve in the negotiation. This can help maintain focus on the most important priorities.

Make sure that the parties understand mutual priorities and objectives. Open and transparent communication is key to the success of the negotiation.

If necessary, document the agreed-upon priorities and objectives in an agreement or contract. This provides a clear record of what has been agreed upon.

Establishing and understanding priorities in a negotiation is essential to finding solutions that meet the most important needs of all parties involved. By focusing the negotiation on these priorities, it is more likely to reach mutually acceptable agreements and effectively resolve conflicts.

Crisis situations can evolve rapidly. Maintain flexibility and adaptability to adjust negotiation strategies as circumstances change.

Flexibility and adaptability are essential attributes in crisis situations and, in particular, in negotiation during a crisis. Since circumstances can change rapidly, it's crucial to be willing to adjust negotiation strategies to address new challenges.

Be willing to consider different perspectives and approaches. Don't cling to a single strategy or solution, as it may be necessary to change course based on new circumstances.

Establish a system to closely monitor the situation's evolution. This may include tracking news, changes in regulations, or shifting conditions that may affect the crisis or negotiation.

Maintain constant and open communication with all parties involved. Ensure that they are aware of any relevant developments and can voice their concerns as they arise.

Priorities may change in a crisis. Reevaluate the needs and concerns of all parties as the situation evolves.

If necessary, adjust the negotiation process to adapt to the circumstances. This could include changes in the schedule, negotiation platform, or meeting format.

If previously considered solutions are no longer viable, seek alternative options. Creativity can be essential in finding effective solutions.

As circumstances change, make informed decisions based on the most recent information. Consult with experts or individuals with specialized knowledge if necessary.

Prepare plans for both the short and long term. Some solutions may be temporary, while others may be more enduring.

Adaptability extends beyond just the technical aspect of negotiation. Consider the emotional well-being of all parties and adjust strategies to address emotions and stress.

Ensure that any related agreements or documentation remain updated to reflect changes in circumstances.

Adaptability and flexibility are crucial in negotiation during a crisis, as they allow for effectively dealing with changing situations and finding solutions that are suitable for new circumstances. Maintaining an open mindset and being willing to adjust strategies is key to achieving success in challenging times.

Once an agreement has been reached, ensure that all parties are committed to its implementation. This may require proper follow-up and monitoring.

Commitment to the agreement is essential to ensure that the resolution of a crisis or conflict is effective and sustainable. Once an agreement has been reached, it's important that all parties involved are committed to its implementation.

Ensure that all terms of the agreement are clearly defined and documented. A clear and well-drafted agreement makes it easier to understand each party's responsibilities.

It is essential that all parties voluntarily accept the agreement without coercion. A forced agreement is less likely to be effectively implemented.

Encourage open and constant communication among all parties. Establish a system for parties to report progress and any issues that may arise.

Establish a monitoring and supervision system to ensure compliance with the agreement. This may include deadlines, milestones, and specific checkpoints.

Define clear consequences in case of agreement breach. Parties should understand the possible sanctions or measures that will be taken if they fail to meet their commitments.

In some cases, it can be useful to provide additional support or resources to help parties comply with the agreement. This could include financial assistance, counseling, or training.

Establish a mechanism to resolve any disputes related to the agreement. This may involve appointing a neutral mediator or arbitrator.

Encourage all parties to actively participate in the agreement's implementation. This may involve assigning specific tasks and responsibility for reporting progress.

If circumstances change or new issues arise, be willing to update and adjust the agreement as necessary.

Recognize and celebrate achievements as parties fulfill their commitments. This can help maintain motivation and commitment.

Maintain transparency at all times and foster trust among all parties. Trust is essential for the long-term success of the agreement.

Properly document the agreement, deadlines, communications, and any changes or adjustments. This provides a clear record and a basis for monitoring.

Commitment to the agreement is essential to ensure that conflict resolution is sustainable and effective. By following these guidelines and maintaining a proactive approach to agreement implementation and monitoring, the likelihood of all parties fulfilling their commitments is increased.

Rather than seeking a quick fix, consider how to address the root of the problem in the long term to prevent future conflicts.

Exploring long-term solutions is a smart strategy in conflict resolution as it addresses the root of the problem and helps prevent future disagreements. Instead of focusing on temporary solutions, consider how to comprehensively address the issues.

Before seeking long-term solutions, it's important to understand what the root of the conflict is. Ask yourself why the conflict occurred and what the underlying causes are.

Instead of focusing on the initial positions, try to identify the underlying interests. This can help you understand why the conflict occurs and how it can be effectively addressed.

Develop a long-term plan to address the underlying causes of the conflict. This may include changes in policies, procedures, or behaviors that contribute to the conflict.

Invite all parties involved to participate in long-term planning. Collaboration is essential to ensure that solutions are effective and mutually acceptable.

Consider the potential risks and benefits of long-term solutions. Evaluate how they will affect all parties and whether they are sustainable over time.

Establish indicators and metrics to measure the progress and impact of long-term solutions. Continuously track to ensure that the desired results are being achieved.

Reflect on past conflict resolution experiences and use the lessons learned to avoid similar issues in the future.

Recognize that long-term solutions may require time and adaptation. Be flexible in implementation and adjust the plan as needed.

Education and effective communication are key to ensuring that all parties understand and support long-term solutions.

Work on building stronger and more collaborative relationships among the parties involved. A foundation of trust and respect can help prevent future conflicts.

If the conflict is due to deficiencies in policies or procedures, work on developing solid policies and procedures that prevent similar problems in the future.

Consider implementing formal mediation and early conflict resolution mechanisms as part of a long-term strategy.

By addressing the underlying causes of a conflict and seeking long-term solutions, you can contribute to a more harmonious environment and prevent future disagreements. This approach is crucial for maintaining healthy and productive relationships over time.

Negotiation in crisis situations can be a complex and time-consuming process. However, it is a valuable tool for finding peaceful solutions and resolving conflicts, especially in sensitive or intensely emotional contexts.

18.Negotiation in Personal and Family Relationships

Negotiation plays a fundamental role in personal and family relationships. Communication is the foundation of any relationship. Practice open and honest communication with your loved ones. Listen actively and express your thoughts and feelings clearly and respectfully.

Open and honest communication is essential in any relationship, whether it's a friendship, a romantic relationship, with family, or in the workplace.

Pay attention when someone is speaking. Make eye contact, nod to show your interest, and avoid interrupting. Sometimes, simply listening to someone can be very supportive.

Don't be afraid to share your own ideas and emotions. Honesty is crucial for building a strong relationship. Don't hold back, but make sure to do it in a respectful manner.

Avoid ambiguity. Communicate your thoughts and feelings clearly and directly to prevent misunderstandings. The clearer you are, the better others can understand you.

Instead of blaming or criticizing, focus your communication on your own feelings and needs. For example, instead of saying, "You're always late and you don't care," you can say, "I feel frustrated when you're late because I value punctuality."

Try to put yourself in the other person's shoes and understand their perspectives and emotions. This helps create an environment of mutual understanding.

Instead of avoiding conflicts, address them openly and respectfully. Seek solutions together instead of blaming or fighting.

In emotional situations, try to stay calm and avoid reacting impulsively. Effective communication requires composure.

If you have criticisms or suggestions, express them constructively. Instead of saying, "You're wrong," you can say, "Maybe we could consider another perspective."

Recognizing your mistakes and apologizing when necessary is an important part of open and honest communication.

Effective communication takes time and effort. Don't expect every conversation to be perfect right away, but work on constant improvement.

Remember that open and honest communication is an ongoing process that requires practice and patience. When a solid foundation of communication is established in a relationship, trust is strengthened, and a strong basis for problem-solving and overcoming challenges together is built.

Try to understand the viewpoints and emotions of others. Empathy will help you establish a deeper connection with your loved ones and resolve conflicts more effectively.

Empathy is a fundamental element in communication and interpersonal relationships. Practicing empathy involves putting yourself in the shoes of others and striving to understand their viewpoints and emotions.

Pay attention to what the other person is saying without judging or interrupting. Ask questions to clarify and delve into their point of view. This shows that you care about what they think and feel.

Ask open-ended questions about how they feel or what's happening in their lives. Listening to their responses and showing genuine interest reinforces the emotional connection.

Try to understand the other person's point of view, even if you don't agree with it. Ask yourself why they might feel the way they do and what personal experiences might influence their opinions.

Acknowledge and validate the other person's feelings, even if you don't share those feelings. Saying something like "I can see you're very upset" shows that you're attuned to their emotions.

Don't assume you know what's going on in the other person's mind. Instead, ask them and give them the opportunity to express themselves.

Sometimes, sharing your own personal experiences can help the other person feel understood and establish a deeper connection. However, make sure your experiences are relevant and don't monopolize the conversation.

Empathy sometimes involves giving the other person time to process their emotions and thoughts. Don't rush to find solutions or answers, especially in distressing moments.

Ask them how you can help or what they need from you. Showing a willingness to provide support demonstrates that you care about their well-being.

We all have biases and assumptions. Recognizing them and being aware of how they may influence your understanding of others is an important step toward empathy.

Empathy is a skill that improves with practice. The more you practice it, the more natural it will become.

Empathy is essential for building strong relationships, fostering understanding, and effectively resolving conflicts. When people feel understood and valued, relationships tend to be healthier and more satisfying.

Instead of focusing on differences, seek common interests. This can help find solutions that benefit both parties and strengthen the relationship.

Empathy is a fundamental element in communication and in interpersonal relationships. Practicing empathy involves putting yourself in the shoes of others and striving to understand their viewpoints and emotions.

Pay attention to what the other person is saying without judging or interrupting. Ask questions to clarify and delve into their point of view. This shows that you care about what they think and feel.

Ask open-ended questions about how they feel or what's happening in their lives. Listening to their responses and showing genuine interest reinforces the emotional connection.

Try to understand the other person's point of view, even if you don't agree with it. Ask yourself why they might feel the way they do and what personal experiences might influence their opinions.

Acknowledge and validate the other person's feelings, even if you don't share those feelings. Saying something like "I can see you're very upset" shows that you're attuned to their emotions.

Don't assume you know what's going on in the other person's mind. Instead, ask them and give them the opportunity to express themselves.

Sometimes, sharing your own personal experiences can help the other person feel understood and establish a deeper connection. However, make sure your experiences are relevant and don't monopolize the conversation.

Empathy sometimes involves giving the other person time to process their emotions and thoughts. Don't rush to find solutions or answers, especially in distressing moments.

Ask them how you can help or what they need from you. Showing a willingness to provide support demonstrates that you care about their well-being.

We all have biases and assumptions. Recognizing them and being aware of how they may influence your understanding of others is an important step toward empathy.

Practice empathy consistently: Empathy is a skill that improves with practice. The more you practice it, the more natural it will become.

Empathy is essential for building strong relationships, fostering understanding, and resolving conflicts effectively. When people feel understood and valued, relationships tend to be healthier and more satisfying.

Define the goals and expectations in the relationship. This can include short and long-term goals, such as future plans, shared values, and family roles.

Setting clear goals in a relationship is essential for maintaining effective communication, fostering mutual understanding, and building a solid foundation.

First and foremost, ensure that both parties are willing to discuss their goals and expectations. Communication is key in this process.

Before discussing common goals, it's important for each person in the relationship to have a clear understanding of their personal goals. This can include career goals, life goals, values, and desires.

Talk about what you expect to achieve in the short and long term in the relationship. This could include financial goals like buying a house, family goals like having children, or personal goals like advancing in a career.

Make sure you both share fundamental values. Values can influence all major decisions in a relationship. Ensure you're on the same page in terms of what's important to you.

Discuss the roles you want to play in the relationship and in the family. This may include discussions about the division of household responsibilities, finances, and child-rearing.

While it's important to set goals, you should also be flexible. Life can change, and it's important to be willing to adapt to new circumstances and challenges.

Once you've discussed your goals, it's helpful to create an action plan to achieve them. This could include concrete steps that both of you need to take to progress toward your goals.

Goals and expectations in a relationship are not static. As life evolves, it's important to regularly review and update these goals. You can do this in periodic conversations to ensure they remain aligned.

When defining goals and expectations in the relationship, it's essential that both parties are committed to working together to achieve them. A relationship is a joint effort.

While working together to achieve your goals, it's important to show mutual respect and support. This will strengthen the relationship and help overcome any challenges that may arise.

Setting clear goals in a relationship can provide a solid foundation and help prevent misunderstandings or unnecessary conflicts. Additionally, working together toward common goals can strengthen the bond between the individuals involved and make the relationship more satisfying and successful in the long run.

Conflicts are inevitable in relationships. Learn to address them constructively, avoiding confrontation and seeking mutually acceptable solutions.

Resolving conflicts constructively is essential for maintaining healthy relationships and strengthening interpersonal bonds.

Start the conversation respectfully and actively listen to the other person. Ensure that both have the opportunity to express their points of view.

Stay calm and avoid negative expressions, sarcasm, and personal attacks. Focus on the problem rather than attacking the person.

Ensure you understand what the central issue causing the conflict is. Often, conflicts arise from misunderstandings or unmet expectations.

Communicate your own needs and desires clearly and specifically. Use "I" instead of "you" to avoid blaming the other person. For example, instead of saying, "You never listen to me," you can say, "I feel frustrated when I don't feel you're listening."

Focus on finding solutions rather than winning the argument. There is often common ground where both parties can agree.

Be willing to compromise on certain aspects and reach compromises. Negotiation is an important part of conflict resolution.

Recognize that each person has their own needs and desires. Don't try to impose your opinions or solutions.

At times, it's helpful to take a break and return to the conversation later when both are calmer and can think clearly.

Conflicts can be opportunities for growth. Reflect on what you can learn from each conflict to avoid similar issues in the future.

If the conflict is particularly challenging to resolve, consider seeking the help of a couples' counselor or therapist. Sometimes, a neutral perspective can be very useful.

After resolving a conflict, show appreciation for the other person's effort and forgive. Holding onto grudges or resentment is not healthy for the relationship.

Remember that, in the context of a long-term relationship, some conflicts are normal. What's important is how they are handled and resolved.

Constructive conflict resolution strengthens relationships by fostering mutual understanding and teamwork. Learning to handle conflicts effectively is a valuable skill that can significantly improve the quality of your personal relationships.

Dedicate quality time to your loved ones. Relationships require attention and care, and spending time together strengthens family and personal bonds.

Quality time is essential for strengthening relationships with your loved ones. Schedule time in your calendar to spend with your loved ones. This can include outings, family dinners, game nights, or other activities that everyone enjoys.

During quality time, try to disconnect from electronic devices. This allows you to be present in the moment and avoid distractions.

When you're with your loved ones, make sure to give them your full attention. Listen to their thoughts, feelings, and concerns, and show genuine interest in what they have to say.

Seek out activities that everyone enjoys and that create meaningful memories. It could be a trip, a hike, an evening of cooking together, or even a deep conversation.

Celebrate special occasions like birthdays, anniversaries, and holidays in a meaningful way. This demonstrates appreciation and love for your loved ones.

Establishing family traditions provides structure and cohesion to the family. These can be small rituals or annual events that everyone looks forward to.

Open your heart and share your thoughts and feelings with your loved ones. Vulnerability can strengthen emotional bonds.

Be present and offer emotional support to your loved ones in times of difficulty. This can be especially important when they are going through personal challenges.

Include all family members in activities and decisions. Ensure that everyone feels valued and heard.

Sharing the experience of learning something new can be exciting and enriching. Consider taking classes or learning new skills with your loved ones.

While group quality time is important, it's also valuable to dedicate individualized time to each family member or loved one. This strengthens personal bonds.

Sometimes, the most memorable moments are spontaneous. Be willing to be flexible and seize opportunities to spend time together, even if they weren't planned.

Don't forget to regularly express your love and appreciation to your loved ones. Affectionate words and actions are fundamental to maintaining a close relationship.

Quality time strengthens family and personal bonds by creating meaningful memories and fostering open and affectionate communication. Prioritizing this time in your life is an investment in your relationships and the happiness of all involved.

Establishing clear boundaries in the relationship is essential to maintaining a healthy and respectful relationship.

Clear boundaries are key to maintaining a healthy and respectful relationship.

Communication is crucial for setting boundaries. Have open and honest conversations with your loved ones about your needs and expectations, and listen to theirs.

Before setting boundaries with others, it's important to know your own boundaries. Reflect on what makes you feel uncomfortable or insecure in a relationship.

When setting boundaries, be clear and specific about what you are willing to accept and what you are not. Avoid ambiguities to prevent misunderstandings.

Maintain consistency in enforcing your boundaries. This helps establish clear expectations and maintain the integrity of your boundaries.

Just as you expect your boundaries to be respected, you should also respect those of others. Empathy and mutual respect are crucial.

Assertively and respectfully saying "no" is fundamental to setting boundaries. Don't feel like you have to please everyone all the time.

Everyone needs personal space. Ensure that both you and your loved ones have time and space for yourselves, even in a close relationship.

Social media and technology can complicate relationships. Set clear boundaries regarding the use of devices and social media to avoid conflicts.

Throughout a relationship, it may be necessary to adjust boundaries as circumstances change. Maintain open communication to adapt boundaries as needed.

If you have difficulty setting or maintaining boundaries in a relationship, consider seeking the help of a therapist or counselor. Sometimes, a neutral perspective can be beneficial.

If someone crosses your boundaries, talk to that person in a respectful but firm manner. Explain how you felt and why the boundary is important to you.

Setting boundaries doesn't mean being selfish or insensitive. It's an important part of maintaining healthy relationships. Don't feel guilty about taking care of yourself and your needs.

Setting boundaries in a relationship is a way to protect your emotional well-being and maintain healthy communication. When both parties respect each other's boundaries, a more harmonious and respectful relationship is fostered.

Relationships evolve over time. Be flexible and adaptable as circumstances and the needs of those involved change.

Flexibility and adaptability are crucial for maintaining healthy and successful relationships over time. Relationships evolve over time due to changes in circumstances and the needs of the people involved.

Maintain ongoing communication with your loved ones. Discuss changes in your lives and in the relationship, as it's essential for understanding and addressing challenges that arise.

Change is inevitable. Learn to view it as an opportunity for growth and evolution rather than a threat.

As people change, so do their needs and desires. Be responsive to the changing needs of your loved ones and be willing to adapt to meet those needs.

Recognize that you, too, evolve over time. You may have new interests, goals, and needs. Communicating these changes is important so others can better understand you.

When differences arise in a relationship due to changes, seek solutions that are mutually acceptable through negotiation and compromise.

A positive and open-minded attitude toward change and adaptability will help you face challenges more effectively.

Don't cling to rigid routines. Allow yourself to be flexible in your daily planning to accommodate the changing needs of the relationship.

Disagreements and mistakes are a part of any relationship. Practicing forgiveness and letting go of the past is important for moving forward and adapting to new circumstances.

Changes can be opportunities for personal and collective growth. Seize these opportunities to learn and evolve together.

As circumstances change, it's crucial to continue showing empathy and respect for the needs and feelings of others.

If changes in the relationship are particularly challenging, consider seeking the support of a therapist or counselor. They can help you navigate the changes and challenges in the relationship.

Flexibility and adaptability are essential for maintaining lasting and healthy relationships. As circumstances change, the ability to adjust and grow together strengthens bonds and promotes a more solid and satisfying relationship.

Offer support to your loved ones in times of need and celebrate achievements and successes together. Mutual support strengthens the relationship and fosters trust.

Mutual support is a fundamental pillar in any healthy relationship. In times of need as well as in times of joy, providing support and celebrating achievements together strengthens the relationship and fosters trust.

Pay attention when your loved ones need to talk or vent. Sometimes, simply listening can be the most valuable support you can offer.

Recognize and validate the feelings of the people around you, even if you don't fully understand their perspective. Saying something like "I understand that you feel that way" shows empathy and understanding.

Ask how you can help, and if possible, provide practical support. Sometimes, just knowing that someone is there to back you up can make a big difference.

Offer comfort and emotional support when necessary. Sometimes, people simply need a safe place to express their emotions.

It's important not only to support during difficult times but also to celebrate the successes and achievements of your loved ones. Rejoicing in the victories of others strengthens the bonds.

Express your gratitude when someone provides you with support. Feeling valued reinforces people's willingness to continue helping.

It's important to be willing to offer support, but also to set boundaries so as not to become emotionally exhausted. Communicate respectfully when and to what extent you can provide help.

Support should be unconditional and not subject to conditions or expectations. You shouldn't expect something in return for the support you offer.

Encourage your loved ones to reach their personal goals and aspirations. Fostering growth and empowerment strengthens the relationship.

When disagreements or conflicts arise, address the situation with empathy and respect. Don't let disagreements affect your willingness to provide support.

If someone in your life is going through a difficult situation that requires support beyond your capabilities, consider seeking guidance from a therapist or counselor.

Mutual support is an integral part of healthy and strong relationships. Offering support during difficult times and celebrating successes creates an atmosphere of trust and affection in which relationships can grow and thrive.

When it comes to important decisions, involve all parties and work together in the decision-making process. This may include financial, educational, or lifestyle decisions.

Joint planning and decision-making are crucial for maintaining healthy relationships and ensuring that all parties involved feel valued and heard.

Maintain open and honest communication with all parties involved in decision-making. Actively listen to their viewpoints and concerns.

Before making important decisions, ensure that everyone has a clear understanding of common goals and objectives. This will help guide decisions in the right direction.

Make sure that all individuals affected by the decision have the opportunity to participate in the decision-making process.

Try to understand and empathize with the perspectives and needs of others. This is essential for reaching mutually acceptable solutions.

Discuss the different available options and their consequences before making a decision. Ensure that all parties understand the implications of each choice.

In joint decision-making, it's sometimes necessary to reach agreements through negotiation and compromise. This involves making concessions in certain areas to reach a solution that works for everyone.

Seek consensus whenever possible. Consensus means that everyone agrees with the decision and is willing to support it.

Don't feel pressured to make important decisions quickly. Taking the necessary time to discuss and consider options can prevent hasty decisions.

Sometimes, it's helpful to seek guidance from a professional or decision-making expert, especially when dealing with complex or sensitive matters.

Once you've made a decision, make sure to document it clearly to avoid future misunderstandings.

Decisions may require adjustments as circumstances change or new information becomes available. Being willing to review and amend previous decisions demonstrates flexibility and adaptability.

Reflect on previous decisions and their outcomes. This will help you make future decisions in a more informed manner.

Joint planning and decision-making are essential for maintaining equitable and satisfying relationships. By involving all parties and working together in the decision-making process, a solid foundation for growth and harmony in relationships is built.

Celebrate individual achievements and special events, such as birthdays and anniversaries. This strengthens emotional bonds and creates meaningful moments.

Celebrating achievements and special events is an important way to strengthen emotional bonds and create meaningful moments in relationships. These moments of celebration and recognition are crucial for showing appreciation and love for your loved ones.

Make sure to communicate with your loved ones to understand which events and achievements are meaningful to them. Ask about their preferences and desires.

Sometimes, a surprise can be an emotionally significant gift. Plan surprise celebrations for your loved ones on special occasions.

Personalize the celebrations according to the interests and personality of the person being honored. This shows that you have thought about what would make them happy.

Express your appreciation sincerely. Use words of gratitude and affection to highlight what you value in the person or achievement you are celebrating.

Gifts can be a tangible way to show appreciation. Choose gifts that have special meaning and consider the recipient's taste.

On special occasions, focus on creating shared memories that all those involved can treasure. Take the time to capture those moments with photos or videos.

Not only celebrate relationship milestones or family events, but also celebrate the individual successes of each person in the relationship. Recognizing personal growth and success is important.

Family traditions can add meaning to celebrations. Maintain and create traditions that everyone enjoys.

Don't overlook important dates, such as birthdays and anniversaries. These are ideal occasions to show appreciation and love.

In addition to words, show your love and appreciation through affectionate gestures, such as hugs, kisses, and quality time together.

Don't wait for major events to celebrate. Celebrate small achievements and happy moments in everyday life.

During celebrations, it's also a good time to express gratitude for mutual support and the strength of the relationship.

Celebrating achievements and special events is an opportunity to strengthen relationships and express love and appreciation. Creating meaningful moments together builds a strong foundation for healthy and satisfying relationships.

Reflect on past experiences in the relationship and use the lessons to improve and avoid future conflicts.

Learning from past experiences in a relationship is essential for growth and ongoing improvement. Reflecting on what has worked and what hasn't in the past can help avoid future conflicts and strengthen bonds.

Talk to your loved ones about past experiences and how they have affected you. Listen to their perspectives and concerns as well.

Reflect on your own behavior and actions in the past. Consider how you could have acted differently or better to avoid conflicts.

Look for recurring patterns in past conflicts or challenges. Identifying patterns allows you to take steps to prevent them from recurring.

Don't be afraid to acknowledge your mistakes and learn from them. Recognizing when you've made a mistake is a sign of maturity and growth.

Not everything in the past is mistakes. Acknowledge and celebrate what has worked in the relationship and continue doing it.

Use your past experiences as a foundation to set improvement goals in the relationship. Define what you would like to achieve together.

Once you've identified areas for improvement, commit to making positive changes. This may involve changing behaviors, attitudes, or communication patterns.

If past experiences have caused resentment or pain, work on forgiveness and the ability to let go of the past to move toward a healthier future.

Sometimes, seeking the help of a therapist or counselor can be useful in addressing past issues and learning to manage them effectively.

Consider each past experience, whether positive or negative, as an opportunity for growth and strengthening the relationship.

Use the lessons from the past to improve communication and decision-making in the present. Ensure that communication is open, honest, and effective.

Remember that a relationship is a long-term investment. Learning from past experiences is an important part of maintaining a lasting and satisfying relationship.

Learning from past experiences in a relationship is a valuable way to promote personal growth and strengthen bonds. By applying these lessons in the current relationship, you can avoid future conflicts and foster a healthier and more enriching relationship.

In situations where negotiation becomes difficult or conflict persists, consider seeking the help of a mediator or a relationship counselor. They can offer neutral guidance and support.

Mediation and counseling are valuable resources when relationships face difficulties and conflicts persist. Both mediators and relationship counselors can provide impartial guidance and support to help the involved parties resolve issues and improve communication.

A mediator acts as a neutral third party without bias toward any of the parties. This helps ensure that all voices are heard impartially.

The mediator facilitates communication between the conflicting parties, helping them express themselves effectively and listen to each other.

The goal of mediation is to reach an agreement or a solution that is acceptable to both parties. The mediator assists in exploring options and reaching compromises.

Most mediation processes are confidential, which encourages openness and honesty in discussions.

Mediation is often more efficient and cost-effective than resorting to legal litigation to resolve conflicts.

A relationship counselor provides a safe environment for couples or individuals to discuss issues and concerns.

Relationship counselors can help identify underlying problems in the relationship that may be contributing to conflicts.

Relationship counselors can teach effective communication skills and help people learn to express their needs and desires healthily.

Counselors can guide the parties involved in conflict resolution and negotiation of mutually satisfactory solutions.

Relationship counseling can provide emotional support to individuals facing challenges in the relationship, which can help reduce stress and tension.

Counselors can help couples set long-term goals for the relationship and work towards their realization.

In both cases, it's important that all parties involved are willing to participate in the process and commit to improving the relationship. Both mediation and relationship counseling can be valuable resources for resolving conflicts, improving communication, and strengthening relationships in situations where negotiation becomes difficult or problems persist.

Personal and family relationships are fundamental in a person's life, and effective negotiation plays a key role in their maintenance and strengthening. Open communication, empathy, and constructive conflict resolution are essential skills for maintaining healthy and harmonious relationships.

19.Ethics in Negotiation

Ethics in negotiation is a fundamental aspect to ensure that business transactions and agreements are fair, respectful, and sustainable.

Honesty is crucial in any negotiation. The involved parties should provide accurate and complete information about the topics under discussion. Lying or withholding information can undermine trust and lead to unethical agreements.

Indeed, honesty is one of the fundamental pillars of ethics in negotiation. Providing accurate and complete information is essential to establish a foundation of trust among the parties involved. When parties are honest about their interests, needs, limitations, and expectations, it facilitates informed decision-making and reduces the chances of future conflicts.

Lack of honesty in negotiation, such as concealing important information or providing deceptive data, can lead to unfair agreements, deteriorate the relationship between the parties, and damage the reputation of the individuals or companies involved. Therefore, honesty is not only an ethical matter but also an effective strategy for building strong and lasting business relationships.

Honesty in negotiation is essential to foster trust, facilitate fair agreements, and maintain integrity in the negotiation process.

Honesty is a fundamental principle in the ethics of negotiation. Providing accurate and complete information is essential to establish a strong foundation of mutual trust among the parties involved in a negotiation.

When parties are honest with each other, it promotes an atmosphere of mutual trust. Trust is crucial in any negotiation, as it allows the parties to feel secure in sharing their interests, needs, and concerns.

Accurate and complete information is crucial for parties to make informed decisions. If inaccurate information is provided or important information is omitted, parties may make decisions based on incorrect data, which can lead to detrimental agreements.

Lack of honesty can undermine the integrity of the parties involved in the negotiation. When parties discover that they have been lied to or that information has been withheld, they are likely to lose trust in the other party and the negotiation process as a whole.

Honesty in negotiation is essential for building long-term business relationships. Parties who feel they have been treated with sincerity and fairness are more likely to continue doing business together in the future.

Honesty in negotiation is not only an ethical principle but also an effective strategy for achieving fair and lasting agreements. Lack of honesty can undermine trust and harm business relationships, while honesty promotes integrity and mutual respect in the negotiation process.

Integrity involves acting consistently with ethical values and principles, even when no one is watching. Parties must commit to abiding by agreements and not seek ways to evade their obligations.

Integrity is another fundamental pillar in the ethics of negotiation. It involves acting consistently with ethical values and principles, even when there is no direct public scrutiny.

Parties involved in negotiation must ensure that their actions and decisions align with ethical values that promote honesty, justice, and mutual respect. This includes not compromising ethical principles for personal or business advantages.

An integral part of integrity in negotiation is compliance with agreements. Once an agreement is reached, both parties are responsible for fulfilling the agreed-upon conditions. Non-compliance undermines trust and the integrity of the process.

Parties should not seek ways to evade their contractual obligations or manipulate the terms of the agreement to gain unfair advantages. Integrity requires adhering to the spirit and letter of the agreements.

Individuals involved in negotiation must take personal responsibility for their actions and decisions. Lack of integrity is evident when parties attempt to attribute responsibility to others or avoid accountability for their actions.

Integrity is essential for maintaining a good reputation in the business world. Companies and individuals known for their integrity are more likely to build strong and long-term business relationships.

Integrity in negotiation is essential to ensure that parties commit to fair agreements and consistently fulfill their obligations. This is beneficial not only from an ethical perspective but also in maintaining strong business relationships and preserving the reputation of the parties involved.

Respect: Parties must treat each other with respect and consideration, regardless of differences that may exist. Respect for the dignity and rights of others is fundamental in ethical negotiation.

Respect is another essential principle in the ethics of negotiation. It involves treating all parties involved with consideration and courtesy, regardless of differences that may exist in terms of culture, opinion, social position, gender, race, or other characteristics.

Respect for the dignity and rights of others is a fundamental component of ethics in negotiation. This means that parties must recognize and value the autonomy and equality of all individuals involved in the negotiation.

Respect involves actively listening to the other parties, paying attention to their perspectives, concerns, and needs. This empathetic listening demonstrates that the opinions of others are valued.

Parties should communicate in a respectful manner, avoiding offensive or derogatory language. Aggressive or disrespectful communication can undermine trust and hinder the construction of mutually beneficial agreements.

In negotiation, it is important to acknowledge and respect cultural, linguistic, and other differences that may exist between the parties. This entails not imposing one's own cultural values or standards.

Respect also involves providing equal opportunities for all parties to express their views and participate in the decision-making process. The opinions of any party should not be marginalized or belittled.

In case of disagreements or conflicts in negotiation, parties should address them in a respectful and constructive manner, rather than resorting to confrontation or disdain.

Respect in negotiation is essential to promote an atmosphere of collaboration and trust. When parties treat each other with respect and consideration, they are more likely to overcome differences and reach fair and mutually beneficial agreements for all parties involved.

Negotiations should be fair and equitable. This means that both parties should have the opportunity to express their interests and concerns, and agreements should be beneficial to both parties as much as possible.

Justice is a fundamental principle in the ethics of negotiation. It implies that negotiations should be fair and equitable for all parties involved.

All parties should have equal opportunities to express their interests, needs, and concerns in the negotiation. This means that no one should be marginalized, excluded, or disadvantaged in the decision-making process.

Parties should enter into negotiations with the intention of negotiating in good faith and with the goal of achieving a beneficial agreement for all parties. They should not use deceptive or manipulative tactics to gain unfair advantages.

Agreements should be equitable and beneficial to all parties as much as possible. This does not mean that all parties get exactly what they want, but it does imply that agreements should be fair and equitable in relation to the interests and needs of all parties.

Attention should be paid to the interests and concerns of all parties involved. Ethical negotiation involves seeking solutions that take into account the perspectives and needs of all parties.

Justice in negotiation involves avoiding the exploitation of one party for the benefit of another. Weaknesses or disadvantages of one party should not be exploited to gain unfair advantages.

Negotiations should be conducted within the framework of applicable laws and regulations. This ensures that the negotiation process adheres to fair legal standards.

Justice in negotiation is essential to ensure that agreements are equitable and beneficial for all parties involved. When justice is practiced, it promotes the building of strong business relationships and reduces the possibility of disputes and conflicts in the future.

Transparency involves providing clear and accessible information about the terms and conditions of the negotiation. Harmful clauses or conditions should not be hidden in complex agreements.

Transparency is a fundamental principle in the ethics of negotiation. It involves the open and clear disclosure of relevant information to all parties involved.

Parties should provide relevant information about the terms and conditions of the negotiation. This includes details about prices, deadlines, obligations, and other important aspects that may affect the involved parties.

Communication in negotiation should be clear and understandable for all parties. Technical terms or ambiguous language that can lead to misunderstandings should be avoided.

Information should be easily accessible to all parties so they can review and understand it before making decisions. This may include delivering documents in writing, presenting information in meetings, or making information available online.

It is important for parties to disclose any conflicts of interest that may affect the negotiation. This ensures that parties are aware of potential influences that could bias the process.

Transparency means that harmful clauses or conditions should not be hidden in complex agreements. All conditions should be presented openly and honestly so that parties can make informed decisions.

Parties should be willing to answer questions and provide clarifications about the information presented. This helps ensure that all parties have a complete understanding of the negotiation details.

Transparency is essential for creating an environment of trust and fairness in negotiation. When transparency is practiced, it reduces the likelihood of misunderstandings, conflicts, and detrimental agreements. Additionally, transparency promotes ethics and integrity in the negotiation process, which, in turn, strengthens long-term business relationships.

Negotiations should be conducted within the framework of the law. It is important to comply with all applicable laws and regulations, both at the local and international levels.

Compliance with the law is a fundamental principle in the ethics of negotiation. It implies that all negotiations should be conducted within the legal framework, adhering to all applicable laws and regulations, whether at the local, national, or international level.

Parties involved in negotiation must respect and comply with all laws and regulations governing the negotiation process and the subject of the agreement. This includes laws related to taxes, intellectual property, competition, consumer safety, and other relevant areas.

Before entering into a negotiation, it is important to conduct legal due diligence to understand the applicable laws and regulations. This helps to avoid potential legal violations.

Parties should be transparent and disclose all relevant information that is subject to legal requirements. Withholding information or violating disclosure regulations can have serious legal implications.

The agreements and contracts resulting from a negotiation should comply with all relevant laws and regulations. This includes drafting contracts that are legally sound and binding.

It is also important for parties to follow ethical practices in their negotiations. This means that, in addition to respecting legality, ethical principles such as honesty, integrity, and respect should be observed.

Compliance with the law is essential to ensure that negotiations are conducted fairly and within an ethical framework. Legal violations can result in serious legal consequences, damage the reputation of the parties involved, and undermine trust in the negotiation process. Therefore, it is imperative for parties to adhere to applicable laws and regulations at all stages of negotiation.

Ethical negotiation seeks to achieve agreements that benefit all parties involved. The focus should not be on exploiting or taking advantage of one party for the benefit of another.

In an ethical negotiation, the parties seek to collaborate in finding solutions that satisfy their mutual interests instead of trying to win at the expense of the other party. The goal is to create a scenario where both parties come out as winners.

Parties must pay attention to the needs and interests of all involved parties. This involves listening, understanding, and valuing what each party aims to achieve in the negotiation.

Agreements should be fair and just for all parties to the extent possible. This doesn't necessarily mean that all parties get exactly what they want, but it does imply that agreements should balance the interests and needs of all parties.

The pursuit of mutual benefits encourages the building of long-term business relationships. When parties feel they have been treated fairly and respectfully, they are more likely to continue doing business together in the future.

Exploiting one party for the benefit of the other is not ethical in negotiation. Parties should not seek unfair advantages at the expense of the other party, as this can damage trust and undermine the integrity of the negotiation process.

Focusing on mutual benefit is essential for building strong business relationships and achieving ethical agreements. By practicing this principle, parties demonstrate mutual respect and strive to find solutions that satisfy the interests and needs of all involved parties.

Respecting the confidentiality of sensitive information shared during negotiations is essential. Parties should agree on how information will be handled and ensure it is not used inappropriately.

Confidentiality is a crucial principle in the ethics of negotiation. It involves respecting the privacy and confidentiality of sensitive information shared during the negotiation process.

Before entering a negotiation, it is common for parties to agree in writing on the terms of confidentiality. This may include signing a non-disclosure agreement (NDA) that establishes guidelines for handling confidential information.

Parties should take steps to protect sensitive information shared during the negotiation. This may include limiting access to information only to those necessary for the negotiation and implementing security measures to prevent unauthorized disclosure.

Confidential information shared in the context of negotiation should not be used inappropriately. This implies not using the information to gain unfair advantages or harm the other party.

The confidentiality agreement generally specifies the duration of the obligation to keep confidential information. After the negotiation, parties may be bound by this obligation for a specified period.

If it is necessary to disclose confidential information to third parties, it should be done in a controlled manner and, in some cases, only after obtaining the consent of the party that provided the information.

At the conclusion of the negotiation, it is common for parties to agree to destroy or return the shared confidential information as stipulated in the confidentiality agreement.

Respecting confidentiality is essential to create an environment of trust in negotiation. Parties must have confidence that the sensitive information they share will not be used against them or disclosed without their consent. Failure to meet confidentiality obligations can have serious legal consequences and harm the integrity of the parties involved. Therefore, it is essential to respect and uphold confidentiality at all stages of the negotiation process.

Coercion and manipulation are not ethical practices in negotiation. Parties should not use threats, undue pressure, or deceptive tactics to gain advantages.

The prohibition of coercion and manipulation is a central principle in the ethics of negotiation. This means that parties involved should not employ tactics that threaten, exert undue pressure, or manipulate the other party to gain unfair advantages.

Ethical negotiation respects the autonomy and decision-making capacity of each party. Coercion and manipulation undermine one party's ability to make informed and voluntary decisions.

Parties should enter into negotiations based on mutual consent and voluntariness. Undue pressure or manipulative tactics can lead to agreements that are not genuinely accepted by both parties.

Threatening or intimidating the other party, whether explicitly or implicitly, is not ethical in negotiation. These practices can create an atmosphere of fear and distrust.

Ethical negotiation involves being honest and clear in communication. Parties should not use deceptive tactics or false information to influence the decision-making of the other party.

Instead of resorting to coercion or manipulation, parties should focus on listening and understanding the perspectives and needs of the other party. Empathy and open communication are essential in ethical negotiation.

Parties must respect the boundaries set by the other party. If one party expresses unwillingness to do something, that decision should be respected instead of attempting to pressure them into changing their mind.

Respecting boundaries is a crucial component of ethics in negotiation. This principle emphasizes the importance of recognizing and respecting the decisions and limits set by the other party involved in the negotiation.

In an ethical negotiation, autonomy and decision-making capacity of each party are respected. Each party has the right to set boundaries and make decisions about what they are willing to do or not do.

Decisions and actions should be based on the voluntary consent of both parties. Coercive, manipulative, or pressure tactics should not be used to try to change the other party's opinion.

Active listening is essential in ethical negotiation. Parties should be willing to listen and understand the needs and limits expressed by the other party.

Respecting boundaries in negotiation is essential to maintain a relationship of negotiation based on mutual respect. When parties respect the autonomy and decisions of the other party, trust is promoted, and strong business relationships are built.

Parties should communicate their own boundaries clearly and respectfully. They should also be willing to listen and understand the boundaries of the other party.

When parties recognize and respect each other's boundaries, they are more likely to seek solutions that satisfy the interests and needs of both parties, which is a beneficial approach in negotiation.

Respect for boundaries in negotiation is essential for creating an environment of collaboration, trust, and mutual respect. This principle contributes to the construction of fair and lasting agreements and ensures that decisions are made freely and voluntarily. In summary, in ethical negotiation, the autonomy and limits of both parties involved are recognized and respected.

The prohibition of coercion and manipulation in negotiation is essential to ensure that decisions are made freely and voluntarily and that agreements are fair and equitable. The use of these practices undermines trust and can damage long-term business relationships. Therefore, ethics in negotiation involves respecting and considering the needs and desires of both parties without resorting to coercive or manipulative practices.

Today, there is an increasing emphasis on social and environmental responsibility in negotiation. Companies and parties must consider the impact of their agreements on society and the environment.

Ethics in negotiation involves behaving fairly, honestly, respectfully, and responsibly, seeking agreements that benefit all parties involved. By following these ethical principles, the building of strong, long-term business relationships is promoted.

20. The Role of Empathy in Negotiation

Empathy plays a significant role in negotiation, as it facilitates effective communication and the building of strong relationships. It involves putting oneself in the other party's shoes, trying to understand their perspectives, needs, and concerns. This, in turn, leads to more effective communication, as the parties can express themselves more clearly and feel heard and understood.

It also plays a fundamental role in improving communication in negotiation. Active listening to the other party is an essential component of empathy. This means paying full attention to what they are saying without interruptions and showing a genuine interest in their perspectives and viewpoints. By doing so, a solid foundation is established for effective communication.

When empathetic, the parties seek to understand the needs and concerns of the other party, which allows them to address the key points of the negotiation more effectively and work together to find mutually beneficial solutions.

Empathy helps reduce misunderstandings. By trying to understand the other party's perspective, potential points of confusion can be clarified, ensuring that both parties are on the same page.

When the parties feel that they are being heard and understood, a foundation of trust is established in communication. Trust is essential for successful negotiation and the building of strong business relationships.

Empathy doesn't only involve listening but also effectively communicating one's interests and needs. When the other party feels heard and understood, they are more receptive to listening and understanding one's interests.

It promotes mutual respect in communication. When the parties show consideration for each other's perspectives and needs, it creates an environment of respect that facilitates collaboration and joint decision-making.

Therefore, empathy is a valuable tool in negotiation, as it improves communication, fosters trust, and enables parties to collaborate more effectively in achieving mutually beneficial agreements. By putting themselves in the other party's shoes and showing empathy, a fertile ground is established for a more successful and ethical negotiation.

It contributes to the building of strong business relationships. When parties show empathy toward each other, a foundation of mutual trust and respect is established, often leading to long-term and collaborative relationships.

The construction of solid business relationships is a fundamental outcome of empathy in negotiation.

It contributes to the creation of an environment where parties trust each other. When parties feel that they are heard, understood, and respected, they are more comfortable sharing information and collaborating.

It promotes mutual respect. When putting themselves in the other party's shoes and showing consideration for their perspectives and needs, mutual respect is built, which is essential for a strong relationship.

Relationships based on empathy tend to be more collaborative. Parties are willing to work together to find mutually beneficial solutions rather than adopting a competitive attitude.

It is also valuable in conflict resolution. It allows parties to address disagreements constructively and seek solutions that satisfy both parties, often leading to more effective and less contentious resolutions.

Relationships based on empathy are usually accompanied by open and honest communication. Parties feel more comfortable expressing their concerns and needs, which facilitates communication and decision-making.

It contributes to the building of long-term relationships. Parties who feel understood and respected are more likely to continue doing business together in the future.

Companies and individuals known for their empathy and strong business relationships often enjoy a good reputation in their respective industries. This can open up additional opportunities and enhance the company's image.

It is essential for the construction of strong and collaborative business relationships. By fostering trust, mutual respect, and open communication, empathy contributes to the creation of lasting relationships in negotiation. These strong relationships are not only beneficial in the short term but can also lead to long-term collaborations and opportunities.

It allows parties to identify common interests or areas of agreement in negotiation. By understanding the needs and concerns of both parties, it is more likely that solutions that satisfy their shared interests will be found.

It plays a fundamental role in identifying common interests in negotiation. Empathy involves putting oneself in the other party's shoes and trying to understand their needs and concerns. By doing so, a deeper insight into what is important to that party in the negotiation is gained.

It promotes open and honest dialogue between the parties. When both parties feel heard and understood, they are more willing to openly and honestly share their interests and goals.

By understanding the perspectives of both parties, it is more likely that areas of agreement or common interests will be identified. This can be a solid starting point for building mutually beneficial solutions.

It can also help overcome obstacles in negotiation. When the other party's concerns and limitations are understood, it is possible to address these issues more effectively and seek solutions that mitigate them.

The identification of common interests through empathy promotes cooperation rather than competition. Parties are more willing to work together to find solutions that benefit both parties.

It is a key element in the construction of win-win agreements, in which both parties benefit. By identifying common interests, it is more likely that solutions that are beneficial to all parties involved will be found.

By recognizing and understanding the interests of both parties, disagreements and conflicts in negotiation can be reduced. This contributes to a smoother and more effective process.

Therefore, empathy not only facilitates the identification of common interests but is also crucial for building mutually beneficial agreements in negotiation. By understanding the needs and concerns of both parties, a strong foundation is established for collaboration and joint decision-making.

It is useful in conflict resolution. It allows parties to address disagreements constructively by actively listening to and understanding the perspectives of the other party, often leading to mutually acceptable solutions.

It involves actively listening to and comprehending the other party's perspectives, needs, and concerns. This approach enables a deeper understanding of the factors contributing to the conflict.

When parties feel heard and understood, it is more likely that negative emotions and hostility associated with the conflict will diminish. Empathy helps to ease tensions and create a more collaborative environment.

It helps parties focus on their underlying interests rather than rigid positions. Instead of debating conflicting positions, they can explore the underlying needs and desires that can lead to more satisfactory solutions.

It can inspire the generation of creative options to resolve the conflict. By understanding both parties' perspectives, it is more likely that solutions satisfying both parties' interests will be identified.

It promotes a more collaborative negotiation in which parties work together to find mutually acceptable solutions rather than fighting to win at the other's expense. It can also help find compromises that partially satisfy both parties' interests. This can be a practical solution when a complete conflict resolution is not possible.

It is not only useful for resolving current conflicts but also for preventing future conflicts. By understanding the other party's perspectives and concerns, it is possible to identify potential areas of conflict and address them before they become significant problems.

It is a valuable tool in conflict resolution in negotiation. By listening, understanding, and showing consideration for the other party's perspectives, it creates a conducive environment for finding mutually acceptable solutions and building strong and lasting business relationships.

In high-tension or conflict situations, empathy can play a significant role in reducing hostility and creating a more collaborative environment. When parties show empathy, negative emotions are softened, making negotiations easier.

Empathy is a valuable resource in reducing tension and managing conflicts in negotiation.

In high-tension situations, emotions can run high, making effective communication and decision-making challenging. Empathy allows parties to recognize and understand each other's emotions, contributing to the reduction of hostility and aggression.

It helps parties shift their focus from rigid positions to underlying interests. Instead of fighting over positions, they focus on understanding both parties' needs and concerns, which can reduce tension by creating common ground for negotiation.

When parties show empathy, a collaborative environment is established instead of a competitive one. Parties are more willing to work together to find solutions that satisfy their shared interests.

It facilitates more effective communication during tense moments. By actively listening to and understanding the other party's concerns, misunderstandings and unnecessary conflicts can be avoided.

It can help identify areas of agreement even in conflict situations. When both parties feel heard and understood, they are more likely to find points of convergence in their interests.

It is an essential component of constructive conflict resolution. It helps address root issues rather than simply treating conflict symptoms, often leading to more lasting and mutually acceptable solutions.

It can also prevent conflicts from escalating. When parties show empathy and are willing to understand the other party's concerns, disagreements are less likely to turn into more serious conflicts.

It is a powerful tool for reducing tension and managing conflicts in negotiation. By demonstrating consideration and understanding of the other party's perspectives and emotions, it creates an environment conducive to the peaceful resolution of differences and the construction of strong business relationships.

It is a fundamental component of ethical negotiation. By putting oneself in the other party's shoes, it fosters respect for their interests and needs, contributing to the creation of fair and equitable agreements. It involves respecting and understanding the interests and needs of the other party. By empathizing with the other party and showing consideration for their perspectives, mutual respect is encouraged.

It helps identify areas of agreement and seek solutions that satisfy both parties' interests. In ethical negotiation, the goal is to achieve agreements that benefit both parties rather than exploiting or taking advantage of one party for the benefit of the other.

It contributes to preventing coercive or manipulative practices, which are unethical in negotiation. By understanding the other party's needs and concerns, it is less likely that tactics seeking unfair advantages will be used.

Ethical negotiation is not limited to the current transaction but focuses on building long-term business relationships. When parties feel respected and understood, they are more likely to continue doing business together in the future.

It promotes negotiation based on voluntary consent. Parties enter into negotiations freely and voluntarily, which is an essential component of ethical negotiation.

In the end, empathy in ethical negotiation is about treating the other party with respect and consideration, recognizing their needs and desires, and working together to achieve fair and equitable agreements. Empathy contributes to building a strong foundation for ethical and lasting business relationships.

It is especially valuable in international negotiation and multicultural contexts. It helps understand cultural differences and overcome potential barriers in communication and understanding.

It is of particular importance in international negotiation and multicultural contexts due to cultural differences and potential communication and understanding barriers. Here's an explanation of why empathy is valuable in these contexts:

In international and multicultural negotiations, cultural differences can influence communication, behavioral norms, and expectations. Empathy allows parties to recognize and respect these differences, which is essential to avoid misunderstandings and conflicts.

It can help overcome language barriers. When parties show interest in understanding and respecting the other party's language and communication, it facilitates communication and minimizes misunderstandings.

It enables parties to build cultural bridges. By putting themselves in the other party's shoes and trying to understand their cultural perspective, meaningful connections can be established, fostering trust and collaboration.

Each culture may have different values, priorities, and expectations in negotiations. Empathy helps understand the specific needs and desires of different cultures, which is crucial for finding solutions that are acceptable to all parties.

It contributes to reducing cultural stereotypes and prejudices. By empathizing with the other party, people are seen as individuals with their own perspectives, rather than making generalizations based on their cultural background.

In international and multicultural contexts, it is a key factor in building strong and lasting business relationships. Trust and mutual respect, facilitated by empathy, are fundamental to long-term success in these contexts.

The lack of empathy in international negotiations can lead to misunderstandings and international conflicts. Empathy helps avoid such situations by facilitating understanding and effective communication across cultures.

It plays an essential role in international negotiation and multicultural contexts by facilitating understanding, effective communication, and the building of strong relationships. It helps parties overcome cultural differences and find solutions that are respectful and beneficial to all involved.

It is essential in negotiation because it contributes to effective communication, the building of strong relationships, and the pursuit of mutually beneficial solutions. By showing empathy toward the other party, an environment of mutual respect is created, which can be fundamental to success in negotiation.

In summary, showing empathy toward the other party in a negotiation involves putting oneself in their shoes, understanding their perspectives, needs, and concerns, and demonstrating a genuine interest in their well-being and goals. This empathy not only reflects an attitude of respect and consideration toward the other party but is also a powerful tool for building a trusting relationship in the negotiation process.

When both parties demonstrate empathy, an environment of mutual respect and understanding is created. This has several significant benefits for success in negotiation:

Empathy fosters trust between parties, as it shows they are willing to understand and take the needs and concerns of the other party seriously. When there is trust that the other party will not try to exploit the situation or take unfair advantage, they feel more secure and open to collaboration.

Empathy facilitates more effective communication. When both parties feel heard and understood, they are more likely to communicate openly and honestly. This allows for clarifying misunderstandings, resolving conflicts, and working together to find mutually beneficial solutions.

Empathy also plays a significant role in conflict management. When disagreements arise, the ability to put oneself in the other party's shoes and understand their perspectives can help find solutions that satisfy both parties without resorting to prolonged disputes.

It is fundamental to building strong and lasting business relationships. When parties feel they have been treated with respect and understanding in a negotiation, they are more likely to want to maintain that relationship in the future. This can lead to ongoing agreements and a long-term partnership.

Empathy is also a catalyst for seeking solutions that meet the interests and needs of both parties. When both parties care about each other's well-being, they are more willing to find compromises and creative solutions that benefit both parties.

Empathy in negotiation is not only a sign of mutual respect but also an effective strategy for building strong relationships, promoting open and honest communication, resolving conflicts, and achieving mutually beneficial agreements. In an environment of ethical and empathetic negotiation, the chances of success are significantly higher.

21.The Importance of Active Listening in Negotiation

Active listening is a fundamental skill in any negotiation process, as it plays a crucial role in its success.

Active listening allows the parties in a negotiation to better understand each other's needs, interests, and concerns. This is essential for finding solutions that satisfy both parties and for avoiding misunderstandings that can hinder the process.

Mutual understanding is one of the main reasons why active listening is essential in negotiation. When the parties involved in a negotiation take the time to listen and understand each other's needs, interests, and concerns, the foundations for a successful agreement are laid.

Active listening enables the parties to uncover the real needs and desires of the other party. This is crucial for designing proposals and solutions that are appealing and beneficial to both parties.

When parties do not practice active listening, they often make assumptions about what the other party wants or needs. These assumptions can be incorrect and lead to misunderstandings or a lack of agreement. Active listening helps eliminate these assumptions and obtain direct information.

A deeper understanding of the other party's needs and concerns can help prevent unnecessary conflicts. When the reasons behind the demands or positions of the other party are understood, it is easier to find solutions that address those concerns without compromising one's interests.

With a deeper understanding, it is possible to design solutions that are specific to the needs of each party. This can result in more equitable and satisfying agreements.

Mutual understanding promotes empathy and the building of long-term relationships. This is especially valuable in business environments where long-lasting relationships can lead to future opportunities and collaborations.

In conclusion, mutual understanding facilitates more effective and collaborative negotiation because it allows the parties to address their concerns and needs more accurately and satisfactorily. Active listening plays a fundamental role in this process by opening the door to a deeper and more meaningful dialogue between the parties involved.

Building relationships: Active listening fosters the building of trusting relationships. When parties feel that they are being heard and understood, they are more likely to collaborate and find solutions that benefit both parties. This is especially important in long-term business relationships.

Undoubtedly, building trusting relationships is one of the most significant advantages of active listening in the context of negotiation. Here are some additional reasons why active listening promotes the building of strong relationships in negotiation:

Active listening demonstrates respect for the other party. When people feel heard, they feel valued and respected, laying the foundation for a more positive and constructive relationship.

Empathy is the ability to understand and share the feelings of another person. Active listening promotes empathy, as it puts you in the other party's shoes and allows you to understand their perspectives and feelings. This helps create an emotional connection and strengthens the relationship.

Effective communication is a key component in building strong relationships. Active listening ensures that communication is two-way, and both parties feel heard. This reduces the likelihood of misunderstandings and disagreements.

When parties feel heard and understood, they are more willing to collaborate in finding mutually beneficial solutions. This is essential in negotiation situations where the goal is to reach an agreement that satisfies both parties.

In long-term business relationships, building a foundation of trust is crucial. Active listening in the early stages of negotiation sets the stage for future smoother and successful interactions, as the parties have established a level of mutual trust.

Even in the strongest business relationships, disagreements and conflicts can arise. The trust and empathy built through active listening can help resolve these conflicts more constructively and less harmfully to the relationship.

Active listening is not only important for achieving a successful agreement in negotiation but also contributes to the building of trusting relationships and the potential for long-term collaborations and business partnerships. The ability to actively listen is an essential component for success in business and in managing long-lasting business relationships.

Sometimes, parties in a negotiation may not reveal all their interests or concerns from the beginning. Active listening can help uncover these hidden interests, opening up new opportunities for a mutually beneficial agreement.

The identification of hidden interests is another important reason why active listening plays a crucial role in negotiation.

Often, parties in a negotiation may have underlying interests or motivations that are not immediately disclosed. Active listening allows negotiators to delve deeper into the conversation and ask open-ended questions that help uncover these hidden motivations.

When hidden interests are revealed, new opportunities arise to find creative solutions that satisfy both parties. Options may emerge that would not have been considered if active listening had not been used to discover these interests.

A negotiator's ability to discover the other party's hidden interests demonstrates a genuine concern for understanding their needs. This can build greater trust between the parties, as it shows that you are willing to make an extra effort to meet their interests.

Discovering hidden interests can help avoid unpleasant surprises later in the negotiation or business relationship. If both parties fully understand each other's motivations and needs, unexpected conflicts are less likely to arise.

Knowing the hidden interests of the other party can help make strategic decisions about the concessions you are willing to make. This allows you to prioritize what is most important to the other party and negotiate more efficiently.

By uncovering hidden interests, the parties can work together more effectively to find mutually beneficial solutions. This fosters an atmosphere of cooperation and collaboration in the negotiation.

Active listening is essential for unraveling hidden interests, enriching the negotiation by allowing both parties to fully understand what motivates the other. This not only facilitates conflict resolution and more informed decision-making but also creates a fertile ground for beneficial and sustainable agreements.

Active listening can help prevent misunderstandings and unnecessary conflicts. By listening attentively and asking questions to clarify points, issues can be addressed before they become insurmountable obstacles.

Conflict reduction is another key benefit of active listening in the context of negotiation. Here are some additional aspects of how active listening contributes to conflict prevention and resolution:

When active listening is practiced, parties can clarify any misunderstandings or misinterpretations of what the other party is saying. This prevents misunderstandings from becoming sources of conflict.

Active listening allows for the identification of disagreements and differences of opinion before they escalate into serious conflicts. This provides an opportunity to proactively address these issues and seek solutions before the relationship deteriorates.

It fosters an environment in which both parties feel comfortable expressing their concerns and opinions. This reduces the likelihood of tensions silently accumulating and erupting into future conflicts.

When practiced, parties can identify and address issues constructively and collaboratively. This helps prevent the escalation of conflicts and maintains a more positive negotiation atmosphere.

It not only helps identify points of conflict but also focuses on finding mutually acceptable solutions. This shifts the focus from confrontation to problem-solving, which is beneficial for both parties.

Conflict reduction through active listening is essential for maintaining a long-term relationship, especially in business situations. Avoiding unnecessary conflicts protects the relationship and facilitates future business interactions.

It is a valuable tool for preventing and resolving conflicts in the negotiation process. By promoting open communication, clarifying misunderstandings, and early identification of disagreements, it significantly contributes to maintaining a harmonious negotiation atmosphere and achieving successful agreements.

Creativity in finding solutions: Active listening fosters an environment in which parties feel comfortable sharing ideas and proposals. This can lead to creative solutions that might not have been considered otherwise.

It can have a significant impact on generating creative solutions in a negotiation.

When parties feel heard and valued, they are more willing to share their unique perspectives and approaches. This can lead to the introduction of fresh ideas and unconventional solutions that might not have emerged otherwise.

It promotes a collaborative environment in which parties work together to find mutually beneficial solutions. Collaboration can inspire new ideas and approaches that better satisfy the needs of both parties.

Open conversation and a willingness to actively listen allow parties to explore joint options and consider solutions that are not limited to their initial demands. This can expand the set of possible solutions and lead to a more satisfactory agreement.

It creates an environment in which parties feel less threatened by innovative ideas or unconventional proposals. This can reduce resistance to adopting novel solutions.

In negotiations, parties often have different perspectives, backgrounds, and experiences. Active listening allows leveraging this diversity of ideas to find more comprehensive and effective solutions.

Creativity in finding solutions can not only lead to the identification of new ideas but also to the optimization of existing agreements. By carefully considering the needs and concerns of both parties, it's possible to refine proposals and reach a more equitable agreement.

It promotes creativity by fostering an environment in which parties feel comfortable sharing ideas and proposals. This can lead to innovative solutions that better satisfy the needs of both parties and improve the quality of the final agreement. Creativity in finding solutions is a fundamental part of effective negotiation.

When parties feel heard and respected, they feel empowered in the negotiation. This can lead to greater commitment and a sense of ownership over the final agreement.

Empowerment of parties is a crucial aspect closely related to active listening in negotiation.

When parties feel heard and respected, they tend to be more engaged in the negotiation process and the final outcome. They feel valued and considered, increasing their willingness to collaborate and work together to reach an agreement.

It allows parties to feel like active participants in the decision-making process. This gives them a sense of ownership over the agreement and proposed solutions, which can make them more committed to their success and fulfillment.

The empowerment derived from active listening can also increase the parties' confidence in the final agreement. When they feel their voices were heard and considered, they are more likely to trust that the agreement meets their needs.

Empowered parties tend to show less resistance to necessary proposals and concessions to reach an agreement. This is because they feel more involved in the decision-making process and view the agreement as a solution they contributed to creating.

They are more likely to collaborate effectively since they feel more responsible for finding solutions that satisfy their interests. This can expedite the negotiation process and increase the likelihood of reaching an agreement.

In business situations and long-term relationships, the empowerment of parties is essential for maintaining a constructive and trusting relationship. When parties feel empowered, they are more willing to continue working together in the future.

In summary, active listening empowers parties by giving them a sense of ownership and control over the negotiation process. This, in turn, can increase commitment, trust, and collaboration, contributing to the likelihood of reaching mutually beneficial and long-lasting agreements. Empowerment is a key factor in negotiation success.

Lack of active listening can lead to one party dominating the negotiation, which can result in an unfair deal. Active listening promotes balance in communication and gives voice to both parties.

Active listening plays an important role in preventing unfair treatment in a negotiation. It involves giving both parties the opportunity to express their views and concerns. This is essential to ensure that decisions are made fairly and equitably, rather than being unilaterally driven by one of the parties.

It promotes an equal voice in negotiation. It ensures that both parties have the opportunity to speak and be heard, preventing one party from dominating the conversation and making unilateral decisions.

In some negotiations, one party may have an advantage in terms of power, resources, or experience. Active listening helps level the playing field by allowing the less powerful party to be heard and have a say in the decision-making process.

Lack of active listening can lead to the exploitation of one party by another. By promoting balance in communication, it prevents one party from unfairly taking advantage of the other.

For an agreement to be considered fair, both parties must feel that their interests and concerns have been taken into account. Active listening is fundamental to achieving this balance and building agreements that are equitable and sustainable.

When parties feel they are being treated fairly and have the opportunity to express their views, trust in the negotiation process develops. Trust is essential for negotiation success.

Lack of fairness in a negotiation can lead to resentment and future disagreements. Active listening helps prevent these issues by ensuring that parties feel they are being treated fairly throughout the process.

Active listening is essential to avoid unfair treatment in a negotiation as it promotes balance in communication and ensures that both parties have a voice and participation in the process. This is essential for building fair and equitable agreements that satisfy both parties and promote trust and collaboration.

The information gathered through active listening provides a solid foundation for making informed decisions during the negotiation. This increases the likelihood of reaching a mutually beneficial agreement.

Improved decision-making is another key benefit of active listening in the negotiation process.

Active listening involves listening attentively and asking questions to deeply understand the needs, interests, and concerns of the other party. This provides detailed and valuable information that is crucial for making informed decisions.

The information gathered through active listening allows parties to more accurately assess the risks and benefits of various options. This is essential for making decisions that minimize risks and maximize benefits for both parties.

The information obtained also influences the choice of negotiation strategies. When the needs and priorities of the other party are understood, it is possible to tailor strategies to reach an agreement that is satisfactory for both parties.

It helps discern which concessions are most important to the other party. This allows parties to focus on critical aspects of the agreement and negotiate more effectively.

By gaining a complete understanding of the other party's perspectives and motivations, the chances of misunderstandings that could negatively affect the negotiation process are reduced.

The information collected through it is essential for designing fair solutions that address the needs of both parties fairly. This increases the likelihood of reaching mutually beneficial agreements.

Informed decision-making reduces uncertainty in the negotiation. When parties have a clearer understanding of their own interests and those of the other party, they can make decisions with greater confidence.

Active listening provides parties with the information they need to make more informed and strategic decisions during the negotiation. This not only increases the likelihood of reaching a beneficial agreement for both parties but also contributes to a more efficient and collaborative negotiation process. It is essential in negotiation because it promotes effective communication, mutual understanding, the building of strong relationships, and the search for solutions that satisfy both parties. By practicing active listening, parties can increase their chances of achieving successful and lasting agreements.

In conclusion: The practice of active listening is fundamental in negotiation and can have a significant impact on the parties' ability to achieve successful and lasting agreements. Here is an elaboration of these concepts: Active listening is not limited to simply hearing what the other party is saying; it involves paying complete attention to their message, understanding it, and showing genuine interest in their perspectives and needs. By practicing active listening, parties demonstrate respect and consideration for the other party. This not only facilitates communication but also creates an atmosphere of trust and mutual respect in the negotiation.

Active listening is a valuable tool for reaching successful agreements. When parties feel heard and understood, they are more willing to openly and honestly communicate their interests and needs. This provides both parties with a clearer view of what is important to the other and creates a foundation for collaboration.

In situations of conflict or disagreement, active listening is particularly beneficial. It allows parties to address each other's concerns and work together to find mutually acceptable solutions. Instead of getting stuck in rigid positions, parties can focus on resolving underlying issues, which often leads to a more effective and less contentious resolution.

Agreements reached through active listening tend to be more lasting. This is because both parties feel heard and understood, giving them a sense of investment and ownership in the agreement. This emotional investment in the agreement promotes its long-term fulfillment and can lead to a stronger and more enduring business relationship.

Active listening facilitates the identification of common interests in the negotiation. By deeply understanding the perspectives and needs of the other party, it is more likely that areas of agreement or shared interests will be found. This is essential for building mutually beneficial agreements.

Active listening also promotes more effective communication in general. When both parties feel heard and understood, misunderstandings are less likely to occur, and unnecessary conflicts are less likely to arise. Open and honest communication is key to successful negotiation. It is an essential skill in negotiation that can increase the likelihood of success and the durability of agreements. By practicing it, parties show respect, promote collaboration, and create an environment of trust in which mutually beneficial solutions are more likely to be achieved.

22.The Influence of Nonverbal Communication in Negotiation

Non-verbal communication plays a crucial role in negotiation. It is often considered that non-verbal communication can be even more important than verbal communication in conveying messages and building relationships during a negotiation.

Facial expressions can reveal emotions and attitudes. During a negotiation, it is important to pay attention to the facial expressions of the participants to understand their emotional reactions and adapt your approach accordingly.

Facial expressions are a fundamental component of non-verbal communication in negotiation.

A genuine smile can indicate liking, satisfaction, or interest. If a participant smiles during a negotiation, it could be a sign that they feel comfortable or agree with the discussion.

A furrowed brow or raised eyebrows can signal confusion, disapproval, or disgust. If you observe this expression in the other party, you may want to clarify or modify your message to address their concerns.

If someone has a blank or expressionless look, it can be difficult to interpret their feelings. In this case, it is important to ask open-ended questions or seek feedback to better understand their perspective.

Avoiding eye contact or looking away can indicate a lack of confidence, insecurity, or dishonesty. If you notice someone avoiding eye contact, you may want to further investigate their motivations or concerns.

A furrowed brow can suggest confusion, disagreement, or concern. It can be helpful to address any concerns or questions that may have led to this expression.

Narrowing the eyes can be a sign of scrutiny or mistrust. It is important to maintain transparency and honesty in your statements to build trust in the negotiation.

If someone looks at you attentively, it could indicate interest or focus. Take advantage of this signal to highlight key points or present arguments effectively.

Some people tend to use facial gestures while speaking, such as nodding or pursing their lips. These gestures can provide additional clues about their agreement or disagreement with what is being discussed.

Facial expressions may vary by culture and individual personality. Therefore, it is essential to consider the context and use non-verbal communication as a guide, but it is always advisable to support it with clear and effective verbal communication to avoid misunderstandings in a negotiation.

Eye contact can convey trust and sincerity. Maintaining appropriate eye contact during a negotiation demonstrates interest and commitment, while avoiding eye contact can be interpreted as a lack of trust or evasion.

Eye contact is a fundamental part of non-verbal communication in negotiation and can have a significant impact on how you are perceived and how you perceive others.

Direct and sustained eye contact is often interpreted as a sign of trust and sincerity. When you maintain eye contact with the other party, you are indicating that you are willing to be transparent and that you feel confident in the conversation.

Maintaining eye contact shows interest and engagement in the conversation. You can convey that you are focused on what the other party is saying and that you value their perspective.

It can also help you emotionally connect with the other party. You can show empathy by looking into the person's eyes and demonstrate that you are willing to understand their needs and concerns.

It is important to remember that norms regarding eye contact may vary by culture. In some cultures, constant eye contact may be perceived as dominant or even confrontational, while in others, it is a sign of respect and sincerity. Therefore, it is essential to be aware of cultural differences and adapt accordingly.

Although eye contact is important, it is also crucial to find a balance. Excessive or overly intense eye contact can make the other party feel uncomfortable or even threatened. On the other hand, lack of eye contact can be interpreted as a lack of trust or evasion. Look for a natural and comfortable balance.

Keep in mind that personal preferences vary. Some people may be more comfortable with less eye contact, while others may expect more. Observing the signals of the other party and adjusting your eye contact as needed is an important skill in negotiation.

Eye contact is a powerful tool in non-verbal communication during a negotiation. It can convey trust, sincerity, interest, and commitment. However, it is essential to be aware of cultural differences and individual preferences and find an appropriate balance that reflects mutual trust in the conversation.

Gestures and body movements, such as crossing arms, gesturing, or leaning forward, can provide clues about a person's attitudes and emotions. These gestures can indicate openness, defensiveness, or impatience.

Gestures and body movements are essential components of non-verbal communication in negotiation, as they can reveal a lot about a person's attitudes and emotions.

Crossing arms is generally interpreted as a defensive or closed-off gesture. It can indicate that the person feels insecure, distrustful, or is protecting their ideas. In a negotiation, crossing arms can be an obstacle to effective communication, as it may suggest a lack of willingness to listen or cooperate.

Hand and arm gestures are common in communication and can be used to emphasize points, show enthusiasm, or clarify ideas. However, excessive or erratic gestures can be distracting or give the impression of nervousness. It is important to use gestures moderately and consistently to support your message.

Leaning forward during a conversation can be a sign of interest and commitment. It indicates that you are focused on the other person and what they are saying. However, you should also be careful not to invade the other party's personal space, as this could be interpreted as aggressive.

Repeatedly looking at the clock or showing obvious signs of impatience, such as tapping your fingers, can indicate that you are anxious for the negotiation to end or that you are not fully engaged in the conversation. This can have a negative impact on the relationship and the results of the negotiation.

An open posture, with relaxed arms and a body position toward the other party, can indicate openness, a willingness to collaborate, and trust. Conversely, a closed posture, with crossed arms and a body position away, can suggest defensiveness or mistrust.

Excessive movement, such as leg swinging or tapping feet back and forth, can indicate nervousness or anxiety. Trying to maintain calm and composure is important during a negotiation.

A firm and appropriate handshake at the beginning of the negotiation can establish a positive impression. Avoid a handshake that is too weak or too strong, as it can be interpreted negatively.

In negotiation, it is crucial to be aware of your own gestures and body movements, as well as those of the other party. Observing these gestures and movements can provide clues about the attitudes and emotions of the people involved, allowing you to adapt your approach and strategy for more effective communication and better collaboration.

Body posture can reflect a person's level of comfort or discomfort in negotiation. Sitting up straight and maintaining an open posture can show confidence, while hunching or crossing legs defensively can indicate distrust or tension.

Body posture is an important aspect of non-verbal communication in negotiation, as it can provide valuable clues about a person's emotional state and disposition. Here are some ways in which body posture can influence a negotiation:

Sitting or standing upright with shoulders back and arms relaxed at the sides is generally interpreted as a sign of confidence and openness. It can indicate that you are willing to listen, collaborate, and engage in the negotiation. This posture tends to be perceived as secure and receptive.

Hunching or crossing legs in a defensive or closed manner can indicate discomfort, distrust, or tension. This posture can make the other party feel that you are on guard or not willing to commit. It can hinder effective communication and the building of positive relationships.

Leaning slightly forward can demonstrate interest and commitment in the conversation. It can indicate that you are focused on what the other party is saying and that you value their perspective. However, you should be careful not to invade the other party's personal space.

Observing changes in someone's posture during a negotiation can provide clues about their emotional reaction as the conversation progresses. If you notice that someone who was sitting upright starts to hunch or cross their arms, they may be experiencing discomfort or disagreement.

Relaxation of body muscles can indicate comfort and confidence, while muscle tension can reflect nervousness or stress. Watch if the person is tensing their arm, leg, or jaw muscles, as this can be an indicator of their emotional state.

The direction in which a person's body is oriented is also significant. If someone is facing you, they are likely interested in what you are saying. Conversely, if their body is turned away or in another direction, it may suggest disinterest or a lack of commitment.

In negotiation, it is essential to pay attention to both your own and the other party's body posture. This will allow you to adapt your approach and strategy as needed to improve communication and collaboration. Keep in mind that postures may vary by culture and personality, so it is important to consider the context and additional signals for a complete understanding.

Tone of voice and speaking speed: The way someone speaks can convey a wealth of information. A calm tone of voice and a slow speaking pace can suggest confidence and control, while a high tone or a fast speaking speed can indicate nervousness or urgency.

Tone of voice and speaking speed are fundamental aspects of verbal communication that are also part of non-verbal communication in negotiation. These aspects can significantly influence a person's perception during a negotiation.

A calm and relaxed tone of voice is often associated with confidence, calmness, and control. It can indicate that you are confident in your arguments and the overall situation. This can be effective in conveying assurance and persuading the other party.

A high tone of voice can suggest nervousness, anxiety, or excitement. It may be interpreted as a lack of confidence or a loss of control in the negotiation. If unintentional, it can convey weakness in your arguments.

Speaking at a slow pace can be effective in conveying confidence and ensuring that your words are clearly understood. It also gives the impression that you are taking your time to consider your words and respond thoughtfully.

Speaking at a fast pace can indicate urgency or impatience. It can give the impression that you are eager to reach an agreement or that you are trying to avoid discussing certain topics in depth. However, it can also convey energy and enthusiasm if used in moderation.

The volume of your voice is also important. Speaking too loudly can be perceived as aggression, while speaking too softly can be seen as lack of confidence or shyness.

The way you emphasize words and phrases through intonation can influence how your messages are interpreted. Proper emphasis can make your key points stand out and be better understood.

Strategic use of pauses and silences can be powerful. It can indicate that you are thinking about what has been said or give the other party an opportunity to reflect. It can also be used to emphasize certain points.

It is important to be aware of your own tone of voice and speaking speed, as well as those of the other party. Adapting your verbal communication according to non-verbal cues and the context of the negotiation can help you build effective relationships and achieve your goals at the negotiation table. The key is to maintain a proper balance and ensure that your communication is clear and consistent with your objectives.

Physical proximity: The physical distance between the parties in a negotiation is also important. Getting too close can be perceived as aggressive, while maintaining distance can indicate a barrier or disinterest. The optimal distance may vary by culture and individual preferences.

Physical proximity is a fundamental aspect of non-verbal communication in negotiation and can have a significant impact on how parties perceive each other and the development of the relationship.

Personal space is the zone of space close to a person and varies by culture and individual preferences. In a negotiation, personal space is important. Getting too close to the other party can make them feel invaded and threatened, which could lead to tension. On the other hand, maintaining too much distance can create an emotional barrier and make the other party feel that you are not interested in the conversation.

Social distance is a broader range of personal space used in social and business situations. Typically, social distance ranges from about 4 to 12 feet. In negotiation, maintaining an appropriate social distance is usually suitable and comfortable for most people.

It is essential to consider that norms regarding personal space may vary by culture. Some cultures may prefer closer proximity in conversations, while others may place greater importance on maintaining a greater distance. Additionally, individual preferences can vary significantly, so it is important to observe the signals of the other party and adjust your physical proximity accordingly.

Observe signs of discomfort from the other party regarding physical distance. If they appear to be moving backward or seem uncomfortable with your proximity, it is important to step back and respect their personal space.

Physical proximity should support your verbal and non-verbal communication. If you are discussing a sensitive or emotional topic, you may want to maintain a greater distance to ensure that the other party feels comfortable and respected.

Physical proximity in negotiation is a crucial aspect of non-verbal communication. Finding a proper balance and respecting cultural and personal preferences of the parties involved is essential for building trust and ensuring effective communication during the negotiation.

Appropriate physical contact, such as a firm handshake, can establish a positive initial connection in a negotiation. However, it's important to be sensitive to cultural differences and personal preferences regarding physical contact.

Physical contact in a negotiation is an important aspect of non-verbal communication and can be an effective way to establish a positive initial bond and show respect to the other party. However, it is crucial to be sensitive to cultural differences and personal preferences related to physical contact.

A firm and appropriate handshake is a common and universal form of physical contact in many cultures. It can convey confidence, respect, and a willingness to collaborate. When shaking hands, it's important for the handshake to be firm but not excessively strong, as an overly strong handshake can be interpreted as aggressive.

Norms regarding physical contact vary widely between cultures. Some cultures are more inclined towards physical contact, such as hugging or cheek kissing, while others are more reserved. Before an international negotiation or when dealing with people from different cultural backgrounds, it's essential to research and respect specific cultural norms related to physical contact.

Even within the same culture, people may have different personal preferences regarding physical contact. Some people may be comfortable with physical contact, while others may prefer to maintain some distance. Observe signals and respect the other party's preferences.

The level of appropriate physical contact can also depend on the context and the relationship between the parties. In a formal business negotiation, a handshake is more common. In more informal situations or when the relationship is close, closer physical contact, such as a hug, may be appropriate if well-received.

You should always wait for the other party's consent before initiating any physical contact. If you're unsure whether a handshake or any other physical contact gesture would be welcome, it's best to ask or wait for the other person to initiate physical contact.

Physical contact, such as a firm handshake, can be an effective tool for establishing a positive relationship in a negotiation. However, it is crucial to be aware of cultural differences and personal preferences regarding physical contact and always respect the boundaries and signals of the other party to ensure that your gesture is appropriate and well-received.

The way you dress and present yourself can influence how others perceive you in a negotiation. Dressing professionally and appropriately for the occasion can convey seriousness and respect for the negotiation process.

Attire and personal appearance are important aspects of non-verbal communication in a negotiation, as they can significantly influence how others perceive you.

Dressing professionally and appropriately for the occasion shows your respect for the negotiation process and the people involved. Professional attire suggests that you take the negotiation seriously and are willing to commit.

Attire may also be influenced by the organizational culture of your company or industry. In some sectors, such as finance or law, a more formal outfit is expected, while in others, such as technology or design, attire may be more informal. Adapting your attire to your company's or industry's culture can help you establish a more effective connection with others.

While professional attire is important, it is also essential to feel comfortable and confident in your choice of clothing. If you feel uncomfortable or disguised, it can negatively affect your confidence and, ultimately, your ability to negotiate successfully.

Make sure your attire is appropriate for the occasion. For example, a formal negotiation may require a suit and tie, while a more informal meeting might allow for a more relaxed approach.

In addition to clothing choices, cleanliness and personal presentation are crucial. Ensure that your clothing is clean and well-pressed, and pay attention to your personal hygiene. A clean and tidy appearance reinforces the impression of professionalism.

The way you dress and present yourself also contributes to your personal brand and the perception others have of you. If you have a specific personal brand or image you wish to project, your clothing and appearance choices should be consistent with that image.

When negotiating internationally, it's important to respect local dress codes and cultural expectations. Research common practices in the country or region where you are conducting the negotiation.

Attire and personal appearance are important aspects of non-verbal communication in a negotiation. Dressing professionally and appropriately for the occasion signals respect and seriousness, but it's also essential to feel comfortable and confident in your choice of clothing. Ensuring that your attire is suitable for the context and the negotiation's cultural norms is crucial for creating a positive impression.

Non-verbal communication, in the context of negotiation, refers to all the signals and messages that people convey without using words, such as gestures, facial expressions, body postures, tone of voice, eye contact, and other physical and behavioral signs. This form of communication is crucial in negotiation because it plays a significant role in several key aspects:

Non-verbal communication influences how the parties involved perceive each other. For example, an open and relaxed posture can convey confidence and a willingness to collaborate, while a closed or tense posture may be perceived as reserved or defensive. Tone of voice and eye contact also affect how someone is perceived. Being aware of how you project yourself through non-verbal communication can help create a positive and favorable impression.

Non-verbal communication plays a crucial role in building trust and empathy in negotiation. Showing empathy through facial expressions or gestures can help establish stronger connections with the parties involved. Additionally, appropriate eye contact and active listening during conversations demonstrate respect and attention, contributing to positive relationships.

Non-verbal signals are a key way to convey emotions and attitudes during negotiation. A genuine smile can express interest or satisfaction, while a furrowed brow or evasive gaze may indicate distrust or dissatisfaction. Understanding how emotions manifest in non-verbal communication can be helpful in adapting negotiation strategy and effectively addressing the concerns of the parties.

Interpreting non-verbal signals: Being able to interpret the non-verbal signals of others is essential to understand their true intentions, needs, and concerns. For example, observing a change in someone's body posture during negotiation may indicate that they feel uncomfortable or uncertain about a proposal. Recognizing these signals allows negotiators to adjust their approach and proactively address concerns.

Non-verbal communication is an integral part of negotiation that is often overlooked. Being aware of how you project yourself and being able to interpret the non-verbal signals of others are valuable skills for success in negotiation. Non-verbal communication can influence perception, relationship building, the transmission of emotions and attitudes, and is a key tool for understanding the underlying dynamics in negotiation. Therefore, paying attention to this aspect of communication can significantly improve the effectiveness of negotiation interactions and increase the chances of achieving successful and lasting agreements.

23.Negotiation in Impasse Situations

Negotiating in impasse situations refers to the stage in which the parties involved in a negotiation have reached a standstill or deadlock, meaning they cannot move forward or reach a mutual agreement. In this situation, it is essential to take specific steps to attempt to overcome the impasse and find a solution that is acceptable to both parties.

Instead of focusing on rigid positions, the parties can reassess and discuss their underlying interests and needs. Often, impasses occur because the parties are entrenched in their initial demands rather than understanding the reasons behind those demands.

Reevaluating interests and needs is a fundamental strategy in negotiation during impasse situations. Instead of focusing on initial demands or rigid positions, the involved parties should try to understand and communicate their underlying interests and needs.

Demands are often specific statements about what each party wants, but those demands are often just a manifestation of deeper needs or interests. By exploring and discussing these underlying interests, the parties can discover areas of agreement or potential solutions that they hadn't considered before.

The parties should ask themselves and each other why they want what they are asking for. What is the reason behind their demand? Identifying interests helps them better understand their own needs.

Asking open-ended questions that encourage communication is essential. Asking questions like, "Why is this important to you?" or "What do you need to achieve with this proposal?" can open the door to a deeper discussion about interests.

Listening with empathy and attentiveness to the other party is crucial. This helps in understanding their interests and needs and demonstrates a willingness to reach a mutually beneficial agreement.

During the negotiation, it is helpful to seek common or overlapping interests of both parties. Identifying areas where the needs of both parties can be met is an important step in overcoming the impasse.

Once the interests and needs are understood, it becomes easier to be flexible and seek solutions that satisfy both parties. This may involve adjusting initial demands or finding compromises that were not considered previously.

Reevaluating interests and needs can be a turning point in negotiations during impasse, as it often allows for innovative solutions and, in turn, facilitates progress toward an agreement. It is essential for both parties to actively engage in this process and maintain open and constructive communication.

Encouraging the generation of new options or solutions can help unlock the negotiation. Innovative ideas that were not considered before may arise.

Generating creative options is a fundamental strategy for overcoming impasse situations in negotiations. Instead of getting stuck in rigid positions or immovable demands, the parties should actively seek new solutions and alternatives that can satisfy their interests and needs innovatively.

Encourage both parties to engage in open and unrestricted brainstorming. At this stage, ideas should not be dismissed, no matter how strange or unconventional they may seem.

Promote lateral thinking, which involves looking at the problem from different angles and considering unconventional approaches. This can help challenge preconceived assumptions and open up new possibilities.

Look for areas of overlap in the interests of both parties. Often, these areas can form the basis for creative solutions that satisfy both parties.

Promoting collaboration and teamwork can lead to innovative solutions. Sometimes, combining the resources, skills, and knowledge of both parties can result in unique solutions.

In some situations, it may be beneficial to involve experts or impartial third parties who bring new perspectives and solutions.

During the options generation stage, it is important not to dismiss any idea immediately. Even ideas that may seem impractical at first can lead to more viable solutions if explored and adjusted properly.

Once various options have been generated, it's time to evaluate and refine them. The parties should consider the feasibility, benefits, and potential drawbacks of each option.

Creativity and flexibility are key in this process. Being willing to think "outside the box" and open to novel solutions is essential for overcoming the impasse.

Generating creative options can result in innovative solutions that satisfy both parties more effectively than rigid initial positions. It's important that the parties are willing to compromise and explore new avenues to resolve the conflict. Collaboration and creativity are essential for finding mutually beneficial solutions.

If the parties are unable to resolve the impasse on their own, the intervention of an impartial and neutral mediator can be beneficial. A mediator can help facilitate communication, reduce tensions, and propose intermediate solutions.

The intervention of an impartial and neutral mediator is an effective strategy for overcoming impasse situations in negotiations.

A mediator can act as a neutral intermediary who facilitates communication between the parties. They can ensure that both parties listen to each other and understand each other's concerns and perspectives impartially.

Emotions can play a significant role in negotiations, and in impasse situations, tensions are often high. A mediator can help reduce tensions and maintain a constructive tone in the negotiation.

A trained mediator can help the parties identify and express their underlying interests and needs, which is often essential for overcoming the deadlock.

The mediator can propose intermediate or alternative solutions that were not previously considered. Since they are a neutral third party, they can offer an objective and creative perspective.

The mediator's impartiality is essential. They must ensure not to take sides with either of the parties and not have any personal interest in the negotiation's outcome.

Most mediation sessions are conducted confidentially, allowing the parties to speak openly and honestly without fear that their statements will be used against them in the future.

A mediator can help the parties assess their alternatives outside the current negotiation. This includes analyzing each party's BATNA (Best Alternative to a Negotiated Agreement), which can provide valuable context for decision-making.

Trust in the mediator's impartiality is essential. Both parties must be willing to accept mediation and trust that the mediator will seek a fair agreement.

The intervention of a mediator can be especially helpful when the parties are entrenched in their positions and cannot move forward. The mediator acts as an objective facilitator who helps the parties find mutually beneficial solutions and reestablish communication. It is important to select a mediator with experience and proper training to ensure an effective mediation process.

Sometimes, taking a step back and a short break can be useful. It allows the parties to calm down, reflect, and return to the negotiating table with a more open mind.

Taking a break is an effective strategy in impasse situations during a negotiation.

In moments of impasse, emotions can run high, and tensions between the parties can be intense. Taking a break allows everyone to step away from the immediate conflict and reduce intense emotions.

A break provides the parties with an opportunity to reflect on the negotiation's status and their own objectives. This enables them to reconsider their positions and perhaps be more open to compromises.

Negotiations can be mentally exhausting. A brief break allows the parties to rest and recharge their capacity for making informed and reasonable decisions.

During the break, the parties can consult with their teams or advisors for additional advice or strategies. This can help reinforce their focus and preparation.

During the break, the parties can recall the importance of their underlying interests and needs rather than focusing on immovable positions.

Time away from the negotiation table allows for a broader perspective on the situation. They can consider the consequences of not reaching an agreement and be more willing to seek creative solutions.

If tension is high and there is a risk of the situation deteriorating further, a break can prevent the negotiation from getting worse.

It is important that the break is brief and well-scheduled. Both parties must agree to take a break and when the negotiation will resume. Furthermore, it is crucial to use the break constructively, i.e., to reflect and return with an open mind and an attitude willing to seek solutions. The goal is not to postpone the conflict but to help the parties effectively overcome the impasse.

In impasse situations, it may be necessary for the parties to consider compromises or concessions to make progress. This involves giving in on certain aspects to reach an agreement on others.

Considering the possibility of compromises or concessions is a fundamental strategy in negotiation, especially when facing an impasse.

Successful negotiation often involves a degree of flexibility. In an impasse situation, both parties may need to make concessions on certain aspects to reach an agreement that satisfies their interests and needs overall.

In many negotiations, intransigence in initial positions can lead to a stalemate. Being willing to make concessions may be necessary to move forward and reach an agreement.

Sometimes, one party has more power or influence than the other in the negotiation. Making concessions can help level the playing field and facilitate a fair agreement.

Willingness to make concessions can be seen as a sign of goodwill and can contribute to building trusted relationships between the parties. This can be especially important if future interactions or collaborations are expected.

By considering which aspects of the negotiation are most important, the parties can prioritize their goals and be willing to make concessions on less critical aspects to achieve an agreement on the most essential ones.

By making strategic concessions, it is possible to overcome obstacles that once seemed insurmountable. This can open the door to mutually beneficial solutions.

Willingness to make concessions must be reciprocal. Both parties must be willing to make concessions on certain aspects for the compromise to be fair.

It is important that concessions are made consciously and calculated. The parties must have a clear understanding of their interests and needs and carefully assess what they are willing to concede and to what extent. It is also important that concessions are mutual and equitable to avoid the feeling that one party is being exploited or treated unfairly. Successful negotiation involves finding a balance that satisfies both parties' interests.

The BATNA (Best Alternative to a Negotiated Agreement) is the best option one party has if the current negotiation is unsuccessful. Evaluating it can help determine whether it is better to abandon the current negotiation and seek other alternatives.

Evaluating the Best Alternative to a Negotiated Agreement is a fundamental strategy in negotiation, especially in impasse situations. Here is more information on how it works and why it is important:

It represents the best alternative that one party has if the current negotiation fails. In other words, it is the option one party can pursue if an agreement is not reached in the current negotiation.

Evaluating it is crucial because it provides the parties with a benchmark to determine whether the proposed agreement is better than their alternatives outside the negotiation. If the proposed agreement is worse than their BATNA, it does not make sense to accept it.

By knowing it and the other party's BATNA as well, the parties can make more informed decisions during the negotiation. They can assess whether the agreement on the table is acceptable compared to their alternatives.

With a solid understanding of it, one party can negotiate with greater confidence and firmness. If they know they have a strong alternative, they will not feel pressured to accept an unfavorable agreement.

If the impasse persists and the agreement on the table is not close to it, it may be time to reevaluate the strategy. This may include leaving the current negotiation and seeking other alternatives that are more favorable.

Preparation is key to evaluating it properly before the negotiation. The parties must identify and plan their alternatives in case an agreement is not reached.

Evaluating it also involves considering the costs and risks associated with the alternative option. It's not just about identifying the best alternative but also understanding its implications.

If both parties communicate their BATNAs clearly and honestly, there can be a mutual understanding of the limitations and possibilities of the negotiation, which can sometimes help overcome the impasse.

Evaluating it is essential for making informed decisions in a negotiation and determining whether it's better to accept the agreement on the table or seek other alternatives. It can be especially useful in impasse situations as it provides an objective framework for making strategic decisions.

Sometimes, the impasse is due to misunderstandings or communication issues. Make sure that the parties are expressing their views and concerns clearly and actively listening to the other party.

Effective communication is a fundamental element in negotiation and is particularly important in resolving impasse situations.

It's crucial that the parties express their views, interests, and concerns clearly and concisely. Avoiding ambiguities and communication errors can help eliminate misunderstandings.

Active listening means giving full attention to what the other party is saying, rather than just waiting for them to finish speaking. This allows for a better understanding of their perspectives and concerns.

Asking open and specific questions can help clarify points of confusion and allow both parties to delve deeper into their arguments.

Showing empathy towards the other party, acknowledging their concerns and perspectives, can help reduce tensions and create a more cooperative atmosphere.

Repeating or summarizing what the other party has said can help confirm that it has been understood correctly and can clarify misunderstandings.

Effective communication goes beyond verbal language. Body language, facial expressions, and tone of voice also play an important role in communication. It's important to be aware of these aspects to convey clear messages and understand the other party's communication.

Seeking feedback from the other party about your own communication can be helpful. This ensures that they are interpreting what's being said correctly and that their concerns are being addressed adequately.

Fostering an environment of open and constructive communication is essential. This involves a willingness to listen, consider other perspectives, and avoid the use of offensive or confrontational language.

If misunderstandings or confusion are identified, it's important to address them directly and work together to clarify the situation.

Sometimes, summarizing and reviewing the key points of the negotiation up to that point can ensure that both parties are on the same page.

Effective communication is a fundamental pillar for overcoming impasse in a negotiation. By addressing communication issues, clearing up misunderstandings, and fostering clear and constructive dialogue, parties can work together more productively to find mutually beneficial solutions.

In some situations, setting a deadline can motivate the parties to find a solution before time runs out.

Setting a deadline is a common strategy in negotiation that can be useful for overcoming impasse.

An impending deadline can motivate the parties to make quicker decisions and commit to the negotiation process. Knowing that time is running out can create a sense of urgency.

Deadlines help focus the mind on the task at hand. Parties may be more inclined to concentrate on finding solutions and reaching an agreement when they know time is limited.

In impasse situations, where parties may be entrenched in their positions, a deadline can prevent the negotiation from deteriorating further and becoming a protracted conflict.

Deadlines can lead to a reevaluation of the situation. Parties may take a step back and consider whether it's worth continuing negotiations or if it's better to explore their alternatives (BATNA) or seek other approaches.

Time pressure can drive parties to make decisions and reach agreements that they might otherwise postpone or avoid.

A set deadline may require the parties to be more organized and efficient in their approach to reaching an agreement.

When parties know that time is limited, they may be more inclined to focus on shared interests and principles, which can lead to more creative and mutually beneficial solutions.

It's important to set realistic deadlines and communicate them clearly to both parties. It's also important to maintain flexibility if an extension is needed due to significant progress in the negotiation. The implementation of deadlines should balance time pressure with the need to ensure that parties have the space to make reasoned decisions. Ultimately, deadline management can help reinvigorate stalled negotiations and move toward an agreement.

Instead of a comprehensive agreement, it may be possible to find partial solutions or provisional agreements that allow progress and resolve some aspects of the conflict.

Exploring partial solutions or provisional agreements is an effective strategy for overcoming impasse situations in negotiation. Instead of insisting on a comprehensive agreement that addresses all aspects of the conflict immediately, this strategy allows parties to progress incrementally and address specific issues.

Partial solutions allow for gradual progress in conflict resolution. Instead of waiting for a complete agreement, parties can make progress by addressing specific aspects of the problem.

By achieving provisional agreements, parties can build momentum and confidence in the negotiation process, often facilitating the resolution of other issues later on.

By addressing individual aspects of the conflict, parties can reduce the complexity of the negotiation, making it easier to focus on practical solutions.

Partial solutions allow parties to make gradual compromises and assess whether the solutions work in practice before reaching a complete agreement.

In an impasse situation, insisting on a comprehensive agreement can lead to a deadlock. Instead, partial solutions allow for progress and keep the negotiation moving.

This strategy is more flexible and allows parties to adjust and adapt their agreements as they progress in resolving the conflict.

It can be especially helpful in addressing immediate and urgent issues while working on the long-term resolution of the conflict.

By achieving provisional agreements and sticking to them, parties can build mutual trust throughout the negotiation process.

It's important that partial solutions are clearly framed and adequately documented to avoid misunderstandings in the future. Additionally, parties should continue working toward a complete agreement and not lose sight of the ultimate goal of the negotiation. Exploring partial solutions can be an effective strategy for unlocking an impasse negotiation and moving toward a more gradual and effective conflict resolution.

In extreme cases, if the impasse persists and parties cannot find a solution, it may be necessary to consider the possibility of escalating to more formal conflict resolution processes, such as mediation or arbitration.

Considering the escalation to formal conflict resolution processes, such as mediation or arbitration, is a strategy that may be necessary when parties cannot overcome an impasse in negotiation. Here are some reasons why this might be an option to consider:

After repeatedly attempting to reach a direct agreement without success, parties may realize that they need external intervention to resolve the conflict.

Mediation and arbitration typically involve impartial and neutral third parties who can help parties overcome their differences. This often reduces tensions and bias in conflict resolution.

Mediation and arbitration are structured processes with clear rules and procedures. This can help ensure that conflict resolution is conducted fairly and efficiently.

Both mediation and arbitration are often carried out in a confidential environment, which can be beneficial for parties who wish to maintain the privacy of their disputes.

In the case of arbitration, decisions are usually binding and mandatory for both parties, ensuring that the conflict is definitively resolved.

Mediators and arbitrators often have expertise in conflict resolution and can provide an objective perspective and specialized knowledge to the process.

If parties have an ongoing relationship they wish to preserve, mediation or arbitration can help prevent permanent harm by keeping the conflict out of the courts.

It's important to note that escalating to formal processes can be costly in terms of time and money and may not be suitable for all situations. Before considering mediation or arbitration, it's advisable to exhaust all other conflict resolution strategies, such as direct negotiation, reevaluating interests and needs, generating creative options, and exploring partial solutions.

Additionally, parties must be willing to engage in good faith in these processes and respect the outcomes, as arbitrators' decisions are usually binding.

Negotiating in impasse situations can be challenging, but with focus, creativity, and effective communication, it is possible to find solutions that satisfy both parties. The key is to be willing to adapt and consider different approaches to overcome the deadlock and reach a mutually beneficial agreement.

Negotiating in impasse situations refers to the circumstances in which the parties involved in a negotiation find themselves at a standstill or deadlock, meaning they cannot move forward or reach a mutual agreement. In such moments, resolving the conflict becomes particularly challenging, as the parties may be entrenched in their initial positions and encounter difficulties in making progress.

Overcoming an impasse in a negotiation requires a combination of focus, creativity, and effective communication. Here's an elaboration on these key elements:

Maintaining a clear focus involves having a clear understanding of the negotiation's objectives and goals. The parties must keep in mind their fundamental interests and needs that they wish to satisfy through the agreement. Sometimes, amid an impasse, parties can lose sight of these core interests due to frustration or tension. By maintaining a focus on their goals, they can prevent the impasse from unnecessarily prolonging.

Creativity in negotiation entails a willingness to think innovatively and consider unconventional solutions. Instead of getting stuck in rigid positions or immovable demands, the parties must be open to exploring new avenues for resolving the conflict. This may involve generating creative options that uniquely satisfy the interests of both parties. Creativity is essential for unlocking impasse situations and discovering solutions that hadn't been considered previously.

Communication is the foundation of any successful negotiation. In impasse situations, effective communication is even more crucial. The parties must express their viewpoints, interests, and concerns clearly and concisely, avoiding ambiguities and misunderstandings. Actively listening to the other party, paying full attention to what they are saying, and demonstrating empathy are essential for understanding their perspectives and building a trustful relationship.

Being willing to adapt to new strategies and consider different approaches is fundamental for overcoming an impasse. This may involve reevaluating interests and needs, generating alternative options, exploring partial or provisional solutions, and, in extreme cases, considering more formal conflict resolution processes like mediation or arbitration. Adaptation is crucial for finding common ground and moving toward a mutually beneficial agreement.

In summary, overcoming an impasse in a negotiation involves a clear focus on the objectives, a readiness to think creatively, effective communication, and the flexibility to adapt and consider alternative approaches. When parties are willing to compromise and explore innovative solutions, it's possible to find resolutions that satisfy both sides, even in the most challenging situations.

24.Negotiation in Teams and Groups

Negotiation in team and group settings is a complex process that involves the collaboration of multiple individuals to reach agreements or resolve conflicts.

Before beginning the negotiation, it's important for the team or group to clearly define the objective they wish to achieve. All members must be aligned regarding what is being negotiated.

Defining a common objective in team and group negotiation involves establishing the purpose to be achieved through the negotiation in a clear and precise manner. It's essential that all team or group members agree and are aligned with this objective. Some key aspects of this stage include:

The objective must be defined in a clear and understandable way for all participants. Everyone should understand what is sought to be accomplished.

It's important for team members to reach a consensus on the common objective. Without consensus, the negotiation is likely to be more challenging and the outcomes less satisfactory.

In cases where multiple issues or interests are at play, the team should prioritize which objective is the most important to address in the negotiation.

Documentation: It can be useful to document the common objective in writing to have a clear reference during the negotiation and avoid misunderstandings.

A well-defined common objective serves as a reference point that guides the negotiation and provides a framework for decision-making. This facilitates the process of finding solutions and agreements that benefit all team or group members. Additionally, it contributes to transparency and alignment among participants, which is essential for effective negotiation.

It's useful to establish basic rules for negotiation, such as speaking times, mutual respect, and active listening. Additionally, assigning roles, like a moderator or facilitator, can help maintain an organized discussion.

Establishing rules and roles in team and group negotiation is fundamental to ensuring an orderly, respectful, and efficient process.

Setting time limits for each member's participation helps prevent lengthy monologues and allows everyone the opportunity to express their opinions.

Establishing rules that promote mutual respect is essential. This includes not interrupting other members, avoiding the use of offensive language, and maintaining a respectful tone in communication.

Encouraging active listening means participants must pay attention to what others are saying instead of waiting for their turn to speak. You can establish rules that promote asking clarifying questions and providing summaries after each intervention.

Setting an agenda can help keep the discussion focused on important topics and avoid unnecessary digressions.

A moderator or facilitator is responsible for maintaining order and structure in the negotiation. They can lead the discussion, manage speaking times, and ensure that established rules are followed.

Designating someone to take notes and record key negotiation points can be useful for documenting what was discussed and the decisions made.

For larger or more diverse teams, representatives or spokespeople can be appointed for different subgroups or interests, simplifying communication and preventing everyone from speaking at once.

In cases of intense conflicts, a neutral arbitrator or mediator can intervene to help parties reach agreements and resolve disputes.

Establishing rules and roles provides a structure that makes negotiation more organized and efficient, while promoting an environment of respect and collaboration. This contributes to a more effective negotiation process and more informed and equitable decision-making.

Communication is essential in group negotiation. It fosters an environment in which all members feel comfortable expressing their opinions and listening to others. It prevents interruptions and respects speaking turns.

Effective communication plays a crucial role in group negotiation by facilitating the exchange of ideas, mutual understanding, and collaborative decision-making.

It encourages group members to listen carefully when others are speaking. Active listening involves paying attention, asking clarifying questions, and showing interest in others' opinions.

It promotes an atmosphere of respect and courtesy. All members should treat each other's opinions with respect, even when they disagree. It avoids interruptions and disrespectful comments.

It establishes clear rules for speaking turns. This ensures that everyone has the opportunity to express their ideas without interruptions. A moderator can be used to manage speaking times.

It encourages participants to ask open-ended questions that promote discussion and in-depth exploration of topics. Open-ended questions invite reflection and dialogue instead of simple yes or no answers.

It promotes clear and direct communication. It avoids ambiguity and ensures that ideas are expressed in an understandable manner.

Effective communication also involves addressing conflicts constructively. Instead of avoiding disagreements, it helps group members address them openly and seek mutually acceptable solutions.

It provides constructive feedback on the ideas and proposals of others. This may include highlighting positive aspects, pointing out areas for improvement, and suggesting alternative solutions.

It encourages group members to put themselves in others' shoes and understand their perspectives and concerns. Empathy contributes to creating an atmosphere of understanding and collaboration.

Consider non-verbal communication, such as body language and facial expressions, as it can also convey important information. Ensure that participants are aware of their own non-verbal language and that of others.

Effective communication in group negotiation promotes an environment of trust and collaboration, facilitating conflict resolution and decision-making that benefits all team or group members.

Instead of solely focusing on positions, it's important for team or group members to identify their underlying interests and concerns. This allows for finding solutions that satisfy all parties.

Identifying underlying interests and concerns is a fundamental aspect of effective negotiation in team and group settings. Initial positions are often incompatible, but by delving into each party's interests and concerns, it's possible to discover creative and mutually satisfactory solutions.

Encourage team members to question their own positions and those of others. You can ask them to explain why they want something instead of just what they want. This helps uncover underlying interests.

Listen attentively when others speak about their positions, interests, and concerns. Pay attention to keywords and nuances in their speech.

Look for interests that may be shared by all parties involved. Identifying common interests can form the basis for finding solutions that benefit everyone.

Once a series of interests and concerns have been identified, it's helpful to prioritize them. Some may be more important than others, which can help determine what concessions are possible.

Based on the identified interests, encourage them to generate options that address these concerns. The more options proposed, the more likely it is to find solutions that work for everyone.

Promote openness to new ideas and approaches. Sometimes, the most effective solutions may differ from the initial positions, and mental flexibility is essential to embrace those solutions.

Ensure that all team members openly and honestly share their interests and concerns. Transparency in communication is essential for finding satisfactory solutions.

It's useful to keep a record of the interests and concerns identified during the negotiation. This provides a useful reference as the process progresses and a solution is sought.

By focusing on interests and concerns instead of rigid positions, teams and groups can find more creative and equitable solutions. This promotes an atmosphere of collaboration and mutual respect, which often leads to stronger and more lasting agreements.

Encourage group members to propose different solutions or alternatives. The more options presented, the more opportunities there are to find a satisfactory solution for everyone.

Generating options is a crucial part of negotiation in team and group settings, as it broadens the spectrum of possible solutions and creates fertile ground for finding satisfactory agreements.

Create an environment that fosters creativity and free expression of ideas. Encourage group members to think innovatively and not immediately dismiss any idea.

A common technique for generating options is brainstorming. Invite participants to propose ideas without censorship, no matter how unusual they may seem at first. Later, these ideas can be evaluated and developed.

Remind group members to focus on underlying interests and concerns rather than initial positions. This can open the door to solutions that go beyond the initial demands.

Encourage diversity in the options. Invite participants to consider different approaches, from changes in timing or scope to alternative solutions that meet key interests.

Once several options have been generated, invite the group to evaluate them together. They can rank the options according to their feasibility, advantages, disadvantages, and their ability to address the interests and concerns.

Often, the most effective solutions stem from combining multiple ideas. Encourage group members to find ways to merge or modify existing options to create stronger solutions.

Consider the long-term implications of the options. Ensure that the solutions not only resolve the immediate problem but are also sustainable and prevent the creation of future issues.

Promote an environment in which all ideas are respected and considered without bias. Openness to a diversity of opinions is essential to finding truly effective solutions.

The generation of options can be an iterative process. It may require several rounds of proposals and revisions before reaching a solution that everyone considers acceptable.

Record all proposed options and evaluations. This helps keep a record of ideas and facilitates decision-making.

Generating options with a spirit of collaboration and creativity can lead to innovative solutions that satisfy all parties involved in group negotiation. The more options presented, the greater the chances of finding a solution that effectively addresses everyone's interests and concerns.

After generating a series of options, the group should evaluate each of them considering their advantages and disadvantages. This will help make informed decisions.

Evaluating the options is a critical stage in the team and group negotiation process. By carefully analyzing the different alternatives, team members can make informed decisions and select the solution that best fits their needs and goals.

Predefine the criteria to be used for evaluating the options. These criteria should be related to the interests and concerns identified earlier. For example, costs, timing, impact on common interests, sustainability, etc.

If some criteria are more important than others, assign weights or ratings to each of them. This will reflect the relative importance of each criterion in the final decision.

Encourage open and candid discussion about the advantages and disadvantages of each option. Invite group members to express their opinions and concerns regarding each alternative.

Evaluate the potential risks associated with each option. Consider potential negative consequences and how they can be mitigated.

Examine whether some options can be combined or if compromises are needed between different alternatives to create a more balanced solution.

Consider the long-term impact of each option. Evaluate how the choice will affect the situation and the long-term interests of the team or group.

If relevant, consult with experts or individuals with specialized knowledge to obtain additional information that can assist in the evaluation.

Evaluate the options both quantitatively and qualitatively, as appropriate. Some advantages and disadvantages may be measurable, while others may be subjective.

After analyzing all the options, categorize them based on their suitability to the established criteria and weights. This will help identify the most promising option.

Once the evaluation is complete, the team should make a decision. It is important that this decision is made consensually or democratically so that all members feel committed to the solution.

Record the results of the evaluation, the criteria used, and the decision made. This provides a useful reference and can be helpful for tracking and accountability.

The evaluation of options is a crucial step to ensure that the final solution is the most suitable and satisfactory for the team or group. By making informed decisions based on careful evaluation, transparency and trust in the negotiation process are promoted.

Prioritizing and Making Decisions: Once the options have been evaluated, the group must prioritize them and make a collective decision. It is important that all members support the final decision.

The stage of prioritization and decision-making is crucial in the negotiation process in teams and groups. Here are the key steps to carry out this phase effectively:

Begin by reviewing the information obtained during the evaluation of the options. This includes the criteria, weights, and the evaluation results.

Provide a space for group members to share their opinions on the options and their personal preferences. Encourage participants to express their arguments and concerns.

Carefully consider the opinions and arguments of all group members. It can be helpful to use consensus techniques or voting to measure collective preference.

Look for points where all or most members agree. These can serve as a basis for making decisions and building consensus.

In cases of significant disagreements, work on finding compromises and solutions that respect the interests and concerns of all parties involved. It can be helpful to explore compromise options or consider combining elements from different alternatives.

Once consensus has been reached or a majority decision has been made, ensure that all group members support the final decision. Active participation and commitment from everyone are essential for the successful implementation of the decision.

Record the final decision, the rationale behind it, and any associated commitments or agreements. This will serve as an official record and help hold all members accountable for implementation.

Communicate the decision to the team or group clearly and effectively. Ensure that everyone understands what the decision was and why it was made.

Follow up to ensure that the decision is implemented effectively and that commitments are met.

After implementation, it is useful to conduct a review to assess the results and learn from the experience. This can help improve future decision-making processes.

Prioritizing and making collective decisions are fundamental to ensuring that the chosen solution is acceptable and sustainable for the entire team or group. Building consensus and the commitment of all members are key elements in this process.

Implementing and Monitoring: Once a decision has been made, it is essential to implement it and monitor it to ensure compliance.

Implementation and monitoring are critical phases in the negotiation process for teams and groups, as they ensure that the decision made is effectively carried out and commitments are met.

Develop a detailed plan that describes how the decision will be implemented. This plan should include specific responsibilities, deadlines, required resources, and concrete steps for execution.

Clearly communicate the decision and the implementation plan to all team or group members and all involved parties. Ensure that everyone understands their role in the implementation.

Define clearly who is responsible for each aspect of the implementation. This includes task assignments and monitoring of progress.

Continuously track the progress of the implementation. This involves monitoring compliance with deadlines, resource utilization, and addressing any issues that arise during the process.

Keep all involved parties informed about the status of the implementation through regular meetings or progress reports. This facilitates transparency and allows issues to be addressed in a timely manner.

If obstacles or challenges arise during the implementation, work together with the team to find solutions. Ensure that barriers are overcome, and progress continues toward achieving the decision.

Sometimes, adjustments to the implementation plan may be necessary as the process unfolds. If circumstances change or better approaches are identified, do not hesitate to adapt the plan.

After the implementation has been successfully completed, evaluate the results and compare the current status with the initial objectives. Determine whether the desired results were achieved and if there were any unexpected impacts.

Gather feedback from team members and all involved parties. This information can help improve negotiation processes in the future.

Once the decision has been successfully implemented and objectives have been achieved, close the process appropriately. Acknowledge achievements and thank team members for their collaboration.

Implementation and monitoring are essential to ensure that the decision made in negotiations translates into concrete actions and positive results. A careful focus on this stage contributes to the effectiveness of the decision-making process and builds trust within the team or group.

In the group negotiation process, conflicts often arise. These should be addressed in a constructive manner, promoting dialogue and the search for mutually acceptable solutions.

Resolving conflicts in a constructive manner is essential in any group negotiation process since disagreements and tensions are inevitable when people with different perspectives and interests come together.

The first step to resolve a conflict is to acknowledge its existence. Foster an environment where group members feel comfortable expressing their concerns and disagreements.

Encourage all parties involved in the conflict to voice their views and concerns. Listen empathetically and without interruptions to fully understand their perspectives.

Ask the conflicting parties about their underlying interests and concerns. Often, conflicts stem from different perceptions of what is important.

Help group members separate the person from the problem. This means focusing on resolving the dispute itself rather than attacking the person with whom the conflict exists.

Promote a collaborative approach where parties work together to find solutions that satisfy their interests. Creativity and flexibility are key in this process.

In cases of intense or entrenched conflicts, consider the possibility of using a neutral mediator. This person can help facilitate communication and guide the parties toward a solution.

You can establish communication rules for the conflict resolution process, such as allowing each party to speak without interruptions, listening without judgment, and avoiding offensive language.

Assist in finding areas of agreement or common interests that can serve as a basis for conflict resolution. Identifying common ground can be an important first step toward reconciliation.

Once a solution has been reached, ensure that commitments and agreements are clear and specific. Document the agreed-upon terms and the actions to be taken.

Monitor the implementation of the agreements. This ensures that the parties fulfill their commitments and that the conflict does not resurface.

After resolving a conflict, reflect on what has been learned and how conflicts can be avoided or managed more effectively in the future.

Conflicts, if managed properly, can be opportunities for growth and improvement in a team or group. Effective conflict management can strengthen group cohesion and increase trust among its members.

After a negotiation, it is important to reflect on the process and the results. This allows learning from the experience and improving the negotiation skills of the team or group.

Learning and improving from the negotiation experience is an essential part of developing negotiation skills in teams and groups.

Reflect on how the negotiation process unfolded in the group. Consider aspects such as communication, collaboration, conflict management, and adherence to procedures.

Analyze the results of the negotiation. Were the objectives achieved, and were satisfactory decisions made? What were the effects of the decisions on the group or the parties involved?

Recognize areas where the group excelled and where there were challenges. This may include identifying effective strategies and areas that require improvement.

Conduct feedback sessions with group members to gather their opinions and perspectives on the negotiation. Ensure that everyone has the opportunity to express their observations.

Identify lessons learned from the negotiation. What worked well? What could have been done differently? Were there mistakes that can be avoided in the future?

Use the feedback and lessons learned to develop improvement plans. This may include implementing new communication strategies, adopting best practices in conflict management, or establishing more effective rules for future negotiations.

Provide training and development opportunities for group members in specific areas of negotiation. Consider workshops, courses, or consultation with experts in conflict resolution and negotiation skills.

After implementing improvements and changes, track and evaluate their effectiveness. Ensure that the improvements are working and make adjustments as needed.

Maintain records of lessons learned and improvements implemented. This will serve as a reference for future negotiations and decision-making processes.

Foster a culture of continuous learning within the group. Encourage members to be open to feedback, share knowledge, and seek opportunities to improve their negotiation skills.

The process of continuous learning and improvement is essential to strengthen the negotiation capability of the team or group over time. Reflection and adaptation are key to addressing future challenges more effectively and achieving more satisfactory results in negotiations.

Negotiating in teams and groups requires effective communication, the identification of common interests, and the willingness to work together to reach agreements. The ability to negotiate in a group setting is valuable in both professional and personal environments as it can lead to more equitable and sustainable solutions.

Mediation tends to be faster than traditional legal processes, such as going to court. In a courtroom, cases can take months or even years to be resolved, due to congestion in the judicial system and complex legal procedures. In contrast, mediation is typically scheduled within weeks and can be resolved in a limited number of sessions, depending on the complexity of the conflict. This allows parties to achieve a quicker resolution of their issues and move forward with their lives or businesses.

Mediation is often more cost-effective than legal litigation. Legal proceedings involve significant costs, such as attorney fees, court expenses, filing fees, and other expenses related to the legal process. In contrast, the costs of mediation are generally lower and more predictable.

The parties share the mediator's fees and other expenses, which is often more affordable than the legal costs associated with litigation.

Mediation is effective in preventing conflicts from escalating to more intense and harmful levels. When parties in conflict participate in a mediation process, they have the opportunity to communicate and better understand each other's concerns and perspectives. The mediator helps maintain constructive dialogue and facilitates the search for mutually acceptable solutions. This can prevent tensions from escalating into more destructive disputes, such as lengthy litigation or more hostile confrontations.

Mediation is often conducted in a confidential environment, allowing parties to freely discuss their concerns without the fear of their statements being used against them in court. This promotes openness and candor, which, in turn, facilitates conflict resolution.

In a mediation process, parties have greater control over the final outcome. Unlike a trial, where a judge makes a decision that may not fully satisfy both parties, in mediation, parties can work together to design an agreement that suits their specific needs and concerns.

Mediation is an efficient and cost-effective process for conflict resolution that promotes open communication and can prevent the escalation of disputes. Its focus on dialogue, collaboration, and parties' satisfaction makes it an attractive alternative to costly and lengthy traditional legal processes.

25.Dispute Resolution and Mediation

Dispute resolution and mediation are fundamental processes for addressing conflicts and disagreements in negotiation settings and groups.

Dispute resolution refers to the process of addressing and resolving a conflict or disagreement between two or more parties. It may involve identifying a mutually acceptable solution that satisfies the needs and interests of all parties involved. Common methods of dispute resolution include negotiation, mediation, arbitration, and legal adjudication. The choice of method depends on the nature of the conflict and the willingness of the parties to collaborate in finding a solution.

Mediation is a specific approach to dispute resolution in which a neutral third party, called a mediator, facilitates communication and negotiation between the conflicting parties. The mediator acts as an impartial facilitator, helping the parties identify their interests and concerns, explore solutions, and reach an agreement. Mediation is voluntary, confidential, and based on the consent of the parties involved. It is particularly effective in disputes where the parties wish to maintain an ongoing relationship or where cooperation is essential.

The mediator encourages open and effective communication between the conflicting parties.

Communication is a fundamental aspect of mediation and plays an essential role in dispute resolution.

The mediator's primary task is to facilitate open and effective communication between the conflicting parties. This involves creating an environment in which the parties feel comfortable expressing their opinions, concerns, needs, and viewpoints.

The mediator actively listens to the parties, paying attention to what they say, how they say it, and the underlying emotions. Active listening is essential for fully understanding the parties' perspectives and concerns.

The mediator may use reframing and clarification techniques to ensure that the parties understand each other. This involves repeating or summarizing what one party has said to ensure it has been correctly understood.

The mediator can establish rules to prevent interruptions during conversations between the parties. This promotes a respectful environment and allows each party the opportunity to speak without interruptions.

In high-tension situations, the mediator can help the parties manage their emotions to make communication more productive. This may include stress and emotion management techniques.

Rather than focusing on rigid positions, the mediator encourages the parties to identify and share their underlying interests and concerns. This helps address the root of the conflict.

Once the parties' interests and concerns are understood, the mediator can help them generate solution options based on those interests. This drives the search for mutually satisfying solutions.

If disagreements arise during mediation, the mediator can facilitate the discussion of these disagreements and work with the parties to find common ground and solutions.

Confidentiality is crucial in mediation. Parties can speak openly without fear that their statements will be used against them outside the mediation process.

The mediator empowers the parties to take an active role in resolving their conflict. They do not impose solutions but assist the parties in making informed decisions.

Effective communication is essential for mediation to be a successful process. It allows the parties to understand each other, collaborate in finding solutions, and reach agreements that satisfy their needs. Furthermore, it promotes the restoration of relationships and the prevention of future conflicts.

It focuses on identifying the underlying interests and concerns of the parties rather than fixating on their initial positions.

Identifying interests is a key element of mediation and an effective strategy for addressing conflicts and disputes constructively. Instead of focusing on the parties' initial positions, which are often rigid statements of what they want, mediation focuses on identifying the underlying interests and concerns that motivate those positions.

A "position" is what one party specifically wants or demands. An "interest" is the reason behind that position, i.e., why one party wants something particular. Interests are the needs, desires, values, or concerns that drive positions.

Consider a dispute between two neighbors over a tree in one neighbor's garden. The first neighbor's position might be "I want you to cut down that tree." But the underlying interest could be the concern about the excessive shade the tree casts in their garden, affecting their ability to grow plants. The second neighbor, on the other hand, might be concerned about privacy and the tree's beauty.

Identifying interests allows the parties to better understand each other's needs and concerns, often leading to more creative and satisfying solutions. It also helps reduce the defensive resistance that can arise when parties cling to their initial positions.

The mediator uses open-ended questions to help the parties explore and express their interests. These questions do not have a "yes" or "no" answer and encourage deeper reflection and conversation.

Active listening is crucial for fully understanding the parties' interests. The mediator listens attentively to what the parties say and looks for clues about their motivations and concerns.

The mediator may summarize and reflect the identified interests to ensure that the parties understand each other. This can also help clarify misunderstandings and areas of agreement.

Once interests have been identified, the mediator can guide the parties in generating solution options that address those interests. This promotes the search for mutually satisfying solutions.

Identifying interests is a powerful tool in mediation because it focuses on the real needs and concerns of the conflicting parties. By understanding and addressing these interests, mediation can lead to more lasting and effective agreements while improving communication and reducing hostility between the parties.

It helps the parties generate solution options and evaluate their merits.

Option generation is an important step in the mediation process and in conflict resolution in general. In this step, the conflicting parties and the mediator work together to create various alternative solutions that can satisfy the interests and concerns of all parties involved.

The process of option generation begins with a "brainstorming" session in which the parties and the mediator collaborate to generate ideas. During this stage, the parties are encouraged to express all possible solutions, no matter how unconventional they may seem.

It is important to explore a wide range of options to ensure that all possibilities are considered. This fosters creativity and can lead to unexpected and effective solutions.

The conflicting parties must be willing to collaborate in option generation. This means they should be willing to listen to and consider each other's ideas, even if they initially disagree.

Once several options have been generated, it is important to evaluate their merits. This involves considering how each option relates to the interests and concerns of the parties and whether it is feasible in practice.

The parties and the mediator can discuss and prioritize the options based on their suitability and acceptability. Some options may be more promising than others, and it is important to focus on those with a high potential for success.

Sometimes, the parties can combine elements from different options to create a more comprehensive and satisfying solution. This flexibility is key to finding a solution that works for everyone.

The parties must work together to reach a consensus or mutual acceptance of one or more options. This means that all parties involved agree and are willing to commit to the solution.

Once an agreement has been reached, it is important to document the agreed-upon solution clearly and completely. This provides a reference for follow-up and implementation.

Option generation is an essential part of the mediation process, as it allows the parties to actively engage in finding solutions that meet their needs and concerns. By promoting collaboration and creativity, this approach can lead to more sustainable and satisfying solutions compared to simply imposing a solution.

Any agreement reached in the mediation process is voluntary and based on the consent of the parties.

The principle of voluntary agreement is fundamental in mediation and in conflict resolution in general. This principle states that any agreement reached in the mediation process must be entirely voluntary and based on the free and informed consent of the parties involved.

The conflicting parties must participate in mediation voluntarily and without coercion. No one can be compelled to accept an agreement against their will.

Mediation should be conducted in an environment where the parties are free from external influences or undue pressures that may affect their ability to make informed decisions.

The parties must receive complete and clear information about the terms of the agreement and its implications before making a decision. This ensures that they make informed decisions.

At any point during the mediation process, the parties have the right to withdraw if they feel they cannot reach a mutually acceptable agreement. No one can be forced to continue against their will.

Confidentiality is essential for the parties to feel free to express their opinions and concerns without fear that their statements will be used against them in other contexts. The information shared during mediation is generally not admissible in subsequent legal proceedings.

Once the parties reach an agreement, it should be documented clearly and comprehensively. The parties should review and understand the terms of the agreement before signing it.

In some cases, the agreement reached in mediation may require legal ratification, which usually involves a court or legal authority reviewing and approving the agreement. During this process, the confidentiality of the agreement's content is still respected, but the agreement may need to be presented to the court for review.

Mediators are also obligated to maintain confidentiality. They cannot disclose information about the discussions or the content of mediation sessions to individuals outside the process without the parties' consent.

Confidentiality contributes to building trust between the parties and the mediator. Knowing that conversations are private and will not be used against them outside the process encourages open and honest communication.

Confidentiality in mediation is an essential component to ensure that the parties feel secure and comfortable during the process. It allows the parties to speak candidly and explore solutions without concerns about negative consequences from the disclosure of information. Confidentiality contributes to the effectiveness of mediation as a conflict resolution approach.

Mediation is a valuable tool for resolving disputes in a wide range of contexts, from family disputes to workplace and business conflicts. It promotes cooperation, effective communication, and the parties' autonomy to reach agreements that satisfy their mutual needs. Additionally, mediation is often faster and more cost-effective than traditional legal processes and can help prevent the escalation of conflicts.

It is a conflict resolution process in which a neutral and impartial third party, known as the mediator, facilitates communication and negotiation between the conflicting parties to help them reach a mutually acceptable agreement. It is used in a variety of situations, from family and neighborhood disputes to workplace conflicts or legal and business matters.

One of the key advantages of mediation is its efficiency in terms of time and costs compared to traditional legal processes.

Mediation tends to be faster than traditional legal processes, such as going to court. In a courtroom, cases can take months or even years to resolve due to court congestion and complex legal procedures. In contrast, mediation is usually scheduled within weeks and can be resolved in a limited number of sessions, depending on the complexity of the conflict. This allows the parties to achieve a quicker resolution to their issues and move on with their lives or businesses.

Mediation is often more cost-effective than legal litigation. Legal proceedings involve significant costs, such as attorney fees, court expenses, filing fees, and other expenses related to the legal process. In contrast, mediation costs are generally lower and more predictable. The parties share the mediator's fees and other expenses, which is often more affordable than the legal costs associated with litigation.

Mediation is effective in preventing conflicts from escalating to more intense and harmful levels. When conflicting parties participate in a mediation process, they have the opportunity to communicate and better understand each other's concerns and perspectives. The mediator helps maintain constructive dialogue and facilitates the search for mutually acceptable solutions. This can prevent tensions from escalating into more destructive disputes, such as prolonged litigation or more hostile confrontations.

Mediation is often conducted in a confidential environment, allowing parties to freely discuss their concerns without fear of their statements being used against them in court. This fosters openness and frankness, which, in turn, facilitates conflict resolution.

In a mediation process, the parties have greater control over the final outcome. Unlike a trial, where a judge makes a decision that may not fully satisfy both parties, in mediation, the parties can work together to design an agreement that fits their specific needs and concerns.

Mediation is an efficient and cost-effective process for conflict resolution that promotes open communication and can prevent the escalation of disputes. Its focus on dialogue, collaboration, and party satisfaction makes it an attractive alternative to expensive and protracted traditional legal processes.

26.Long-Term Strategic Negotiation

Strategic long-term negotiation is an approach used to achieve sustainable and beneficial agreements over time, especially in business relationships, alliances, partnerships, or any other form of ongoing collaboration. In this approach, the long-term impact of decisions is considered, and solutions that foster a lasting and mutually beneficial relationship are sought. Here are some key guidelines for strategic long-term negotiation:

Instead of seeking short-term transactional agreements, strategic long-term negotiation focuses on building and maintaining strong and trust-based relationships. It recognizes that robust relationships can generate ongoing benefits over time.

The emphasis on relationships in strategic negotiation is a philosophy that places considerable importance on building and maintaining solid and trust-based relationships between the parties involved in a negotiation. Unlike short-term transactional negotiations where the primary goal is to close an immediate deal, strategic long-term negotiation considers strong relationships as essential for generating continuous benefits over time.

The foundation of any solid relationship in negotiation is trust. Parties trust that they will fulfill their commitments and care about mutual benefit over time.

Parties involved in strategic negotiation communicate openly and transparently. This involves sharing relevant information and maintaining constant dialogue to understand the needs and concerns of both parties.

Instead of solely focusing on gaining advantages for one party, strategic negotiation seeks solutions that benefit both parties. Collaboration in the search for mutually beneficial solutions is encouraged.

Over time, circumstances can change, and strategic negotiation recognizes the importance of being flexible and adapting to new situations. This helps maintain strong relationships even in changing situations.

Instead of thinking about a single transaction, strategic long-term negotiation focuses on developing a long-term relationship. This involves considering not only the current agreement but also how future interactions can be beneficial for both parties.

The goal is for both parties to benefit over time. It's not about one party gaining at the expense of the other; it's about building a relationship where both parties thrive.

Strategic negotiation with a focus on relationships seeks more than short-term agreements; it aims to establish a solid foundation for ongoing and mutually beneficial collaboration. This approach is based on the belief that strong relationships are a valuable asset and can generate sustainable benefits over time.

To achieve long-term agreements, it is essential to understand the interests and objectives of both parties. This involves focusing on underlying interests rather than initial positions.

Understanding interests is a fundamental aspect of strategic long-term negotiation. Instead of focusing solely on the initial positions or demands of the parties involved, this approach concentrates on discovering and addressing underlying interests. Here are some reasons why understanding interests is crucial in long-term negotiation:

By understanding the underlying interests of both parties, it is more likely to discover shared needs, goals, or values. This can pave the way for creating solutions that benefit both parties, known as a "win-win" approach.

When parties understand the interests behind the positions, it is easier to resolve conflicts and disagreements. Often, initial positions can be incompatible, but underlying interests can offer opportunities to find solutions that satisfy both parties.

By showing a genuine interest in understanding the interests of the other party, a solid foundation for a trusting relationship is built. People usually appreciate when they feel their needs and interests are being considered.

Understanding interests allows parties to be more flexible in seeking solutions. Instead of being rigidly tied to specific positions, parties can adjust their approaches to better accommodate mutual interests.

Focusing solely on positions can lead to short-term agreements that are not sustainable in the long run. By understanding interests, more enduring and mutually beneficial agreements can be negotiated.

To conduct negotiation based on understanding interests, it is important to ask open-ended questions, listen attentively to the other party, and explore the reasons behind their demands and positions. This approach requires patience and empathy but can result in more satisfactory agreements and stronger long-term relationships.

Strategic long-term negotiation promotes collaboration instead of confrontation. Parties work together to find solutions that meet their mutual interests and avoid competitive tactics that may undermine the relationship.

Promoting collaboration instead of confrontation is a distinctive feature of strategic long-term negotiation. Instead of adopting a competitive and confrontational approach, this approach seeks cooperation and the joint pursuit of mutually beneficial solutions.

Collaboration is based on the "win-win" idea. Parties seek solutions that satisfy their mutual interests rather than trying to maximize their gains at the expense of the other party.

Collaboration allows parties to address problems and challenges more effectively. Working together to find creative and viable solutions can lead to stronger and more satisfactory agreements.

Conflict reduction: By avoiding competitive and confrontational tactics, the likelihood of conflicts and disagreements in the negotiation process is reduced. This contributes to a more harmonious working environment.

Collaboration enables parties to be more flexible and adapt to changing circumstances or needs over time. This is crucial in long-term negotiation, where conditions may evolve.

Collaboration involves mutual respect and consideration of the other party's needs and perspectives. This contributes to an environment of respect and cordiality in the negotiation.

To promote collaboration in long-term strategic negotiation, parties can use techniques such as joint thinking, seeking mutual interests, and exploring creative solutions. Instead of viewing negotiation as a competition where only one party wins, it is considered an opportunity for both parties to work together in achieving sustainable mutual benefits over time.

Integrative negotiation seeks to "expand the pie" rather than simply divide it. It aims to create mutual value by generating solutions that benefit both parties, rather than competing for a fixed slice of the pie.

Integrative negotiation focuses on expanding the value available in a negotiation rather than seeing it as a division of a fixed "pie." Instead of competing for a limited share of resources or benefits, parties seek to create solutions that benefit both, creating a larger "pie" in the process.

This is achieved through a collaborative approach and the identification of shared interests. Some additional characteristics of integrative negotiation include:

Rather than solely focusing on the parties' initial positions, integrative negotiation focuses on understanding underlying interests. This allows for better solutions that meet the needs and goals of both parties.

Collaboration and communication: Collaboration and open, continuous communication are essential in integrative negotiation. Parties work together constructively to solve problems and develop mutually beneficial solutions.

Parties explore a wide variety of options and approaches to find more creative and customized solutions. This involves thinking outside conventional boundaries and considering different approaches.

Integrative negotiation tends to build strong and trusting relationships, as parties seek to collaborate rather than compete. This can lead to more sustainable and lasting agreements.

The primary goal is to achieve an agreement that benefits both parties, rather than a unilateral gain. It seeks a balance where both parties can benefit.

Integrative negotiation is an approach that seeks to optimize value and benefits for all parties involved in a negotiation. By focusing on creating mutual value, this approach can lead to more satisfactory and lasting solutions, building strong relationships in the process.

Open, honest, and continuous communication is essential in long-term strategic negotiation. Parties must be willing to share information, expectations, and concerns effectively.

Effective communication is a fundamental pillar in long-term strategic negotiation. The quality of communication between the involved parties plays a crucial role in building strong relationships, problem-solving, and achieving mutually beneficial agreements.

Open and honest communication contributes to the establishment of trust between the parties. When parties feel comfortable sharing information, they are more secure in the relationship and the negotiation process.

Effective communication allows parties to better understand the needs, desires, and concerns of the other party. This is essential for identifying shared interests and finding mutually beneficial solutions.

Disagreements and conflicts are common in any negotiation process. Effective communication is essential for addressing these conflicts constructively and reaching solutions.

Continuous communication helps establish and maintain clear expectations between the parties. This prevents misunderstandings and disagreements along the way.

In long-term negotiation, circumstances can change over time. Effective communication allows parties to adapt and adjust their strategies as conditions and needs change.

Effective communication promotes collaboration. Parties can work together more effectively to find creative solutions and jointly address problems.

Through open communication, parties can identify opportunities that might otherwise go unnoticed. This can lead to the creation of mutual value and innovative solutions.

Effective communication is essential for building and maintaining strong relationships over time. Solid relationships are a valuable asset in long-term negotiation.

To encourage effective communication in long-term strategic negotiation, parties must be willing to actively listen, ask questions to clarify information, and be transparent about their own needs and concerns. Open and honest communication is a key vehicle for success in this type of negotiation.

For a long-term agreement to be successful, both parties must be committed to fulfilling the agreed-upon terms. This requires ongoing monitoring and timely problem resolution.

Focusing on compliance with the agreed-upon terms is essential in long-term strategic negotiation. For a long-term agreement to be successful and to endure over time, both parties must be committed to fulfilling the commitments made.

Compliance with the terms of the agreement demonstrates to both parties that they are reliable and can count on each other. This contributes to strengthening trust in the relationship.

Compliance with agreements is essential for maintaining strong and long-term relationships. When both parties fulfill their commitments, the relationship is strengthened, and the foundation is laid for future successful interactions.

Compliance with the agreed-upon terms ensures that the agreement is sustainable in the long run. When expectations and commitments are met, the risks of conflicts and breakups are minimized.

Timely and effective compliance with the agreed-upon terms helps to avoid conflicts and misunderstandings. When issues arise, a focus on compliance allows them to be addressed constructively and resolved promptly.

Compliance with the agreed-upon terms ensures that both parties continue to enjoy the mutual benefits originally expected from the agreement. This is especially important in long-term negotiations where sustainable benefits are sought over time.

To ensure the compliance of long-term agreements, parties can establish tracking systems, set clear metrics, and maintain constant communication to resolve any issues that may arise. It is also important that both parties are committed to effectively resolving issues and are willing to adapt and adjust the agreement when necessary to address new circumstances or needs. In summary, compliance is essential for the sustainability and success of long-term agreements in strategic negotiation.

Long-term strategic planning is fundamental. Parties must consider how their agreements will affect their long-term goals and strategies.

Long-term strategic planning is essential in long-term strategic negotiation. When parties are committed to building strong and lasting relationships, it is important to consider how agreements will impact their long-term goals and strategies.

Long-term strategic planning allows parties to identify and align their common objectives. This facilitates collaboration to achieve mutual goals over time.

By considering agreements in the context of a long-term vision, parties can ensure that they are making decisions consistent with their long-term goals and strategies.

Long-term planning allows parties to anticipate possible risks and opportunities that may arise in the future. This allows them to be prepared to address challenges and seize opportunities effectively.

Long-term planning also involves the ability to adapt to changes in the environment and the parties' needs. It may be necessary to adjust agreements as circumstances evolve.

Long-term strategic planning includes defining key performance indicators and metrics to measure progress toward long-term goals. This allows for the evaluation of the success of agreements and adjustments as necessary.

Long-term planning contributes to the durability of the relationship, as parties can anticipate challenges and work together to overcome them.

To conduct effective long-term strategic planning in negotiation, parties should:

Set clear long-term goals and objectives.

Identify areas of collaboration and opportunities for mutual value creation.

Anticipate potential obstacles and risks as agreements are implemented.

Define metrics and criteria for success to evaluate progress and compliance over time.

Long-term planning in strategic negotiation helps ensure that agreements are sustainable, beneficial, and consistent with the parties' goals and strategies over time.

Circumstances can change over time, so flexibility is essential in long-term strategic negotiation. Parties must be willing to adapt and adjust agreements when necessary.

Flexibility and adaptability are fundamental qualities in long-term strategic negotiation. Given that circumstances can evolve over time, the ability to adapt and adjust agreements is essential to maintain strong and successful relationships.

Economic, political, technological, and social factors can change over time, which can affect the dynamics of negotiation and existing agreements. Adaptability allows parties to adjust to these changes.

As the needs and objectives of the parties evolve, it may be necessary to modify agreements to ensure they remain mutually beneficial.

Adaptability is important for addressing unexpected challenges in a timely manner. When unexpected issues arise, flexibility allows parties to find creative and effective solutions.

Inflexibility in negotiation can lead to tensions and relationship breakdowns. Adaptability, on the other hand, can help overcome obstacles and strengthen the relationship.

Changing circumstances can also present opportunities that parties can seize if they are flexible enough to adapt their agreements.

To be flexible and adaptable in long-term strategic negotiation, parties can follow these principles:

Maintain open and constant communication to stay informed about changes and challenges that may arise.

Be willing to reevaluate and, if necessary, renegotiate the terms of the agreement as circumstances evolve.

Be creative and open to considering alternative solutions when current agreements are no longer effective.

Establish processes and tracking systems that allow for continuous adaptation of agreements.

Flexibility and adaptability are essential for long-term success in strategic negotiation, as they enable parties to effectively address changes and challenges and build lasting relationships.

Parties must establish metrics and criteria to assess performance and compliance with the agreement over time. This allows for continuous adjustments and improvements.

Continuous measurement and evaluation are fundamental elements in the management of long-term agreements in strategic negotiation. Establishing metrics and criteria to assess performance and compliance with the agreement over time provides a basis for informed decision-making, identifies areas that require attention or improvement.

Continuous assessment allows parties to adapt and adjust agreements as circumstances change or new opportunities arise. Metrics help identify areas where processes can be improved and issues resolved effectively over time.

To establish an effective system of continuous measurement and evaluation in long-term strategic negotiation, parties can follow these steps:

Identify specific metrics to be used for evaluating performance and compliance with the agreement.

Establish Key Performance Indicators (KPIs): Set relevant KPIs that align with long-term objectives.

Utilize tracking and data collection systems to measure and assess progress and compliance.

Schedule regular reviews to analyze results and make data-driven decisions.

Maintain open and constant communication about progress and results between the parties.

Use measurement and evaluation results to make adjustments and improvements to the agreement and processes as necessary.

Continuous measurement and evaluation not only help ensure long-term compliance with agreements but also contribute to building strong relationships and achieving mutually beneficial outcomes over time.

Since disagreements can arise even in long-term relationships, it's important to address them constructively and seek solutions that do not jeopardize the relationship.

Constructive conflict resolution is an essential component in managing long-term relationships in strategic negotiation. Since disagreements can arise in any relationship, it is crucial to address them effectively to prevent them from endangering the relationship.

By addressing conflicts constructively, parties can prevent disagreements from harming the long-term relationship. This contributes to maintaining a solid foundation for ongoing collaboration.

Effective conflict resolution allows the identification and addressing of underlying issues that may be affecting the relationship or performance. This leads to more effective solutions.

Conflicts can be an opportunity to improve communication between the parties. By openly and honestly discussing concerns and disagreements, mutual understanding can be strengthened.

Conflict resolution can lead to the adaptation and improvement of agreements and processes. Sometimes conflicts reveal areas where improvements can be made.

Handling conflicts constructively and reaching mutually satisfactory solutions can strengthen trust between the parties.

To achieve constructive conflict resolution in long-term strategic negotiation, these principles can be followed:

Encourage open and respectful communication among the parties involved in the conflict.

Listen with empathy and understanding to the other party to comprehend their perspectives and concerns.

Seek shared interests and mutually beneficial solutions instead of focusing on opposing positions.

Work together to find solutions that address issues and meet the needs of both parties.

Remember the value of the long-term relationship and be willing to compromise in its preservation.

Constructive conflict resolution not only contributes to maintaining strong and successful relationships but can also lead to improvement and mutual growth over time. It is an essential component of long-term strategic negotiation.

Long-term strategic negotiation is based on the idea that lasting and beneficial relationships are more valuable than short-term gains.

27.Negotiation in the Digital and Virtual World

Negotiation in the digital and virtual world has experienced a significant increase in importance and frequency in recent years due to the growing influence of technology and globalization.

Most negotiations in the digital and virtual world take place through communication platforms such as email, instant messaging, video conferencing, and social media. It's important to be clear and concise in written communication and ensure the use of an appropriate tone.

Virtual communication platforms play a crucial role in online negotiations.

Email is a common tool for business communication and negotiation. It's important to draft emails clearly and concisely, with an informative subject and a professional tone. It can also be used to send attachments.

Messaging applications like WhatsApp, Slack, or Microsoft Teams allow for quick and real-time communication. They are ideal for quick questions, informal discussions, and maintaining constant communication flow with team members.

Platforms like Zoom, Microsoft Teams, Skype, and Google Meet are essential for virtual meetings. They provide a face-to-face experience through webcams and allow for real-time interaction, which is crucial for in-depth discussions and real-time negotiations.

Some negotiations may take place on social networks like LinkedIn or Twitter. These platforms allow for direct contact with professionals and can be useful for establishing business relationships, sharing information, and staying updated on industry trends.

Applications like Google Docs, Trello, and Asana enable real-time collaboration on documents, tasks, and projects. These tools are useful for negotiation planning, tracking, and related project management.

Remember the importance of adapting the communication channel to the type of negotiation and the preferences of the parties involved. Additionally, clarity, conciseness, and the appropriate tone are fundamental to avoid misunderstandings and ensure effective communication in virtual negotiations.

In a global digital environment, it's crucial to understand and respect cultural differences. Negotiation norms and expectations can vary widely from one country to another.

Consideration of culture and diversity is essential in negotiations in a global digital environment.

Before engaging in negotiations with people from different cultures, it's important to research cultural norms, business practices, and the other party's expectations. Understanding how they communicate, make decisions, and negotiate in their culture can help you avoid misunderstandings.

Learning to communicate effectively with people from different cultures is fundamental. This includes being aware of differences in language, tone, body language, and courtesy norms. Avoid assuming that the communication norms of your own culture apply universally.

In international negotiations, flexibility is key. You may need to adapt your negotiation approach and style to accommodate the cultural preferences and values of the other party. Adaptability can help you build strong relationships and generate trust.

Respect for diversity is fundamental. Avoid making judgments based on cultural stereotypes and show openness and respect for others' perspectives and values. Empathy plays a significant role in building successful intercultural relationships.

Perceptions of time can vary by culture. Some cultures are more future-oriented and punctual, while others may place greater emphasis on personal relationships and be more flexible about schedules. Being aware of these time management differences is essential.

Courtesy norms can vary widely among cultures. Some cultures value formal politeness, while others prefer a more direct approach. Learn how to show respect appropriately in the cultural context in which you are negotiating.

In some cultures, negotiations are conducted in groups or teams, rather than as an individual process. Understand whether the other party is following a group negotiation dynamic and be prepared for it.

If you are negotiating in a language different from your own or that of the other party, make sure to have reliable translation services to avoid linguistic misunderstandings and confusion.

Consideration of culture and diversity in digital negotiations is essential for building strong relationships and achieving successful agreements. Cultural sensitivity and adaptability are key skills in a global digital environment.

The security and privacy of information are critical concerns in virtual negotiations. Use secure methods for sharing confidential information and guard against cyber threats.

The security and privacy of information are of utmost importance in virtual negotiations, as any leakage or unauthorized access to confidential data can have serious consequences.

Use secure communication channels, such as encrypted email services and end-to-end encrypted messaging apps. Ensure that communications are private and cannot be intercepted by unauthorized third parties.

Protect your online accounts and documents with strong and unique passwords. Use two-factor authentication whenever possible to add an extra layer of security.

Always encrypt sensitive data before sharing it online. Encryption ensures that data is unreadable to anyone without the decryption key.

Keep your devices (computers, phones, tablets) updated with the latest security updates and use antivirus and anti-malware software to prevent cyberattacks.

Use secure network connections, such as Virtual Private Networks (VPNs), especially when accessing confidential information or conducting video conferences. VPNs encrypt internet traffic, making it more secure.

Educate all parties involved in virtual negotiations about best online security practices. Make them aware of cyber threats, such as phishing, and how to recognize them.

Limit access to confidential documents and data only to those who need to know. Use access management systems and appropriate security policies.

Ensure that all involved parties are aware of privacy policies and confidentiality agreements. Set clear expectations for how confidential information will be handled and protected.

Keep your applications and operating systems up to date with the latest security patches. Vulnerabilities in outdated software can be exploited by attackers.

Regularly back up critical data to be able to recover it in case of a cyberattack or information loss.

Cybersecurity is an ongoing process. Maintain a high level of awareness and vigilance at all times.

Security and privacy should be a priority at all stages of virtual negotiation, from initial communication to agreement signing. Prevention and preparedness are essential to maintain the integrity of information and protect the interests of all involved parties.

Keeping a clear record of conversations and agreements is essential in virtual negotiations. This can help prevent misunderstandings and future conflicts.

Documentation and tracking are fundamental in virtual negotiations to ensure clarity, avoid misunderstandings, and resolve conflicts.

Use a centralized system to store and organize all negotiation-related documentation, such as emails, notes, agreements, shared documents, and meeting minutes. You can use project management tools or cloud storage to keep all files accessible and organized.

If you hold virtual meetings or video conferences, assign someone the responsibility of taking detailed minutes. Minutes should include key points discussed, decisions made, and actions agreed upon. Share these minutes with all parties involved to confirm that everyone is on the same page.

Record the date and time of all communications and agreements, as this may be important for determining when certain milestones were reached or for setting deadlines.

After each important conversation or meeting, send an email summarizing the key points discussed, agreements reached, and next steps. Request that all parties confirm their understanding and agreement in writing.

If documents are shared online, make sure to keep a record of different versions. Label and archive each version to avoid confusion about which is the latest version.

Use project management or online collaboration tools to track tasks and deadlines agreed upon during the negotiation. This helps ensure that all parties fulfill their commitments.

When reaching significant agreements, it's advisable to formalize them in a written document, such as a contract or memorandum of understanding. Ensure that all parties sign and have copies of this agreement.

Formalizing agreements in writing is a fundamental practice in virtual negotiations, as it provides clarity and protection for all involved parties.

Make sure the agreement contains all the terms and conditions agreed upon during the negotiation. This includes details about products or services, timelines, prices, responsibilities, and any other relevant information.

Organize the agreement in a clear and logical manner. You can use headers, bullet points, and numbered paragraphs to make it easy to read and reference.

Use clear and easy-to-understand language. Avoid using jargon or confusing terminology that may lead to misunderstandings.

Consider including clauses that address unforeseen scenarios or changes in circumstances. These clauses can be helpful for dispute resolution and adapting to changing situations.

All parties involved in the agreement should sign and date it. This indicates that they agree with the specified terms and conditions.

In some cases, it may be necessary to have a witness or a notary to validate the agreement, especially if it's a legally binding contract.

Make sure that all parties involved receive copies of the signed agreement. You can do this in printed or electronic format, depending on the parties' preferences.

Store the agreement in a secure and accessible location for all parties. Cloud storage solutions are useful to ensure document availability and security.

Once the agreement is in effect, it's important to track its compliance. Establish a tracking system to ensure that all parties fulfill their commitments.

Include dispute resolution clauses in the agreement that describe how disagreements or issues will be addressed in the future.

If modifications to the agreement are needed in the future, be sure to document them and obtain consent from all parties involved before implementing the changes.

Written agreements are an essential tool to protect the interests of all parties in a virtual negotiation and provide a solid foundation for cooperation and conflict resolution. Clarity and formality in documenting agreements are crucial for negotiation success.

Comply with relevant record retention regulations and policies. Some industries and jurisdictions may have specific requirements regarding how long certain records should be kept.

Record retention is a critical aspect of managing documentation and information security in virtual negotiations. Compliance with record retention regulations and policies is essential to ensure legal compliance and data protection.

Research and understand the specific record retention regulations and requirements of your industry and jurisdiction. These requirements can vary widely and may be subject to changes over time.

Establish clear internal policies for record retention. Define what types of records should be retained, for how long, and how they should be stored and disposed of at the end of their lifecycle.

Classify records based on their importance and relevance. Not all records are equal, and some may require long-term retention while others may be disposed of more quickly.

Ensure that records are stored securely, whether in paper or electronic format. Cloud storage solutions can be helpful to ensure record integrity and availability.

Set up a deadline tracking system for records. Ensure that records are retained for the required time and disposed of in a timely manner once the retention period is met.

When it's time to dispose of records, ensure that it's done securely. This may involve physically destroying paper documents or securely deleting electronic data.

Conduct regular internal audits to ensure compliance with record retention policies and to identify potential areas for improvement.

In complex situations or when there are doubts about record retention requirements, consider seeking legal or compliance advice to ensure that you're in compliance with current regulations.

Record retention is important not only for complying with regulations but also for protecting your organization's interests and maintaining an accurate record of transactions and agreements. Proper record management is crucial in virtual negotiations, where documentation and communication are primarily digital.

Perform regular reviews of the documentation and the progress of the negotiation with all parties involved. This helps identify and address any issues or deviations early in the process.

Regular reviews are a fundamental practice in negotiation management as they help maintain control and transparency in the process and allow for early problem identification and resolution.

Set a specific schedule for conducting regular reviews. This could be weekly, bi-weekly, monthly, or based on the negotiation's duration and complexity. Ensure that all parties involved are aware of these review dates.

Keep a record of the negotiation's progress over time. This includes the status of agreements, pending tasks, and identified issues. Use project management tools or shared documents to document this progress.

Before each review, establish a clear agenda indicating the topics to be addressed and the review's objectives. Make sure all parties are aware of the points to be discussed.

Invite all parties involved in the negotiation to participate in the review. This ensures that everyone is aligned and has the opportunity to raise concerns or deviations.

During the review, consider potential risks and obstacles that may arise in the future. Identify strategies to mitigate these risks and overcome obstacles.

If issues or deviations are identified during the review, work together with the parties involved to find solutions. Ensure that everyone is committed to addressing the problems, and corrective actions are established.

If necessary, adjust the negotiation strategy based on changes in circumstances or new developments. Make sure all parties agree to these adjustments.

As changes are made or new agreements are reached, update the relevant documentation and ensure that all parties have access to the latest version.

During the review, track the agreed-upon actions and ensure they are being carried out as planned.

Encourage open and honest communication during reviews. All participants should feel comfortable expressing their concerns and opinions.

Regular reviews are a fundamental part of successful negotiation management. They help keep the process moving efficiently and ensure that the involved parties are informed, committed, and aligned in achieving negotiation goals.

Transparency is key in virtual negotiation. Share information openly and honestly, and ensure that all parties are informed about the negotiation's status.

Transparency is essential in any negotiation process, whether virtual or in-person. Open and honest communication fosters trust and collaboration among the parties involved.

Transparency helps build and maintain trust among the parties. When all parties feel that information is shared honestly and openly, they are more willing to commit and cooperate.

Lack of information or opaque communication can lead to misunderstandings and confusion. Transparency reduces the likelihood of misinterpretations and ensures that all parties have a clear understanding of the situation.

When parties have access to relevant and up-to-date information, they can make informed decisions more efficiently. This speeds up the negotiation process.

Transparency contributes to the building of long-term business relationships. Parties that have experienced transparent negotiation are more likely to want to collaborate in the future.

When disagreements or conflicts arise in the negotiation process, transparency facilitates problem-solving. All parties can openly discuss their concerns and work together to find solutions.

Transparency also promotes shared responsibility. Parties can clearly understand their roles and responsibilities in the process and ensure that everyone is committed to achieving negotiation goals.

To maintain transparency in virtual negotiation, consider the following practices:

Share relevant information in a timely and comprehensive manner.

Ensure that all parties have access to the same information.

Promote open communication and encourage parties to ask questions and express concerns.

Provide regular updates on the negotiation's status.

Address concerns directly and honestly.

Use secure communication channels to protect the confidentiality of sensitive information.

Transparency is a key value in virtual negotiations and significantly contributes to their success and the quality of business relationships.

Effective documentation and tracking are essential for establishing a solid foundation for virtual negotiations. This not only helps prevent misunderstandings but also provides a strong record for future disputes or the need to track agreed-upon commitments.

In virtual environments, it's common for parties to communicate at different times. This can lead to asynchronous negotiations where responses are not immediate. Patience is important in this context.

Asynchronous negotiation is a common feature of communications and negotiations in virtual environments. Since parties may be in different time zones or have different schedules and availabilities, responses may not be immediate. Here are some key considerations for addressing asynchronous negotiation:

From the outset, communicate to all parties involved the expectations regarding response times and how the negotiation will take place in an asynchronous environment. This may include agreements on response deadlines and the use of specific communication channels.

Because conversations may extend over a period of time, it's important to be clear and concise in written communication. Use clear language and structure your messages in a way that makes it easy for others to understand your points.

Use organizational tools, such as key point lists or shared documents, to ensure that information remains organized and easy to find for all parties.

Leverage technological tools to facilitate asynchronous communication, such as email, messaging apps, shared documents, and online collaboration platforms.

Recognize that parties may need time to review and respond to messages. Avoid excessive pressure or setting unrealistic expectations for immediate responses.

When possible, establish specific deadlines for responses or milestones in the negotiation. This can help keep the process on track and ensure that important deadlines are met.

In asynchronous negotiation, it's important to avoid hasty interpretations or assuming that a lack of immediate response is a negative signal. Parties may need time to reflect or consult before responding.

Since conversations may span a longer period of time, it's essential to document discussions and the progress of the negotiation. Additionally, keep track of agreed commitments and tasks.

When communicating asynchronously, pay attention to the privacy and security of shared information, especially if it involves confidential data.

Asynchronous negotiation can be effective and efficient, but it requires a different approach compared to real-time negotiations. Patience and clear communication are key to effectively addressing this type of negotiation.

Online collaboration tools like Google Docs and Trello can be helpful for planning and tracking negotiations, allowing parties to work efficiently together on shared documents.

Online collaboration tools are essential in virtual negotiations as they enable parties to work efficiently together, even when they are in different geographical locations or time zones. Here are some of the most common online collaboration tools and how they can be useful in the context of negotiation:

Google Docs: Google Docs is an online word processing platform that allows multiple people to collaborate on a document in real-time. It's useful for creating and jointly editing proposals, contracts, and other important documents. You can also track changes and view the edit history to keep a record of modifications.

Trello: Trello is a project management tool that uses boards, lists, and cards to organize tasks and projects. You can create boards dedicated to the negotiation and share them with involved parties, making it easy to track negotiation stages and pending tasks.

Microsoft Teams: Microsoft Teams is a collaboration platform that combines messaging, video conferencing, and real-time document sharing and editing. It's ideal for real-time communication and collaboration on important documents.

Slack: Slack is a business messaging app that allows real-time communication in specific channels. You can create channels dedicated to the negotiation and share documents or links to related resources.

Asana: Asana is a project management tool that facilitates the organization of tasks and deadlines related to the negotiation. You can assign tasks, set deadlines, and track progress.

Dropbox or Google Drive: These cloud storage solutions enable you to securely store and share documents. You can create shared folders containing all negotiation-related documents and resources.

Zoom or Microsoft Teams for meetings: These video conferencing platforms are essential for conducting real-time virtual meetings. You can discuss important issues, present proposals, and make decisions online.

Evernote is a note-taking tool that allows you to capture, organize, and share relevant information for the negotiation, such as notes, images, and voice recordings.

Miro or Microsoft Whiteboard: Some tools provide virtual whiteboards that enable real-time collaboration on diagrams, charts, and mind maps.

The choice of tool will depend on the specific needs of the negotiation and the preferences of the parties involved. The key is to leverage these tools to maintain an organized record of information, facilitate collaboration, and ensure that all parties are synchronized in the negotiation process.

In videoconferences, non-verbal communication still plays an important role. Pay attention to your body language and your counterpart's cues to better understand their emotions and attitudes.

Non-verbal communication remains relevant in videoconferences and plays a crucial role in interpreting emotions, attitudes, and the effectiveness of communication. Here are some guidelines for paying attention to non-verbal expression in videoconferences:

Maintain eye contact: Keep eye contact with the camera of your computer or device instead of looking down at the screen. This creates the impression that you're looking directly at the people in the videoconference and shows attentiveness.

Monitor your body language: Maintain an open and relaxed posture, avoid crossing your arms, and convey interest and attention through gestures like nodding when you agree.

Use facial expressions effectively: Your facial expressions are a significant part of non-verbal communication. Smile when appropriate and show empathy through your expressions.

Employ hand gestures purposefully: Use hand gestures effectively to emphasize important points or to indicate clarity in your words. Avoid nervous or distracting gestures.

Pay attention to your voice and tone: Speak clearly and enthusiastically, adjusting your tone to effectively convey your message.

The environment in which you're in during the videoconference can communicate a lot. Ensure that the background is professional and free from distractions.

When you're not speaking, use the mute function to prevent background noise that may distract or interrupt the conversation.

In addition to your own non-verbal language, observe the non-verbal cues of other participants in the videoconference. You can detect signs of boredom, interest, confusion, or other emotions that help you adjust your communication.

"Remember that the rules of non-verbal expression can vary by culture. What may be interpreted in one culture can be perceived differently in another.

Record your own video conferences or seek feedback from colleagues or friends on your non-verbal expression to improve your skills.

Non-verbal communication in video conferences is an important skill for effectively interpreting and conveying information and emotions. Paying attention to these aspects can enhance the quality of negotiations and collaboration in virtual environments.

Artificial intelligence is increasingly being used in virtual negotiations to analyze data, automate repetitive tasks, and provide useful real-time information.

Artificial intelligence (AI) and automation are playing an increasingly important role in virtual negotiations and various aspects of business management. Here are some ways in which AI and automation can benefit virtual negotiations:

AI can analyze large volumes of data to identify patterns, trends, and opportunities that can be valuable in decision-making during a negotiation. This may include analyzing financial, market, or past performance data.

Chatbots and virtual assistants can provide real-time assistance to parties involved in a negotiation. They can answer common questions, provide information about products or services, and even help with scheduling meetings or gathering information.

Repetitive tasks, such as data collection and organization, sending meeting reminders, and generating reports, can be automated through AI. This allows people to focus on more strategic and creative tasks.

AI can provide real-time reports and analysis on the progress of the negotiation, the status of agreements, and other key indicators. This enables parties to make more informed decisions.

In international negotiations, AI-powered translation can facilitate communication between people who speak different languages.

These technologies allow for voice conversations to be transcribed into text and for the understanding of instructions and questions in natural language. This can be useful in documenting agreements and interacting with automated systems.

AI can analyze the emotions and attitudes of the parties involved in the negotiation based on language used, tone, and other indicators. This can help negotiators adapt their approach as needed.

AI can use predictive models to forecast possible negotiation outcomes based on historical data and current variables. This can assist in strategic decision-making.

AI also plays a significant role in detecting and preventing cyber threats, which is critical for protecting the confidentiality of information in virtual negotiations.

AI can personalize interactions and communications with parties involved in the negotiation based on their preferences and specific needs.

It is important to remember that while AI and automation can provide many advantages in virtual negotiations, it is also essential to maintain a balance with human communication, empathy, and ethical decision-making. AI can be a valuable tool for enhancing the efficiency and effectiveness of virtual negotiations, but it does not replace the need for emotional intelligence and human decision-making.

As technology advances, ethical issues arise in virtual negotiations, such as the authenticity of shared information and the use of artificial intelligence in decision-making.

Ethics plays a crucial role in digital negotiations, as advanced technologies can pose specific ethical challenges. Here are some important considerations regarding ethics in virtual negotiations:

Maintaining the authenticity and truthfulness of shared information in digital negotiations is fundamental. Information should not be manipulated or distorted for unfair advantages. Honesty and integrity are fundamental pillars of ethical negotiations.

Transparency is essential in digital negotiations. Parties should be informed clearly and comprehensively about relevant information and agreement conditions. Hiding information or using deceptive tactics can be ethically unacceptable.

Handling privacy and data protection is crucial in virtual negotiations. You should ensure compliance with applicable privacy regulations and protect confidential information properly.

Before using technologies like artificial intelligence or automation in negotiations, you should obtain informed consent from all parties involved. Parties should understand how their data will be used and to what extent decisions will be based on AI.

Decisions made through AI should be fair and just. Bias and discrimination in automated decision-making should be avoided. Ethics in AI involves ensuring that all parties are treated fairly and equitably.

When sharing documents and resources during negotiations, you should respect the intellectual property rights of third parties. You should not use or distribute protected material without permission or violate copyright.

Although AI can provide valuable information, the ultimate responsibility for decisions lies with people. You should not evade your ethical responsibility by delegating important decisions to technology.

Empathy and consideration for the emotions and needs of the parties involved are important in digital negotiations. Cold and dehumanized interactions can have a negative impact on the relationship and the ethical perception of the negotiation.

Ensure compliance with all legal regulations and rules related to digital negotiations, such as privacy and data protection laws.

Promote ethical training and awareness among participants in virtual negotiations. Everyone should understand the ethical implications of decisions and the use of technology in the negotiation process.

Ethics in digital negotiations are essential for building strong business relationships and ensuring that parties involved are treated fairly and respectfully. Ethics should be a guiding principle in all business interactions, regardless of the platform or technology used.

Negotiating in the digital and virtual world presents unique challenges but also offers opportunities for efficient communication and effective collaboration in a global environment. Adapting to these new forms of negotiation is essential for success in an increasingly connected world."